"We tend to look at church growth through the lens of numbers and vision strategy. In this book, Ian Duncum helpfully explores a more holistic understanding of church health by looking at and assessing local church health and growth through tested consultancy ministry. This is an incredible aid to understanding church growth and wellbeing. These insights come from his years of experience in church consultancy and compelling analysis of data. A wonderful addition to healthy church life."

—**ROSS CLIFFORD**
Principal of Morling Theological College, Sydney; author of thirteen books, including *Taboo or To Do?* and *The Cross Is Not Enough*

"As we grapple with missional leadership and congregational transformation in the Western world, we desperately need reliable assessments, valid metrics, and practical tools for understanding and fostering church health and growth. Sometimes churches need a consultant to come alongside to ask diagnostic, curious, and subversive questions. But sometimes consultants need someone else to ask diagnostic, curious, and subversive questions of their processes. Ian Duncum has been asking insightful questions for twenty years as a pastor and church consultant and now offers a timely in-depth analysis of church consultancy in a group of Australian Baptist Churches. *The Impact of Church Consultancy* is a gift and resource for churches, pastors, denominational leaders, and consultants to learn about the necessary dance between pastor and congregational system that fosters church health and lays the groundwork for church growth."

—**DARREN CRONSHAW**
Head of Research and Professor of Missional Leadership with Australian College of Ministries (Sydney College of Divinity); pastor of Auburn Life Baptist Church; author of *Credible Witness* (2006), *Sentness* (with Kim Hammond, 2014) and *Dangerous Prayer* (2017)

"It's very helpful to see empirical evidence that supports the good work of the church consultancies offered by the Baptist Association of NSW/ACT. Thank you, Ian Duncum for this important contribution to the life of our churches."

—**MICHAEL FROST**

Director, Tinsley Institute, Morling Theological College, Sydney; author or editor of seventeen books, including *The Shaping of Things to Come* (with Alan Hirsch), *Exiles*, *The Road to Missional* and *Surprise the World!*

"Ian Duncum's book is an important study of the impact of church consultancies on church health and growth. When church consultancies are done well, they help churches become healthy, be revitalised, embrace fresh purpose and vision, and grow missionally. This is a valuable and timely book."

—**GRAHAM HILL**

Lecturer in Applied Theology, Morling Theological College, Sydney; Founding Director of The GlobalChurch Project; author or editor of five books, including *Healing Our Broken Humanity* (with Grace Ji-Sun Kim, 2018), *Global Church* (2016), and *Salt, Light, and a City* (Cascade, 2017)

"Ian Duncum has done our NSW & ACT Baptist movement a great service in the conducting and reporting of this research. The NSW & ACT Baptist Association has had a longstanding commitment to the value of church consultancies in assisting churches to navigate to greater health and vitality, and for proactive reflection and development. Now we have added clarity about their value, and how this may be further enhanced as we continue to seek to best serve the churches across our movement. His research has value for ongoing reflection in our movement and beyond. I highly commend it to the reader."

—**STEVE BARTLETT**

Director of Ministries, NSW & ACT Baptist Churches, Australia

The Impact of Church Consultancy

Australian College of Theology Monograph Series

SERIES EDITOR GRAEME R. CHATFIELD

The ACT Monograph Series, generously supported by the Board of Directors of the Australian College of Theology, provides a forum for publishing quality research theses and studies by its graduates and affiliated college staff in the broad fields of Biblical Studies, Christian Thought and History, and Practical Theology with Wipf and Stock Publishers of Eugene, Oregon. The ACT selects the best of its doctoral and research masters theses as well as monographs that offer the academic community, scholars, church leaders and the wider community uniquely Australian and New Zealand perspectives on significant research topics and topics of current debate. The ACT also provides opportunity for contributors beyond its graduates and affiliated college staff to publish monographs which support the mission and values of the ACT.

Rev Dr Graeme Chatfield
Series Editor and Associate Dean

The Impact of Church Consultancy

Explore the Impact of One Model of Church Consultancy on Church Health and Church Growth in NSW/ACT Baptist Churches

IAN G. DUNCUM

WIPF & STOCK · Eugene, Oregon

THE IMPACT OF CHURCH CONSULTANCY
Explore the Impact of One Model of Church Consultancy on Church Health and Church Growth in NSW/ACT Baptist Churches

Copyright © 2019 Ian G. Duncum. All rights reserved. Except for brief quotations in critical publications or reviews, no part of this book may be reproduced in any manner without prior written permission from the publisher. Write: Permissions, Wipf and Stock Publishers, 199 W. 8th Ave., Suite 3, Eugene, OR 97401.

Wipf & Stock
An Imprint of Wipf and Stock Publishers
199 W. 8th Ave., Suite 3
Eugene, OR 97401

www.wipfandstock.com

PAPERBACK ISBN: 978-1-5326-6793-0
HARDCOVER ISBN: 978-1-5326-6794-7
EBOOK ISBN: 978-1-5326-6795-4

Manufactured in the U.S.A.   02/13/19

The author can be contacted via email at duncum@internode.on.net.

This book is dedicated to my amazing family: my wife Joanne, partner in life and ministry, and our sons Jeremy and Joshua.

Contents

Permissions | xi
Preface | xiii

1 Introduction | 1
    Personal Interest | 2
    Methodology | 3
    Qualifications and Limitations | 4
    Usage Conventions and Definitions | 6

2 Church Health | 7
    Introduction | 7
    Definition | 9
    Systems Theory | 10
    Faithfulness to the Purposes of the Church | 14
    Theology of Church Health | 23
    Measurement of Church Health | 33
    The Emerging Missional Church as a Response to Postmodernity/Cultural Shifts | 38
    Conclusion | 44

3 Church Growth | 49
    Definition | 49
    History and Theology of Church Growth | 49
    Measurement of Church Growth | 64
    Conclusion | 65

4 Church Consultancy | 70
    Definition | 70
    Literature Survey/Approaches to Church Consultancy | 71
    Theology of Church Consultancy | 75
    A Rationale of, and Indicators for Using, Church

    Consultancy | 80
     A Model of Church Consultancy | 82
     Other Consultancy Models | 90
     Conclusion | 92
5 Data Analysis | 97
    Church Consultancy Case Studies | 97
    Analysis of Interviews | 120
    Analysis of Core Vitality Indicators | 125
    Evaluation and Interpretation of Results | 140
6 Conclusion | 143
    Recommendations | 150

Appendix A	Interview Questions	153
Appendix B	Request for Permission for Research	156
Appendix C	Interview Participant Information Sheet	159
Appendix D	Interview Participant Consent Form	162
Appendix E	NCLS Category by Church	164
Appendix F	Diagnostic Flowchart for Intragroup and Individual Intervention	165
Appendix AA	Church A Consultancy Report Summary	169
Appendix BB	Church B Consultancy Report Summary	175
Appendix CC	Church C Consultancy Report Summary	179
Appendix DD	Church D Consultancy Report Summary	183
Appendix EE	Church E Consultancy Report Summary	187
Appendix FF	Church F Consultancy Report Summary	190
Appendix GG	Church G Consultancy Report Summary	194
Appendix HH	Church H Consultancy Report Summary	199
Appendix II	Church I Consultancy Report Summary	205
Appendix JJ	Church J Consultancy Report Summary	208

Bibliography | 213

List of Tables

Table 1: Consultancy Objectives | 119

Table 2: Coded Health Indicators from Interviews | 121

Table 3: Initial Analysis Descriptives | 125

Table 4: Initial Analysis ANOVA | 127

Table 5: Scores Over Six Cross-Tabulation | 130

Table 6: "Weaker Churches" Descriptives | 132

Table 7: "Weaker Churches" ANOVA | 133

List of Figures

Figure 1: Interview Responses by Health & Growth Indicators | 121

Figure 2: Interview Responses by Church | 122

Figure 3: Comparison of Change in Core Qualities | 129

Figure 4: Comparison of Change in Core Qualities "Weaker Churches" | 135

Figure 5: Change in Attendance | 137

Figure 6: Comparison of Change in Attendance Measures "Weaker Churches" | 138

Permissions

SCRIPTURE QUOTATIONS ARE FROM the New Revised Standard Version Bible, ©1989 National Council of the Churches of Christ in the United States of America. Used by permission. All rights reserved worldwide.

NCLS Research, North Sydney has kindly granted permission for:

- The use of NCLS Research data generally
- National Church Life Survey Form 2006 (AP)
- Initial Analysis Descriptives
- Initial Analysis ANOVA
- Weaker Churches Analysis Descriptives
- Weaker Churches Analysis ANOVA

Morling Press has kindly granted permission for the part of chapter 5 which appeared in a different form. See Duncum, Ian. "From Stuck to Growing: Examining the Place of Church Consultancy in Revitalising Churches." In *Congregational Transformation in Australian Baptist Church Life: New Wineskins Vol. 1*, edited by Darren Cronshaw and Darrell Jackson. Macquarie Park: Morling Press, 2015.

Preface

FOR YEARS I HAVE been on a quest to identify the factors that contribute to church health. I have read many books, experimented in the churches I have pastored, and engaged in various training opportunities. One of the highlights for me has been to train as a church consultant under Rev. Les Scarborough and Tim Dyer of John Mark Ministries. It has been my great privilege to see many churches transformed through such consultancy processes. Another opportunity was to embark on a Doctor of Ministry course. This book endeavors to synthesize both experiences and share some of what I have learnt, both in the field and in the study, with a wider audience.

This research evaluated the pre- and post-consultancy "snapshots" of ten churches. These "snapshots" of vitality indicators and attendance figures were taken four to five years apart, and were compared with churches that have not undertaken church consultancies. This was enhanced by interviews with some of the pastors of the consultancy group of churches, reflecting on their perceptions of the ways in which the church consultancy impacted the health and growth of their church.

Results of this study indicated statistically significant correlations between increased church health and the churches that have undertaken church consultancies. Correlations between church growth and church consultancy were marked but not statistically significant. However, the results warrant further research with a larger sample size.

I thank those who inspired this book, my doctoral supervisors, especially Dr Graham Hill, the many (including the generous assistance of the Australian College of Theology) who helped create this book, the pastors and churches who assisted with this research, and the countless churches who graciously invite me to consult with them. It is my prayer that the fruit of successful consultancies will result in transformed churches that seek to effectively serve and reach their local communities for Christ.

Ian G. Duncum
Sydney

1

Introduction

OVERALL CHURCH ATTENDANCE IN Australia is declining: between 1950 and 2007 monthly or more frequent "church attendance has declined from 44% to 17%" of the Australian population, and the underrepresentation of younger generations in churches relative to the wider community does not bode well for future attendance.[1] Within NSW and ACT Baptist churches, the focus of this research, field staff from Ministry Support and Development estimate that approximately one hundred churches (of over 300) are under "serious stress" in terms of poor church health and long-term viability.[2] Growth in Baptist churches over the decade to 2006 has been assessed as zero.[3] Growth in Baptist churches relative to population growth over the same period has been assessed at –9 percent in NSW and –4 percent in ACT.[4]

There is little doubt that God desires healthy, growing churches. But the pathway to vitality and to increase, especially in terms of vital connections with the surrounding community, is often less clear, and sometimes results in "the sure-fire solution" presented at the latest round of conferences.

To these issues of church decline and poor health there have been many solutions offered in books, articles, and seminars, with little effect apparent. Church consultancy is neither a quick fix, nor sure-fire, nor the

---

1. Powell, *Why Innovation Is Needed in Church Life*, 1.
2. Clendinning, *Report on the Current State of Baptist Churches in NSW and ACT*.
3. Pratt, *Baptist Churches Research Project*, 6.
4. Pratt, *Baptist Churches Research Project*, 8.

only pathway to church health and growth. It is but one tool of many for church health and growth. More importantly, it is a process that assists churches in their journey towards church health.

Many pastors and church leaders want to know what tools, processes, and strategies are the most effective for church health and growth. These questions will be explored in the scope of this current research project. To date, there has not been any significant Australian quantitative, retrospective research that explores the impact of church consultancy specifically on either church health or church growth. And there has been little research on the effectiveness of church consultancy worldwide. This study seeks to carry out such research.

1.1 Personal Interest

Having been in pastoral ministry since 1992, I have sought to discover the factors that contribute to the health of churches, and to identify the dynamics that are most conducive to the growth of a church. In this time, I have grown to recognize that churches have their own particular "personalities" with concomitant strengths and weaknesses. These strengths and weaknesses firstly need to be discerned, then leadership needs to be given to a process that enhances the health and growth of a church.

I have been a church consultant since 1998. It has been a great privilege to receive extensive training in this avenue of service and to come alongside churches who for the most part have been struggling or feeling stuck, and I have learned much along the way. I have valued opportunities to reflect with fellow church consultants on what has worked well and what might have been done differently to assist churches. These conversations have also been the fertile soil in which the seeds of this project have germinated. In these conversations, the questions that consultants have asked, "Does church consultancy work?" and, "Are we making a difference?" deserve a considered response. My hope in carrying out this research is that some answers to these questions may emerge, not merely for the sake of consultants, but so that vital churches can make significant inroads into their local communities with the gospel.

This project aims to explore the process of church consultancy and its contribution to church health and church growth. It is hoped that the efficacy of church consultancy for church health and church growth will become evident as a result of this study.

1.2 Methodology

The research methodology is divided into two parts: quantitative and qualitative.

Twenty church consultancies were carried out between November 2001 and December 2002 by the Baptist Churches of NSW/ACT Consultancy Team.[5] Of these twenty churches, 50 percent or ten (this is over 3.3% of all Baptist churches in NSW/ACT) had reliable data for both NCLS-2001 and NCLS-2006, enabling a retrospective comparison of their numerical growth and health or quality indicators over a four-to-five-year interval post-consultancy. In this way, the impact of the consultancy on the church will be evaluated, and any correlation between church consultancy and church growth and health will be identified.[6] Two separate statistical analyses were carried out using this data.[7] Firstly, churches undergoing a consultancy in this time period were compared with NCLS data from all non-consultancy churches that had undergone both NCLS-2001 and NCLS-2006. Secondly, those non-consultancy churches with weaker NCLS quality indicators were compared with the nine weakest consultancy churches.

Church consultancy reports were also analyzed for each of these ten churches.

In order to seek to confirm and interpret the quantitative data obtained from consultancy churches, interviews were carried out with five people who were senior/sole/associate pastors of the churches that form this study at the time of the consultancies. They were asked for their responses regarding perceived increases or decreases in church vitality or health since the church consultancy. They were also asked for their perceptions regarding whether church attendance had increased or decreased in the time interval since the church consultancy. Two churches where the researcher had carried out a church consultancy were excluded from interviews. This was done to protect the honesty of answers and to avoid any perception of an unequal relationship.

---

5. Data only includes Baptist churches which are affiliated with the Baptist Union of NSW/ACT.

6. Data for both consultancy churches and non-consultancy churches is obtained from churches who participated in NCLS-2001 and NCLS-2006 (205 Baptist Union NSW/ACT churches in 2001, 150 Baptist Union NSW/ACT churches in 2006).

7. See 5.3 Analysis of Core Vitality Indicators.

It was helpful to interview pastors who were very involved in the actual consultancy process, who oversaw the implementation of the consultancy recommendations, and, for those who continued to pastor the church for some time after the consultancy, who were very familiar with the various aspects that contributed towards the health and growth of the church.

Participants in interviews were given a Participant Information Sheet outlining the project and a letter of consent beforehand.[8]

Interviews were conducted on a structured basis, with responses to questions asked at Appendix A coded as follows:

Response	Code
grown	1
about the same	0
declined	-1

Ethical protocols, including obtaining consents were observed throughout.[9] Code names were used to preserve confidentiality with interviewees. Where details are given that may identify the church or the community, they are disguised.

1.3 Qualifications and Limitations

In approaching a project of this type, several limitations need to be expressed.

First, as a retrospective study, this project is mainly descriptive in its nature. While some conclusions may be drawn about the efficacy of church consultancy for church health and church growth, this project is not primarily prescriptive.

---

8. See Appendices D and E.
9. See Appendices D and E.

Secondly, this project relates to the study of NSW/ACT Baptist Churches. While a wider body of literature regarding church growth, church health, and church consultancy are explored, the project data concerns church consultancies carried out in ten NSW/ACT Baptist churches, and the health and growth of NSW/ACT Baptist churches more generally.[10] Any inference of the wider applicability of church consultancy to other denominations should be done carefully and with the recognition of the impact of different church polity and structures on such extrapolation.

Thirdly, this project relates to one model of church consultancy. There are a number of models that are used in Baptist churches, as well as in other denominations, both in Australia and around the world. It is not within the scope of this study to outline these models. While this model does not have a particular name, it has been championed by practitioners from John Mark Ministries in Australia. It should be noted, in relation to this point and to the previous point, that this church consultancy model is currently being used in a large number of denominations in Australia, such as Anglican and Presbyterian churches.

Fourth, this project seeks to explore the impact on church health and church growth. While there may be other positive impacts of this model of church consultancy such as individual growth in process skills by pastors and lay leaders, these are not the focus of this study.

Fifth, this project is limited to churches that have had a church consultancy in a particular time period. These churches are therefore not necessarily representative of all churches that have had church consultancies. This brings with it a limitation of the number of churches that are included in the study and may impact the statistical reliability of data as a result.

Sixth, this project is limited to churches who have invited a church consultancy. That means that this group of churches is not representative of all churches, since they tended to have "weaker" church health. However, this group of consultancy churches will be compared to all other Baptist churches in NSW/ACT for which data is available. This concept of typicality will be explored in more depth in the second statistical

---

10. More specifically, these are churches associated with the Baptist Union of NSW/ACT. It is acknowledged that there are Baptist Churches not so associated, but the researcher could not obtain data for these churches or for churches from other denominations.

analysis when comparing "weaker" consultancy churches with "weaker" non-consultancy churches.

Seventh, this project is exploratory, recognizing both the usefulness and the limitations of quantitative analysis in social research, and the implied difficulty of drawing definitive conclusions on the impact of church consultancy on church health and church growth.

1.4 Usage Conventions and Definitions

Terms are used such as "pastor" where other denominations may use the words "minister" or "priest." This merely reflects the churches and denomination that comprise this study. It does not minimize the valuable contribution that other denominations have made in this field, both in Australia and beyond, and where it is appropriate readers are encouraged to insert the terms with which they are familiar.

In a similar way, the churches that comprise this study all had male pastors. This was not intentional and was merely the result of churches that had invited church consultancies within the specified time period, and that had reliable NCLS-2001 and NCLS-2006 data. The use of the term "he" in this context is therefore not intended to minimize the valuable contribution made by female pastors in NSW/ACT Baptist Churches and in other states and denominations.

NCLS is used to refer to National Church Life Survey, and NCLS-2001 and NCLS-2006 are used to refer to surveys carried out in those years. Where the National Church Life Survey team is referred to, they are designated as the "NCLS Team."

Other definitions are placed in the chapters in which they most properly belong.

2

Church Health

2.1 Introduction

RICK WARREN STATES "I believe the key issue for churches in the twenty-first century will be church health, not church growth . . . Focusing on growth alone misses the point. When congregations are healthy, they grow the way God intends."[1]

Symptoms of church unhealth or dysfunction include: inward-looking churches that do not engage missionally with their community, schisms, splits, discord, attenders leaving churches, churches that collapse or die, and the undermining of a church's witness in the community. Some US denominational leaders estimate that "20 percent of our churches are functioning as living organisms and bearing substantial fruit . . . between 35 to 50% are dysfunctional, bearing no fruit at all."[2]

Collateral damage involves hurt and discouraged pastors, relational stress in pastoral families, and pastors that leave the ministry. Hart asserts that "the emotional hazards facing pastors are far and away more challenging than in any other profession."[3] One expression of this church-pastor stress is evidenced in 6 percent of pastors at some time having been fired, and 19 percent being forced to resign by "a small faction" of about ten people.[4] Compounding this unhealth, for those forced to resign, 63

---

1. Warren, *The Purpose Driven Church*, 17.
2. Anderson and Mylander, *Extreme Church Makeover*, 13.
3. Hart, "Unhealthy Trends in the Church."
4. Miller, "What Pastors Are Saying," 1.

percent of the time the church was not told why, and 62 percent were aware that the church had forced out other ministers in its past.[5] Eighty percent of pastors say they have insufficient time with their spouse and that ministry has a negative effect on their family, and thirty-three percent of pastors state that being in ministry is an outright hazard to their family.[6] The results of church unhealth encompass pastoral depression and burnout, with forty-five percent of pastors experiencing this to such an extent that they needed to take a leave of absence, and forty percent of pastors considered leaving the pastorate in the past three months.[7]

In many ways this lack of health is not surprising. People, both pastors and church attenders, are human and at least sometimes dysfunctional. Their families of origin and current families are imperfectly functional. There is no such thing as a perfectly healthy church because of human sin. This sin spoils peoples' interactions and sense of unity with one another, gets in the way of having a clear, shared corporate identity as a church, stifles mission to the surrounding community, and is a barrier to agreement on how to achieve that mission—a church's purpose, priorities, and goals.

The locus of church health is neither the pastor nor the congregation; they are intertwined, and each influences the other. Healthy pastors tend towards creating healthy churches.[8] Toxic people[9] and churches with systemic dysfunction[10] tend towards a negative impact on pastors (and others). The considerable body of literature devoted to the topic of clergy stress and forced termination is one general indicator of a lack of health in churches.[11] However, looking at church health or pastoral health in isolation is counterproductive, since it is in the relationship

---

5. Miller, "What Pastors Are Saying," 1.
6. London and Wiseman, *Pastors at Greater Risk*, 22.
7. London and Wiseman, *Pastors at Greater Risk*, 172.
8. Hart, "Unhealthy Trends in the Church."
9. Shelley, *Well-Intentioned Dragons*; Rediger, *Clergy Killers*.
10. Johnson and VanVonderen, *The Subtle Power of Spiritual Abuse*; Steinke, *How Your Church Family Works*.
11. Kaldor and Bullpitt, *Burnout in Church Leaders*; Greenfield, *The Wounded Minister*; Warren, *The Cracked Pot*; Roukema, *Shepherding the Shepherd*; London and Wiseman, *Pastors at Greater Risk*; Dollard et al., *Occupational Stress in the Service Professions*; Train, *A Strategy of Maintaining Personal Care in Ministry*; Lehr, *Clergy Burnout*; Thorndike, *Gratitude and Human Flourishing*; Lewis et al., "Clergy Work-Related Psychological Health, Stress, and Burnout"; Abernathy, *Self-Care for Pastors*.

between the pastor and the church where either health is fostered, or disease arises.

2.2 Definition

Health is defined as:

> (1) The state of the organism when it functions optimally without evidence of disease or abnormality. (2) A state of dynamic balance in which an individual's or group's capacity to cope with all the circumstances of living is at an optimal level. (3) A state characterized by . . . psychological integrity, ability to perform personally valued family, work, and community roles; ability to deal with physical, biologic, psychological, and social stress; a feeling of well-being, and freedom from the risk of disease and untimely death."[12]

This definition points us towards a condition, not just of the absence of disease nor a narrow focus on the physical only, but that of flourishing, experiencing well-being; encountering intrapersonal and interpersonal peace and justice; integrity, wholeness and fulfillment. Such concepts are captured by the Hebrew word, מעלאהס.[13] These formulations of health are very relevant when applied to church health: optimal functioning, experiencing well-being, responsiveness to the surroundings, a clear sense of purpose, and navigating stressful situations resiliently are some important indicators of a church's health.

There is some reluctance in church health literature to too closely equate church health with growth. This recognizes that one may have a healthy church that finds growth more difficult because of external challenges such as an older community profile and/or negative population growth.[14] It also acknowledges that growing churches may not experience health, and Schwarz's research shows that while church health is a good predictor of church growth, church growth is not necessarily a good predictor of church health.[15]

There is wide variance amongst authors in terms of the focus of congregational health. Throughout the literature on church health, there

---

12. Stedman, *Stedman's Medical Dictionary*, 382.
13. Yoder, *Shalom*.
14. Kaldor et al., *Shaping a Future*, 191–204.
15. Schwarz, *Natural Church Development*, 46–48.

appear to be three (sometimes overlapping) groupings: those who draw from the sociologically-based models of systems theory, those who, broadly speaking, work from ecclesiology in defining church health in terms of faithfulness to the purposes of the church, and those who suggest that the current models of church are flawed or rendered culturally ineffective in a postmodern world and that the "emerging missional church" (EMC) is the appropriate model of church seeking to operate effectively in that postmodern culture.

2.3 Systems Theory

Although the seeds of general systems theory may be traced back further, biologist Ludwig von Bertalanffy is considered to be the founder of general systems theory.[16] This theory has been applied to many disciplines, including family therapy,[17] and organizations.[18] These two applications of systems theory have been important contributors in the quest to understand how churches work and how they can reach their full potential and health.

E. Mansell Pattison notes the benefits of a healthy church for individuals who comprise it when he states that "the church can and should . . . be the social system that produces a whole, holy, person."[19] Pattison sees the church's contribution to its health and the health of attenders as:

> The church as a living system functions best when it provides leadership, commitment, behavioral sanctions, organization, goals and tasks, association, behavioral taboos, and outside connections. These are crucial functions of the healthy and health-engendering system, and must be regarded as optimum contributions of the effective church.[20]

Edwin Friedman applied Bowen's family therapy to faith communities in seeing problems as system-wide.[21] He views the concepts of systemic balance, process and content, the non-anxious presence,

---

16. Bertalanffy, *General System Theory*.
17. Bowen, *Family Therapy in Clinical Practice*.
18. Senge, *The Fifth Discipline*.
19. Pattison, *Pastor and Parish*, 12.
20. Pattison, *Pastor and Parish*, 27.
21. Friedman, *Generation to Generation*, 198.

over-functioning, triangles, and the symptom-bearer, as important in assessing and fostering systemic health.[22]

Friedman focuses on self-differentiation as the means to effective leadership of the system: "If a leader will take primary responsibility for his or her own position as 'head' and work to define his or her own goals and self, while staying in touch with the rest of the organism, there is a more reasonable chance that the body will follow."[23] Similarly, Ronald Richardson underlines the importance of a church leader's self-differentiation (i.e. they are separate from the system but connected to it), and the significance of the leader assessing and reducing anxiety within that system.[24] This assessment will come through an awareness of the impact of birth order on leadership, triangulation (of people seeking to draw others into alliances), and an individual's level of functioning as compared with others in the system.[25] Peter Steinke sees congregational health in terms of avoiding "diseases" and "viruses" such as murmuring, anxiety, accusation, deceit, and triangulation, and of embarking on a journey of ongoing learning.[26]

Dennis Campbell draws heavily on Senge's *The Fifth Discipline*[27] but places it firmly in a church context when he insists that a healthy congregation must be a learning, dialoguing community, and that the means to doing this will be through using three tools that he develops: appreciative inquiry, congregational culture analysis, and scenario planning.[28] Denise Goodman focuses exclusively on healthy behaviors to develop a congregation's capacity to manage or transform conflict in constructive, rather than anxious ways.[29] Scazzero and Bird maintain that the transformation of individuals and churches will only occur when emotional health is integrated with spiritual maturity, and they outline a process for discipling towards this goal.[30]

---

22. Friedman, *Generation to Generation*, 202–19.
23. Friedman, *Generation to Generation*, 229.
24. Richardson, *Creating a Healthier Church*, 85–89.
25. Richardson, *Creating a Healthier Church*, 114–57.
26. Steinke, *Healthy Congregations*, 54–75.
27. Senge, *The Fifth Discipline*.
28. Campbell, *Congregations as Learning Communities*.
29. Goodman, *Congregational Fitness*.
30. Scazzero and Bird, *The Emotionally Healthy Church*.

A system is simply "a set of forces and events that interact; that mutually influence one another."[31] Systems thinking resists a simplistic cause-and-effect understanding of the parts of an organization, or individual relationships within it, to pan back to a big picture perspective on the whole.[32]

Such a picture has some resemblances to the way a family interacts; "they have "hidden lives" comprised of forces and dynamics that operate below the surface . . . [which are] especially invisible to those who are in the system."[33] Friedman notes the family-like systemic complexity for clergy who "are simultaneously involved in three distinct families whose emotional forces interlock: the families within the congregation, our congregations, and our own."[34] Paul often used family language to describe the church (God's family: Matt 25:40, Rom 8:29, 1 Cor 8:12, Gal 1:2, Gal 6:10, Eph 3:15, 1 Pet 2:17; and God's household: Matt 10:25, John 8:35, Eph 2:19, 1 Tim 3:15, 1 Pet 4:17), along with the relationships that Christians share with one another (brother, sister, mother, father). All organized groups, including churches, have leaders ("parents") and followers ("children"), and so imitate the family form in one way or another.[35]

Systems thinking can provide useful insights about leadership. Pattison considered the pastor as "a shepherd of systems."[36] Seeing a pastor's leadership in this light means that it goes beyond pulling the levers that may bring growth, to identifying points of stuckness or trauma in the church's history that may need addressing in order to facilitate health, then working through such points. In many such situations, this may be best done by an intentional interim pastor[37] or an outside consultant.

So, an important focus of family system theory is how the church and pastor function in relation to each other. That is, is the pastor underfunctioning, overfunctioning, or functioning appropriately? Is the congregation overfocused on the clergy, trying to draw them into overfunctioning in an effort to compensate for its dependent, underfunctioning stance? Steinke asserts that in contrast to an overfocus on clergy, a

31. Steinke, *How Your Church Family Works*, 4.
32. Rendle, *Leading Change in the Congregation*, 55.
33. Galindo, *The Hidden Lives of Congregations*, 12.
34. Friedman, *Generation to Generation*, 1.
35. Stevens and Collins, *The Equipping Pastor*, 78–85; Cosgrove and Hatfield, *Church Conflict*, 12–14.
36. Pattison, *Pastor and Parish*, 50.
37. Nicholson, *Temporary Shepherds*.

mission-focused church has a clear focus on its identity and destiny.[38] Some rightly call this passivity and overinvestment in the clergy an addiction. Bandy puts the process of becoming free starkly when he writes:

> It is very hard for a group of addicts to admit an addiction. It means recognizing absolute helplessness to liberate themselves by their own power. It also means recognizing no emergency capital assistance from denominational offices, no expert consultants, no new program gimmicks, and no "messianic" pastoral call to a new minister who will liberate them from their addictions. Nothing human will liberate them from their addictions . . . only God.[39]

Senge discusses our human tendency towards defensiveness when confronted with information that is new or at odds with our worldview and extends this into how organizations respond (or don't respond) to a similar challenge. An organization has the opportunity to be open to its continually changing environment (rather than closed to it), and to continually adapt, learn, and change as a result of this feedback.

> A learning organization is a place where people are continually discovering how they create their reality. And how they can change it.[40]

Drawing on systems theory, Arch Hart lists the characteristics of a healthy church as a foundation or starting point: it has very few power struggles, is free of sabotage tendencies, avoids secrecy like the plague, is relatively unfragmented (unity), confronts conflict up front, emotions are embraced and encouraged, people do not invade each other's boundaries, does not tolerate troublemakers, little defensiveness—leaders are open to constructive criticism, not a closed system, low organizational anxiety (an anxious leader destabilizes the whole system), and leaders are well differentiated but maintain a non-anxious presence.[41]

---

38. Steinke, *Healthy Congregations*, 44–45.
39. Bandy, *Kicking Habits: Welcome Relief for Addicted Churches*, 150.
40. Senge, *The Fifth Discipline*, 13.
41. Hart, "Building a Healthy Church."

2.4 Faithfulness to the Purposes of the Church

Another group of those who write about church health define it as faithfulness to the purposes of the church. There are some commonalities among authors as to what constitutes and contributes to church health. However, there are also some divergent views about what those purposes are.

It should also be noted that in these points raised by numerous authors there is a variety, not just in purposes, but in type, ranging from what many authors see as being timeless, clear biblical purposes of the church such as worship (Matt 4:10), fellowship (Eph 2:19), discipleship (Col 1:28), ministry (Eph 4:12), and mission (Matt 28:19–20), through to practicalities such as videotaped baptism testimonies and streaming videos on the internet.[42]

Most of these authors have a particular emphasis which is highlighted by the headings.

2.4.1 Absence of Disease

Peter Wagner puts health in the absence of disease category when he outlines nine diseases that can afflict the health of any church: ethnikitis—a changing community; ghost-town disease—an aging population; people-blindness—a resistance to the homogeneous principle of church growth; hyper-cooperativism—an overcommitment to interdenominational and inter-congregational cooperative evangelism; koinonitis—an overemphasis on internal relationships; sociological strangulation—a disease of the growing church where facilities limit growth possibilities; arrested spiritual development—a lack of maturity; St. John's syndrome—when church involvement is largely going through the motions; and hypopneumonia—a below normal level of the presence and power of the Holy Spirit.[43]

While Wagner may give us some helpful clues about church health, his emphasis on the absence of disease is at odds with the definition of health above in that it does not incorporate optimal functioning, experiencing well-being, responsiveness to the surroundings, a clear sense of purpose, and navigating stressful situations resiliently. It also conflicts

---

42. Stanley and Young, *Can We Do That?*, 37.
43. Wagner, *The Healthy Church*.

with this definition of health: "The state of complete physical, mental, and social well-being and not merely the absence of disease or infirmity."[44] Health is much more than the absence of disease, and in a church setting, much more than the absence of problems, issues, or conflict. Wagner also carries his assumptions about the effectiveness of the homogenous unit principle: while it may be a pragmatic way of working in cross-cultural mission situations, US and Australian research has questioned the principle's effectiveness in growing churches in a multicultural society (see sections 3.2 and 3.3.1).

2.4.2 Preaching and Theology

Mark Dever emphasizes his strong reliance and focus on the Bible in *Nine Marks of a Healthy Church*: expositional preaching, biblical theology, biblical understanding of the good news, biblical understanding of conversion, biblical understanding of evangelism, biblical understanding of church membership, biblical understanding of church discipline, biblical understanding of church leadership, and concern for promoting Christian discipleship and growth.[45] While there is much that is commendable in terms of growing people's understanding, this appears to be a less rounded definition of church health than many of the others in this section, since it does not explicitly address the interpersonal components of a healthy church.

2.4.3 Mission

Bruce and Marshall Shelley prioritize identifying the culture of the local community and reaching that community in outlining the seven steps that are required to create a healthy blend of effectiveness and faithfulness in a church: identify prevailing values and lifestyles in their ministry context; determine common values with people they would reach; design attractive programs to serve the people they would reach; be sensitive and receptive to the unchurched; "charm" these seekers into a more mature and explicit expression of Christian discipleship in worship, membership, and outreach; reshape the values and lifestyles of new members;

---

44. Encyclo Online Encyclopedia, *Health*.
45. Dever, *Nine Marks of a Healthy Church*.

and enlist them in outreach.[46] In a similar way, Anderson includes relating positively to one's environment, and incorporation of newcomers as a context for reaching the local community.[47] These authors work from the viewpoint of increasing secularization and do not grapple with the postmodern cultural milieu in a way that EMC authors have (see section 2.7), with many of those authors calling for new models of church rather than revitalizing existing churches to be more effective. So, Steve Bruce posits in his provocatively titled book, *God is Dead*,[48] that the secularization of the West, particularly in the UK and Europe, is irreversible. Similarly, a US survey "reveals that one out of every three adults (33%) is classified as unchurched—meaning they have not attended a religious service of any type during the past six months," a huge increase from 21 percent in 1991.[49]

2.4.4 Church Revitalization

George Barna studied a number of declining churches that were revived or restored to health in order to ascertain what common factors were present in enabling that turnaround and arrived at the following:

- the pastor is to create a bond of credibility and trust with the congregation
- a pastoral love of people
- the presence of the Holy Spirit and an openness to his working
- a new pastor must be brought in to lead a revolution, release the past, and focus on the future
- define and plan outreach
- equip the congregation for effective, targeted ministry
- pastor must be a strong leader
- pastor must be hardworking
- widespread and heartfelt prayer

---

46. Shelley and Shelley, *The Consumer Church*, 226.
47. Anderson, *A Church for the 21st Century*, 125–42.
48. Bruce, *God Is Dead*.
49. Barna, "Unchurched Population Nears 100 Million in the U.S."

- pastor's sermons were a higher quality than what the congregation had received in the past
- seeking an objective, outsider's perspective on the church
- having great staff members
- having a core of supportive zealots in the congregation
- a long-term pastor.[50]

Undoubtedly, the senior pastor is a key element in leading a church to turn around, but the heavy focus on the senior pastor in Barna's book is almost messianic in proportions. It would be helpful for Barna to explore some of the factors within a church that may predispose it towards (or against) a turnaround, such as Saarinen's life cycle of a church, along with appropriate interventions at each stage of that life cycle.[51]

2.4.5 Discipling

With a strong emphasis on making disciples and equipping attenders for ministry, Bill Hull sketches seven steps to transform a church: seek renewal, develop principled leadership training, transform existing leadership, cast the vision, sacrifice forms for function, create community, and truly do evangelism.[52] Similarly, Sue Mallory sees church health arising from becoming an equipping church which values and lives out prayer, the priesthood of all believers and the vision of the church as contained in Ephesians 4, servant leadership, team ministry, intentionality, and proactive response to change.[53] Equipping attenders for growing in their faith, ministry, and mission in the community will result in transformation:

> Transformational churches are deeply committed to the essential foundations of discipleship: worship, community, and mission. They practice and make disciples through vibrant leadership, prayerful dependence, and relational intentionality—in their context with a missionary mindset.[54]

---

50. Barna, *Turn-Around Churches*, 42.
51. Saarinen, *The Life Cycle of a Congregation*, 15–22.
52. Hull, *Seven Steps to Transform Your Church*.
53. Mallory, *The Equipping Church*, 198.
54. Stetzer and Rainer, *Transformational Church*, i.

This emphasis on discipling, so long as it is kept in balance with the other elements for vitality, will be important in a cultural context where people are increasingly unchurched before conversion, and require a longer period of time to grow to maturity, develop their ministry, and engage in local mission. No longer can churches rely on "ready to go" mature Christians walking through their doors, and churches must engage in the hard work of relational discipling, either one-to-one or in small groups.[55]

2.4.6 Quality of Interpersonal Relationships

Stephen Macchia focuses heavily on relationships when he outlines his ten characteristics of a healthy church as: God's empowering presence, God-exalting worship, spiritual disciplines, learning and growing in community, a commitment to loving and caring relationships, servant-leadership development, an outward focus, wise administration and accountability, networking with the body of Christ, and stewardship and generosity.[56] While including characteristics and practices in common with many other authors, Donald MacNair helpfully includes a vital distinctive that has often been overlooked by authors in the "faithfulness to the purposes of the church" stream, but is often discussed in "systems" literature: that is "the absence of major divisions."[57] Eddie Gibbs goes a step further than this when he includes the following in his list of twelve indicators of a missional church: behaves Christianly toward one another, practices reconciliation, people hold themselves accountable to one another in love, and practices hospitality.[58]

Rowland Croucher adds some unique insights to the health qualities that others emphasize when he underlines: justice, love, training to recognize and deal with spiritual abuse, affirmation of diversity, tolerance of ambiguity, leadership that honors God and gives training and opportunities to people in using their spiritual gifts, leaders welcoming 360-degree feedback and having multiple regular systems for complaints/

---

55. Comiskey, *Leadership Explosion*; Comiskey, *Home Cell Group Explosion*; Comiskey, *From 12 to 3*; Comiskey, *Cell Church Solutions*; Collinson, *Making Disciples*; Webb, *Small Group Leadership as Spiritual Direction*; Kirk et al., *Small Group Leaders' Handbook*; Fryling, *Seeking God Together*; Malphurs, *Strategic Disciple Making*; Spitzer, *Making Friends, Making Disciples*; Hull, *The Disciple-Making Church*.

56. Macchia, *Becoming a Healthy Church*.

57. MacNair, *The Practices of a Healthy Church*, 31.

58. Gibbs and Coffey, *Church Next*, 52.

suggestions from everyone, ministerial code of ethics/conduct is in place, church leaders are accountable to a mentor/spiritual director/supervisor, governance should maximize empowerment of giftedness while providing accountability, and occupational health and safety/duty of care issues are addressed.[59]

Rebecca Hanson also identifies the quality of interpersonal relationships as a significant predictor of whether a church is healthy or unhealthy.[60] In particular, open and honest communication, supportive and inclusive care, and a lack of controlling behaviors such as manipulation or the inappropriate use of shame or guilt are seen as areas which impact the health of a church.[61]

In practice, the area of interpersonal relationships is probably one of the most critical areas of health for a church at many levels. Anderson asserts, "Incorporation of newcomers may be one of the most identifiable and measurable signs of health in a church. Healthy churches assimilate new people into the life and leadership of the congregation."[62] The friendliness of the welcome that people receive will often determine whether they remain at the church or try another church.[63] And those who developed friendships through immediately commencing involvement in small groups, rather than just worship services, were five times more likely to remain in the church five years later.[64] The reverse of this is that breakdown in interpersonal relationships is a significant indicator of poor church health; "congregations that have experienced major conflict are quite likely to have declined in attendance."[65]

2.4.7 Balance of Purposes

Darrell Robinson outlines twelve components of a total church life strategy: vision, commitment, leadership, unity, membership involvement, celebrative and joyful worship and praise, prayer, fellowship, organization,

---

59. Croucher, "Measuring a Church's Health"; Croucher, "Best Practices in a Healthy Church."
60. Hanson, "Healthy Church or Unhealthy Church?"
61. Hanson, "Healthy Church or Unhealthy Church?"
62. Anderson, *A Church for the 21st Century*, 135.
63. Oswald and Leas, *The Inviting Church*, 25.
64. Rainer, *Surprising Insights from the Unchurched*, 120.
65. Hadaway, *FACTs on Growth*, 8.

equipping, pastoral care and ministry, and evangelizing.[66] Ken Hemphill lists eight characteristics of effective churches that mirror the purposes of the church outlined in Scripture: supernatural power, Christ-exalting worship, God-connecting prayer, servant leaders, kingdom family relationships, God-sized vision, passion for the lost, and maturation of believers.[67] Rick Warren focuses on balancing the purposes of the church (worship, ministry, evangelism, fellowship, and discipleship)[68] for achieving health: "Church growth is the natural result of church health. Church health can only occur when our message is biblical and our mission is balanced. Each of the five New Testament purposes of the church must be in equilibrium with the others for health to occur."[69] To Warren such health is not theoretical or an ideal, but can be measured: "the health of a church is quantifiable. For example, I can measure how many more people are involved in ministry this month than last month."[70] Dale Galloway defines eleven characteristics of a healthy church as: clear-cut vision, passion for the lost, shared ministry, empowered leaders, fervent spirituality, a flexible and functional structure, celebrative worship, small groups, seeker-friendly evangelism, loving relationships, and evaluation.[71]

Christian Schwarz's survey across five continents isolates the following eight quality characteristics: empowering leadership, gift-oriented ministry, passionate spirituality, functional structures, inspiring worship, holistic small groups, need-oriented evangelism, and loving relationships.[72]

Eric Geiger and Thom Rainer observe that many churches have become overloaded and unbalanced with programs that do not align with their particular church's purposes. They suggest that churches would benefit from: designing a simple process or pathway for people to grow, placing their key programs along this process, uniting all ministries around this process, and beginning to eliminate things outside this process.[73] In

---

66. Robinson, *Total Church Life*, 4.
67. Hemphill, *The Antioch Effect*.
68. Warren, *The Purpose Driven Church*, 103–7.
69. Warren, *The Purpose Driven Church*, 49.
70. Warren, "Comprehensive Health Plan," 25.
71. Galloway et al., *Making Church Relevant*.
72. Schwarz, *Natural Church Development*, 79.
73. Geiger and Rainer, *Simple Church*, 232–72.

other words, making clarity of identity and vision the priority and seeking to align all else around that.

2.4.8 Regional Denominational Leadership and Church Health

In an effort to examine church health and growth from a wider perspective than that of a local church, Bill Easum investigated how regional denominational leadership could foster that health in local churches. He sent out emails to over fifteen thousand clients looking for examples of success in church transformation and reproduction as a result of input from denominational judicatories. Easum received over two hundred responses, with only a handful actually showing growth in their region.[74] However, from these responses, along with his wide experience as a church consultant, he arrived at the following keys to transformation of existing churches and reproduction of churches: leadership from the judicatory in developing and resourcing healthy established congregations rather than propping up failing existing churches, a focus on developing reproducing church planting systems along with developing leaders for this movement who have a vision for the city, church planting, and multi-site churches.[75]

2.4.9 Conclusion

The authors above outline a number of purposes of the church and in so doing demonstrate a variety of emphases. Insofar as a church purpose propounded above represents a call by an author to return to, or reform around, a biblical principle, value or expression of the church, that is most helpful. What is less valuable are calls rooted in mere pragmatism (this technique worked for me), appeals that do not take into account the vast differences in demographics (this works in my location), entreaties regarding ecclesiologies (this works in my denomination), or other restricted factors. In short, purposes that are limited geographically, culturally, chronologically (i.e. it may have worked last decade but not this decade), or in some other way, are not timeless, overarching principles, and become less useful when thinking about church health on a broader

---

74. Easum, "Transformation and Reproduction Across Denominational Lines."

75. Easum, "Transformation and Reproduction Across Denominational Lines," 9–10.

scale. The ability to "step back" theologically and practically and dialogue with others on the same thought journey is therefore enormously important. Although many purposes may be stated in different words, there appears to be a sense of overlap, though not consensus, by many of the above authors around core health or vitality indicators. For example, Woolever and Bruce list ten "strengths" of US congregations as: growing spiritually, meaningful worship, participation in the congregation, having a sense of belonging, caring for children and youth, focusing on the community, sharing faith, welcoming new people, empowering leadership, and looking to the future.[76]

Woolever and Bruce's work, based as it is on research by Australia's NCLS team,[77] reflects the vitality indicators or qualities arrived at by the NCLS team through their years of research in Australia, New Zealand, United Kingdom, and United States, and extensive survey of church health and church growth literature. The NCLS team have further nuanced this and identify the following nine core qualities of healthy and vital churches: an alive and growing *faith*, vital and nurturing *worship*, strong and growing *belonging*, a clear and owned *vision*, inspiring and empowering *leadership*, open and flexible *innovation*, practical and diverse *service*, willing and effective *faith-sharing*, and intentional and welcoming *inclusion*. Additionally, NCLS has identified three quantitative measures of the missional impact of churches: *young adult retention*—the proportion of the children of attenders still attending a church; *newcomers*—the percentage of newcomers at a church; and *attendance change*—patterns of growth or decline in the number of people attending a church over time.[78]

There is however, the absence of a major focus on justice and poverty alleviation in church health (or church growth) literature. This omission does not adequately reflect Jesus' ministry (e.g. Luke 4:18–19) or the weight of over two thousand biblical verses which make our mission and responsibility with the poor, marginalized, and oppressed abundantly clear (e.g. Micah 6:8 and Matthew 23:23 include justice and mercy as part of our mission).

One valid critique of the church health movement is an overfocus on a church as a self-contained entity and the examination of the health

---

76. Woolever and Bruce, *Beyond the Ordinary*, 13–108.
77. Woolever and Bruce, *Beyond the Ordinary*, 138.
78. Bellamy et al., *Enriching Church Life*, 10–29.

of that church in isolation. Just as a healthy organism grows, reaches out, and reproduces, so one health indicator of a local church is whether it has planted new churches, and especially new church plants that in turn plant others: "reproducing church planting systems."[79] Planting new churches is a strong focus of the New Testament (e.g. Acts 5:12–14; 8:1–4; 9:31; 11:26; 14:21–25; 17:1–4, 10–12). Werning and Garrison are amongst the few who emphasize church planting in their list of health characteristics of churches.[80]

Among authors on church health, there is both a diversity and an overlap regarding the purposes of the church and associated health or vitality indicators. However, many assertions regarding these purposes are not substantiated by research. Some commonality by authors cited above emerges around the nine qualitative NCLS indicators, which are supported by the NCLS team's extensive, multi-country research in thousands of churches. This appears to be one of the better snapshots of church health and vitality, and will be explored further in section 2.6 below.

2.5 Theology of Church Health

Church health or vitality is an important subject in the New Testament. For example, Christ appraises the seven churches of Asia Minor (Rev 2–3), and Paul spends the bulk of his letter to the church at Corinth evaluating their spiritual vitality (1 Cor). Some of the specific evidences of that lack of church health are detailed in 2 Corinthians 12:20 (NRSV):

> For I fear that when I come, I may find you not as I wish, and that you may find me not as you wish; I fear that there may perhaps be quarrelling, jealousy, anger, selfishness, slander, gossip, conceit, and disorder.

There are many areas of theology that bear on church health. The primary driver of individual spiritual health and therefore corporate health is a personal, dynamic relationship with Jesus. As Frost and Hirsch rightly affirm:

> But we both remain convinced that it is Christology that remains even more foundational and therefore the primary issue.

---

79. Easum, "Transformation and Reproduction Across Denominational Lines"; Comiskey, *Planting Churches That Reproduce*.

80. Werning, *12 Pillars of a Healthy Church*; Garrison, *Church Planting Movements*, 22.

We have elsewhere asserted that it is Christology (the exploration of the person, teachings, and impact of Jesus Christ) that determines our missiology (our purpose and function in the world), which in turn determines our ecclesiology (the forms and functions of the church).[81]

Recognizing the centrality of applied Christology (or discipleship) in any discussion of church health or church consultancy, a brief examination of the nature of human sin, the process of sanctification, ecclesiology, and missiology follows.[82]

2.5.1 *The Nature of Human Sin*

Human sin is a critical factor in the health or lack of health of a local church. Based on the understanding that humanity is intended to reflect the nature of God, sin represents a falling short of that standard,[83] and more:

> Sin is to be defined primarily in relation to God. It is disobedience, unbelief, ignorance, the positive assertion of usurped autonomy, and the wicked deviation from, or violation of, God's righteous will and law. The breach of a right relationship with God carries with it the disruption of a right relationship with others and the disintegration of the self.[84]

So not only does sin negatively impact a person's relationship with God and their self, it has dramatic social consequences. Self-centeredness results in competition with others (Jas 4:1–2), a diminished ability to transcend our own desires to empathize with others (Phil 2:3–5), a rejection of any authority that seeks to restrict our actions (this is especially pertinent in many conflicts involving clergy and church leaders or attenders), and a reduced ability to love as people look to our own desires rather than the best interests of others.[85]

The universality of human sin, even for those who have made a Christian commitment, is underlined by 1 Kgs 8:46, Ps 143:2, Eccl 7:20,

---

81. Frost and Hirsch, *ReJesus*, 5–6.

82. A more extensive treatment of missiology can be found in section 3.2, History and Theology of Church Growth.

83. Erickson, *Christian Theology*, 562.

84. Bromiley, "Sin," 518.

85. Erickson, *Christian Theology*, 618–9.

and Rom 3:23. This means that dealing in sound ways with sin and its relational impacts is an essential driver of church health.

2.5.2 Sanctification

Sanctification is the process of growing in holiness, in the sense of being set apart for a particular purpose, belonging to God (Hebrew שָׁדֵק) (1 Cor 1:2; 1 Pet 2:9).[86] It can also mean moral goodness in terms of how people live their lives (Eph 4:1).[87]

Fundamental to the area of church health is the level of sanctification, or lack of it, that is occurring in a local church, particularly amongst its pastoral and other leadership. Because of the progressive nature of sanctification (Phil 1:6), it is incomplete in any believer or church. While sanctification is something that God does through the Holy Spirit (Gal 5:16), Christians are exhorted to cooperate with God in that process (Phil 2:12–13).

2.5.3 Ecclesiology

Ecclesiology is a theology of the church. The Greek word ἐκκλησία refers to "a gathering or assembly of persons."[88] Ecclesiology recognizes that different emphases, or in Brown's language, "proportions," characterize how church is thought about and practiced in various denominations:

> In short, a frank study of NT ecclesiologies should convince every Christian community that it is neglecting part of the NT witness. I do not mean that all churches can or should give the same importance to each NT witness, for our respective histories have oriented us (probably irrevocably) to different proportions in our evaluation of the Scriptures.[89]

And further that this in part arises because a well-defined and developed ecclesiology is not apparent in the New Testament:

> In this book I have not dealt with different models of the church in the NT because no one of the biblical authors discussed

---

86. Erickson, *Christian Theology*, 968.
87. Erickson, *Christian Theology*, 969.
88. Erickson, *Christian Theology*, 1031.
89. Brown, *The Churches the Apostles Left Behind*, 149–50.

intended to offer an overall picture of what the church should be. Had an author wanted to present a model, we can be sure that a more complete and nuanced ecclesiology would have emerged in the respective writing.[90]

Nevertheless, some nascent ecclesiological emphases do begin to emerge as the NT writers seek to give shape to the growing and multiplying churches of the NT.[91]

Firstly, an exploration of the interplay between ecclesiology and church health will be undertaken, then a survey of Protestant and Free Church ecclesiologies carried out, and finally the interplay between ecclesiology and this model of church consultancy will be considered[92].

2.5.3.1 Ecclesiology and Church Health

Of particular relevance to church health is the tension, explored on an individual level above in 2.4.1, between the church as a "fellowship of regenerate believers" who display purity and devotion to God, and being "made up of imperfect human beings" who will not be perfected until Christ's return.[93] London and Wiseman express the current crisis starkly:

> Now dysfunctional family relationships are so common that a high percentage of individuals in every congregation carry scars from a fractured childhood. They look to the church as their most convenient help. When churches ignore these pains in persons in their fellowship, the unresolved issues pop up in strange and unexpected ways. Like an acre of dandelions, the crop gets worse when ignored.[94]

One of the significant purposes of Christian community is to be a place where people learn to love one another (Matt 22:39), and where through the love and challenge of others, broken people are brought to increasing levels of wholeness and godliness. In situations of poor health in a church, people encounter greater brokenness and a distancing in their relationships. Hart maintains that a contributing factor in poor church health is that "for the past 50 years the church has majored

---

90. Brown, *The Churches the Apostles Left Behind*, 146.
91. See 2.5.3.1 below.
92. See chapter 4 for a detailed treatment of this model of church consultancy.
93. Erickson, *Christian Theology*, 1049.
94. London and Wiseman, *Pastors at Risk*, 45.

on salvation and minored on sanctification."[95] Paul makes it clear that individual actions can do much more than harm individuals spiritually. So, because such actions threaten the health or well-being of the church (and God's reputation in the world), they must be dealt with (1 Cor 5; 6:12–20; Eph 4:17–25; 5:3–20, n.b. 7, 11; Rom 16:17–18). This is because the church is not merely a human institution but is established by God to carry out his will on earth, both in terms of being a demonstration of God's character and unity in its corporate life (Rom 12:9–13; 1 Cor 1:10; 1 Cor 12:25; 13:1–8; Eph 4:2–3, 13–16), and through carrying out God's mission in the world (Matt 28:18–20). Matthew 18:15–35 acknowledges that Christians will fall short of this ideal. Sin, taking offence, and conflict will arise between individuals, but when it does Matthew encourages a healthy process to resolve that conflict and limit its escalation within the church. Further, extending and receiving forgiveness is consistent with our status as those who have been forgiven by the King (Matt 6:15).

As shown previously, the church is a locus for either healthy or unhealthy interpersonal relationships to play out. It is especially critical that pastors, as a significant catalyst of either health or unhealth in a church (1 Cor 4; 2 Cor 6:12–13; 2 Cor 12:10–21; 1 Pet 5:1–3), recognize and deal with areas of sin, their dark side, "personal issues that may plague them in their exercise of leadership,"[96] or their family of origin dysfunctionality.[97] Some ways in which these areas can be dealt with is through their relationship with God through prayer and in their honest interactions with trusted peers and counsellors. The foregoing is also true for those within the congregation, especially those who are in leadership. 1 Timothy 3:1–12 and Titus 1:6–9 underline the significance of character and growth in godliness as requirements for leadership. Given the regularity in which churches find serious conflict erupting, it is instructive that being temperate and self-controlled is mentioned often in these passages. Such characteristics have a dampening effect on the incendiary nature of conflict, as leaders refrain from responding in a reactionary or anxious way.

One of the points at which tensions and unrealistic expectations appear to arise in churches is in the balance between clergy and lay ministry. A biblical recognition of the spiritual gifts and interdependence of

---

95. Hart, "Building a Healthy Church."
96. McIntosh and Rima, *Overcoming the Dark Side of Leadership*, 9.
97. London and Wiseman, *Pastors at Greater Risk*, 45.

church attenders (Rom 12:4–8; 1 Cor 12:4–30; 1 Pet 4:9–11) and the role of leadership to equip believers in discovering, growing, and using their gifts (Eph 4:7–12; 2 Tim 2:1–2) will contribute towards a healthy church where pastor and people are not overwhelmed, but are engaged in and enjoying mutual ministry, and impacting the surrounding community missionally.

In all the above, the importance of church leadership having a biblical ecclesiology, communicating this regularly through preaching and other means, and providing ways for people to grow in demonstrating God's character and living out God's mission individually and as a church, will be an important contribution towards church health.

2.5.3.2 Protestant and Free Church Ecclesiologies

Since this research project is focused on NSW/ACT Baptist churches, it may be helpful to explore some of the ecclesiologies that lie behind such churches. The four widely agreed on Protestant marks of the church, derived from the Nicene Creed, are expanded on by Oden:

> The ekklesia is *one* because it shares in a single body, *Corpus Christi*, the risen Lord. It is being made *holy* by participating by faith in the perfect holiness of the Son through the power of the Spirit. It is universal or *catholic* because it offers the whole counsel of God to the whole world. It is *apostolic* because it is sent into the world even as the Son was sent. These are reliable marks of the church.[98]

Snyder questions the "adequacy of the classical marks, particularly as they relate to issues of revival, renewal, and the institutional failings of the church," especially in their ambiguity and their "inadequate biblical grounding."[99] He then asserts that "if we consult the full range of Scripture, we see that the church is *both* one and diverse; *both* holy and charismatic[100]; *both* universal and local; *both* apostolic and prophetic."[101] These complementary qualities can be more or less present at various times, and the second set of qualities more closely reflects the "organic

---

98. Oden, *Life in the Spirit*, 297.
99. Snyder, "The Marks of Evangelical Ecclesiology," 83–84.
100. See also Moltmann, *The Church in the Power of the Spirit*, 294–313.
101. Snyder, "The Marks of Evangelical Ecclesiology," 87–88.

movement" of the New Testament,[102] while the first set more closely reflects the "organized institution" of the Constantinian or Christendom church.[103] Therefore Begbie makes the following observation concerning the emerging missional church movement's connection with ecclesiology:

> For here is a movement . . . challenging long-running assumptions and forms of church life and mission deemed to be inadequate to the postmodern condition—top-down professional management, centralized organizational structure, control through tight hierarchies, strong ties to places and buildings, and so forth.[104]

Begbie goes on to note five features of Wright's ecclesiology that appeal to the EMC movement: *integral* to God's saving action; *eschatological*, both in the sense of the church providing to the world a foretaste of God's coming kingdom, and in providing a vision for the church of missiological impetus and engagement with the world; *cosmically situated* as God's purposes for his creation are enacted through his redeemed community; *material* in that Christ's bodily resurrection destroys any Platonist sacred/secular division that privatizes Christianity, blocking engagement with its surrounding society; and finally *improvisatory*, as the church responds by the Spirit to diverse circumstances.[105]

Snyder proposes four categories arising from the elements and style of church services: "Anglo-Catholic, revivalist, Pentecostal-charismatic, rock concert [a combination of revivalist and charismatic exemplified by Willow Creek Community Church], or some combination of these four."[106] This is a narrow and liturgical approach to ecclesiology, especially given the current drive to find an ecclesiology that is better contextualized to a postmodern culture. However, to his credit Snyder recognizes five primary sources underlying Protestant ecclesiologies:

---

102. In some New Testament writings, the fledgling church emphasizing one of these qualities more than others can be seen, so "charismatic" in Luke/Acts (Brown, *The Churches the Apostles Left Behind*, 146) and 1 Corinthians (Chester, "The Pauline Communities," 107), and "unity" or oneness by John (Smalley, "The Johannine Community and the Letters of John," 95).

103. Snyder, "The Marks of Evangelical Ecclesiology," 88.

104. Begbie, "The Shape of Things to Come?—Wright Amongst Emerging Ecclesiologies," 185.

105. Begbie, "The Shape of Things to Come?—Wright Amongst Emerging Ecclesiologies," 186-97.

106. Snyder, "The Marks of Evangelical Ecclesiology," 77-78.

1. The Anglo-Catholic and Reformed/Lutheran-Catholic heritage
2. The Radical Reformation and Free Church tradition
3. The revivalist tradition
4. American democracy
5. American entrepreneurship.[107]

In this sense Snyder encourages us to see the formation of various evangelical ecclesiologies as both sociologically and theologically derived. Also, the church is influenced by its contemporary social context and therefore moves responsively (albeit imperfectly) between the opposite polarities of "organic movement" and "organized institution."

The ecclesiological roots of Baptist churches, in the Free Church tradition, value volunteerism, soul competency, freedom of religion and a rejection of any control or coercion of the state, and the autonomy of the local church.[108] While different writers place emphasis on various of these characteristics, even having slightly different sets of Baptist distinctives, many have seen volunteerism as the root of these. The high value placed on local and global mission is frequently revisited in this research.

Kärkkäinen characterizes Free Church ecclesiologies as the fellowship of believers, premised on unmediated access to God and salvation, volunteerism, and the priesthood of believers.[109] Following Volf,[110] Kärkkäinen maintains that "Protestant Christendom of the future will exhibit largely a Free Christian form."[111]

The priesthood of all believers in Christ is realized as Christians in Baptist churches engage in ministry within the church and mission to unbelievers outside of the church, free of any state restraint or compulsion. Miroslav Volf's masterful dialogue of Protestant Free Church ecclesiology with Catholic (Ratzinger) and Orthodox (Zizioulas) ecclesiologies argues that:

> The structure of Trinitarian relations is characterized neither by a pyramidal dominance of the one (so Ratzinger) nor by a hierarchical bipolarity between the one and the many (so Zizioulas),

107. Snyder, "The Marks of Evangelical Ecclesiology," 93–96.

108. Churches, as autonomous entities, are responsible for their own life, growth, and health.

109. Kärkkäinen, *Introduction to Ecclesiology*, 62–67.

110. Volf, *After Our Likeness*, 13.

111. Kärkkäinen, *Introduction to Ecclesiology*, 59.

but rather by a polycentric and symmetrical reciprocity of the many.[112]

As well as the clear implications for the place of clergy in Protestant Free Church ecclesiology, a significant marker for church health and growth arises out of the practice of this understanding of Trinitarian relationships:

> The symmetrical reciprocity of the relations of the Trinitarian persons finds its correspondence in the image of the church in which all members serve one another with their specific gifts of the Spirit in imitation of the Lord and through the power of the Father. Like the divine persons, they all stand in a relation of mutual giving and receiving.[113]

While it may be difficult to identify a particular distinctive of Protestant Free Churches that supersedes all other traits, this mutual serving of one another reflecting the relationship between the members of the Trinity is at the forefront for Volf. While the foregoing Protestant Free Church distinctives may be shared, to a greater or lesser extent, across other denominations and traditions, the Baptist recognition of the competency of believers to minister within, and do mission outside, the church, rescues its ecclesiology from a sterile clericalism or captivity to ruling elders, and has the potential to unleash massive reserves of ministry in churches (so chapter 2 church health), along with a great missional advance (so chapter 3 church growth), and to take responsibility for the life of their church as they carry out recommendations from a church consultant (so chapter 4 church consultancy). Achieving this potential, enabling new vitality and growth in churches, and calling churches to the biblical mandate for their life and mission is a primary objective of church consultancy.

2.5.3.3 Ecclesiology and Church Consultancy

The practice of church consultancy within various ecclesiologies will be briefly explored. This model of church consultancy, detailed in chapter 4, is used in a wide variety of denominations and, at least theoretically, this model is meta-ecclesiological. In practice, this either necessitates

---

112. Volf, *After Our Likeness*, 217.
113. Volf, *After Our Likeness*, 219.

consultants being able to set aside their own ecclesiology, or, more commonly, consultancy teams that work exclusively within their own denominational setting. Even so, denominations reflect a variety of eccesiologies, and this is true in NSW/ACT Baptist churches. Consultancies in NSW/ACT Baptist churches have included a wide variety of church styles and resulting church practices, including a variety of EMCs, charismatic expressions of church, and those tending towards Sydney Anglican and independent Baptist expressions. While these nuances are present, many of the core elements of a Protestant Free Church ecclesiology are intact.

Snyder's liturgical-ecclesiological typologies are clearly seen and present in a variety of Baptist settings. That is, revivalist, Pentecostal-charismatic, and rock concert, with Anglo-Catholic rare in Baptist churches. This is important when it comes to this research, because while it is carried out in a Baptist denomination, this provides some indication of church consultancy's applicability in other denominations. There are presently church consultancy teams in many denominations and states who are actively using this model. NCLS has been used and refined in a number of denominations and ecclesiological settings so that its vitality indicators are relevant in such settings. NCLS will be explored further at 2.6.1 and elsewhere in this research.

2.5.4 Missiology

God is a missionary God (Ps 86:9–10). This mission is shared by each person of the Trinity, as the Son underwent incarnation (John 1:1–18) and death on a cross (Matt 27), and as the Spirit worked in the lives of individuals and the church to empower (Acts 1:7–8), gift (1 Cor 12:4–11), enable testifying (John 15:26–27; 1 Cor 12:3), convict (John 16:8), witness in its caring and love through its corporate life (Acts 2:42–47; 4:32–37), and guide in mission (Acts 8:29, 39–40; 10–11; 13:1–5; 16:6–10). God calls his people, firstly Israel (Gen 18:18–19; Mic 4:1–4), then the church to declare his glory amongst all the nations and call people to repentance and allegiance to him (Matt 28:16–20; Mark 16:14–18; Luke 24:44–49; John 20:19–23; Acts 1:4–8; 1 Pet 2:9; Rev 7:9).

Churches will enjoy health and the favor of God as they deal graciously and effectively with human sin, individually and corporately, as they pursue sanctification and increasing godliness, as they strive for church life that reflects a biblical pattern in love, unity, and mutual ministry, and as they participate in God's mission in the world.

2.6 Measurement of Church Health

Measurement of church health, vitality, or quality characteristics can be valuable for a local church in early intervention of problems, and for tracking progress over time.

Some correlation by church health authors emerges around a number of core qualities of church health or vitality. These core qualities of church health can, to some extent, be measured (these core qualities and their measurement will be expanded on below). From this measurement of quality or vitality characteristics an attempt can be made at the local church level to address deficiencies in church health and foster greater strength in areas of sound health.

There are two tools particularly worth noting that seek to coalesce or distill these quality characteristics from the suggestions made by authors above. These instruments seek to measure church health or vitality in local churches across a number of countries and produce apparatuses that can be used by local churches to assess and improve their health. They are NCLS/International Congregational Life Survey and Natural Church Development (NCD).

2.6.1 National Church Life Survey/International Congregational Life Survey

The NCLS Team have isolated the following nine core qualities of healthy and vital churches: an alive and growing *faith*, vital and nurturing *worship*, strong and growing *belonging*, a clear and owned *vision*, inspiring and empowering *leadership*, open and flexible *innovation*, practical and diverse *service*, willing and effective *faith-sharing*, and intentional and welcoming *inclusion*.[114] Additionally, NCLS has identified three quanti-

---

114. Each core quality score is derived from one NCLS-2006 question (see www.ianduncum.com.au for the survey form)—the percentage of people who answered one particular option for one particular question (except for core quality 7) as follows:
    CQ1 An alive and growing faith—percentage who answered option c to q. 17.
    CQ2 Vital and nurturing worship—percentage who answered option a to q. 23.
    CQ3 Strong and growing belonging—percentage who answered option a to q. 5.
    CQ4 Clear and owned vision—percentage who answered option c to q. 48.

tative measures of the missional impact of churches: *young adult retention*—the proportion of the children of attenders still attending a church; *newcomers*—the percentage of newcomers at a church; and *attendance change*—patterns of growth or decline in the number of people attending a church over time.[115]

NCLS reports on these indicators, which reveal a congregation's strengths, weaknesses, and numerical change relative to previous surveys. These are also compared with other congregations in their denomination, and to all churches. Additionally, demographic data regarding a congregation's attenders is compared with the demographics of the surrounding community (from Australian Bureau of Statistics census data) to aid effective connection with, and outreach to, the local community.

This instrument has been based on research replicated and finessed in twenty-two denominations and over fifteen years in Australia (through four church surveys in 1991, 1996, 2001, and 2006), and subsequently expanded to include four countries with the International Congregational Life Survey. This survey is unique in its breadth and its depth; "No similar body of published work existed to describe worshipers and congregations in New Zealand, England or the United States [or Australia before the NCLS]."[116] In its breadth: more than 1.2 million worshippers in over 12,000 congregations in four countries participated in the International Congregational Life Survey (ICLS). The ICLS was an expansion and revision of the previous surveys conducted in Australia.[117] And in its depth:

> The NCLS methodology effectively overcame one of the primary shortcomings of many other large congregational surveys, the reliance on input from just one person in each congregation. The traditional key-informant approach has both validity and

---

CQ5 Inspiring and empowering leadership—percentage who answered option a to q. 47.

CQ6 Imaginative and flexible innovation—percentage who answered option a to q. 51.

CQ7 Practical and diverse service—average of the number of options answered by attenders to q. 37.

CQ8 Willing and effective faith-sharing—percentage who answered option a to q. 40.

CQ9 Intentional and welcoming inclusion—percentage who answered option a to q. 42.

115. Bellamy et al., *Enriching Church Life*, 10–29.

116. Bruce et al., "An International Survey of Congregations and Worshipers," 4.

117. Bruce et al., "An International Survey of Congregations and Worshipers," 4.

reliability limitations. Chief among these are the bias introduced (1) when one person is asked to speak for a group with varied beliefs, opinions and experiences, and (2) when one individual is asked to provide information about organizational goals or values that might not be clear to all members. Including all worshipers in the survey provides a more accurate view of the variety and complexity of congregational life.[118]

By way of comparison, Natural Church Development (NCD) surveyed a small group of thirty in each of one thousand congregations.[119]

2.6.2 *Natural Church Development*

Christian Schwarz's Natural Church Development survey across five continents isolated the following eight quality characteristics: empowering leadership, gift-oriented ministry, passionate spirituality, functional structures, inspiring worship, holistic small groups, need-oriented evangelism, and loving relationships.[120] Schwarz's research has been met with acclaim and critique.

Philip Hughes values Schwarz's emphasis on qualitative growth as a pathway to quantitative growth, the ease of use of his material, and affirms that " . . . most churches will find that reflection on [the characteristics that Schwarz suggests] will be helpful and stimulating."[121]

Much of the criticism against Natural Church Development has been methodological. Yeakley and Ellas expressed that Schwarz's writings were "fatally flawed, pseudo-scientific, and that he did not follow scientific methods."[122] Similarly, Astley in his review asserts that Natural Church Development " . . . does not contain the technical report that could allow a judgement to be made of the validity and reliability of the research instrument used, and of the statistical analysis employed. In the absence of this information it is impossible to assess the scientific status of the hypotheses presented here."[123] George Hunter III's critique is that "Natural Church Development does not provide enough data . . .

---

118. Bruce et al., "An International Survey of Congregations and Worshipers," 4.
119. Hughes, "Natural Church Development—The Schwarz Method," 1.
120. Schwarz, *Natural Church Development*, 79.
121. Hughes, "Natural Church Development—The Schwarz Method," 1.
122. Yeakley and Ellas, "Natural Church Development," 83.
123. Astley, "Reviews the Book 'Natural Church Development,'" 260.

to understand the basis of the conclusions. Schwarz does not report the (statistical) significance level of his conclusions; without the significance level, empiricists tell us, no statistical study should be relied upon."[124] Significant methodological concerns are raised by Bill Tenny-Brittian:

1. There is no statistical or experimental data to back up NCD's claim that focusing on the "minimum factor" is the most effective way to improve the health or ministry of the church. This is speculation.
2. The statistical analysis of the data provided by NCD to show the validity and reliability of their process does just the opposite.
3. NCD does not measure conversion growth nor does it play any role in the NCD survey.[125]

Other criticisms coalesce around the conclusions that Schwarz draws, and their basis. The provision of sufficient information to allow others to replicate Schwarz's research is a concern expressed by René Erwich[126] and Hunter.[127] Hunter also argues against the "health causes growth" relationship asserted by Natural Church Development; that it "only presents correlations [between health and growth] which are alleged, but not sufficiently demonstrated."[128] Hughes[129] and Erwich also question the reliance on only internal data: "Since the goal is to measure the quality of the life of the church, the question is whether this can be achieved by sole analysis of the insider perspective. This is even more endangered by the fact that only 30 members and a pastor receive a questionnaire . . . Is there an outsider perspective?"[130] While NCLS and the Christian Research Association have surveyed (Australian Community Survey) a large sample of the general Australian population to determine

---

124. Hunter, "Examining the 'Natural Church Development' Project."

125. Tenny-Brittian, *The Complete Ministry Audit vs. Natural Church Development*, 1.

126. Erwich, "Missional Churches: Identical Global 'Plants' or Locally Grown 'Flowers?,'" 184.

127. Hunter, "Examining the 'Natural Church Development' Project," 11.

128. Hunter, "Examining the 'Natural Church Development' Project," 11.

129. Hughes, "Natural Church Development—The Schwarz Method," 1.

130. Erwich, "Missional Churches: Identical Global 'Plants' or Locally Grown 'Flowers?,'" 185.

this outsider perspective and the attitudes toward church of those who do not attend, no similar survey has been completed for NCD.[131]

A third critique revolves around contextual factors.[132] Hughes maintains that Schwarz "ignores the differences between ministry in urban and rural contexts, or in socio-economically poor or wealthy city suburbs."[133] However, when it comes to differences between countries, Hughes notes that "Schwarz' research in Australia is extremely limited... Research such as that provided by the NCLS can be more specific about the characteristics that are important in the Australian context,"[134] and Bill Tenny-Brittian raises his concern:

> The "adjustments" to the scoring of the data that are made in order to reflect the cultural differences between countries is something of a mystery as NCD will neither release the specific formulae nor even a clear picture of what factors are used to make these adjustments. NCD was normed on churches in Germany and there is no information provided that would clearly suggest that those norms are valid for churches as a whole... [135]

A fourth area of criticism is the lack of theological basis for Schwarz's research and missiological derivations. Exclusion of community service and poverty alleviation from the measures of church health[136] and "no priority concern for justice, or peace, or reconciliation between peoples, or for the health of the planet"[137] bring a disjuncture between Schwarz's picture of church health and the church's biblical mandate.

And lastly critique has been leveled from the practical value to local churches. Hughes concludes that: "Schwarz's approach is sometimes too general [for churches] to know how to remedy their weaknesses or build on their strengths,"[138] and Easum, drawing on his wide experience as a church consultant across many US denominations, deduces that NCD

---

131. Hughes et al., *Exploring What Australians Value*.

132. Erwich, "Missional Churches: Identical Global 'Plants' or Locally Grown 'Flowers?,'" 186.

133. Hughes, "Natural Church Development—The Schwarz Method," 1.

134. Hughes, "Natural Church Development—The Schwarz Method," 1.

135. Tenny-Brittian, *The Complete Ministry Audit vs. Natural Church Development*, 1.

136. Erwich, "Missional Churches: Identical Global 'Plants' or Locally Grown 'Flowers?,'" 187.

137. Hunter, "Examining the 'Natural Church Development' Project," 16.

138. Hughes, "Natural Church Development—The Schwarz Method," 1.

"mostly helps healthy, growing churches," criticizes the lack of depth in the training of NCD consultants, and concludes that most of the churches that have an NCD consultation don't grow.[139]

NCD is commendable in that it seeks to distill these quality characteristics from those suggested by many authors above. In addition, it has undertaken significant research and measurement of church vitality in local churches across a number of countries, and has produced tools that may be used by local churches to assess and improve their health. Of particular note is the distinction that Schwarz makes in his research between growth and quality: while generally a strong relationship exists between them, such is not always the case (i.e. a church can be growing but low in its quality index).[140] However, the significant concerns that have been raised regarding methodology (especially the small sample taken within each church, which is numerically constant/decreasing in proportion as church size increases), conclusions, data transparency and replicability, contextual factors, theology/missiology, and the questions raised about the practical value to local churches, detract from the contribution that NCD brings to church health generally, and to individual local churches that may have benefitted from using this tool.

2.7 The Emerging Missional Church as a Response to Postmodernity/Cultural Shifts

There is a significant body of work that is based on the premise that "tinkering with congregational life is of minor importance because the future of the congregation is largely determined by the context in which it finds itself."[141] This context can include demographics of the local community, national trends, or wider cultural trends such as the emergence of "postmodernity."

In terms of the emergence of "postmodernity," Middleton and Walsh comment on the modern worldview: "We are in a world of natural resources that can be known objectively by means of the scientific method and controlled by technological power . . . According to the modern worldview we know what reality is, and we know how to investigate,

---

139. Easum, "Transformation and Reproduction Across Denominational Lines," 8.
140. Schwarz, *Natural Church Development*, 20–21.
141. Kaldor et al., *Shaping a Future*, 13.

understand and control it."[142] In a world torn by such things as war, violence, poverty, the global food crisis, and the global financial crisis, the failure of modernity's promise: to usher in a better world on the back of human autonomy, science, technology, and economic growth, is obvious.

The search for a worldview which may both more effectively explain our world, and provide a more realistic way forward, has given rise to the emergence of postmodernity. However, a variety of definitional nuances have been profered in the stream, and the emergence of postmodernity is not to universal acclaim or agreement, with authors such as Rosenau[143] and Spiro[144] arguing that postmodern proponents such as Derrida[145] and Rorty[146] evidence internal inconsistencies in their arguments and do not provide a hopeful alternate way forward in their critiques of modernity.

The postmodern era is "an era after a modern one" and postmodernism is therefore "a theory that involves a radical reappraisal of modern assumptions about culture, identity, history, or language."[147] Postmodernism is described as "a worldview characterized by the belief that truth doesn't exist in any objective sense,"[148] rather than truth being absolute, it is "relative to the community in which we participate."[149]

The modernist approach has also been used in approaching church life and mission, and is perhaps best typified by the Church Growth Movement: our scientific research indicates that if "x" is done, "y" growth will be achieved. So, just as many in Western culture are zealously re-evaluating modernist foundations, so also in the church many assumptions of modernity, along with their corresponding practices, are being questioned. One result of this is that the church, rather than being at the center of society, is now on its fringe:

> Much of western culture is experiencing a culture shift—from Christendom to post-Christendom. This is obvious in Europe and Australasia and increasingly apparent in many parts of

142. Walsh and Middleton, *Truth Is Stranger than It Used to Be*, 19–20.
143. Rosenau, *Post Modernism and the Social Sciences*.
144. Spiro, "Postmodernist Anthropology, Subjectivity, and Science," 759–80.
145. Derrida, *The Gift of Death; and, Literature in Secret*; Derrida, *Jacques Derrida: Basic Writings*.
146. Rorty, *Objectivity, Relativism, and Truth*; Rorty, *Truth, Politics and "Post-Modernism."*
147. Merriam-Webster Online Dictionary, "Postmodern."
148. McDowell and Hostetler, *The New Tolerance*, 208.
149. Grenz, *A Primer on Postmodernism*, 8.

North America. After centuries of cultural dominance, the churches are now back on the social margins where they were in the early centuries. Our story, language and practices are becoming unfamiliar."[150]

So, in this culture of a multiplicity of worldviews and no overarching metanarrative, how does the church communicate the biblical narrative in a way that connects with people? This is the question that is raised by emerging church proponents, particularly "reconstructionist" authors, dissatisfied with current forms of church and proposing more informal, incarnational, and organic church forms.[151] They assert that the strength of postmodernity's sociocultural impact is so great that it must irrevocably change the way that Christians do church and mission. Consequently, Frost and Hirsch maintain that the problem lies in our theology, and particularly our ecclesiology, that drives our praxis. That is, instead of churches being attractional, dualistic, and hierarchical, they need to be missional, messianic, and apostolic.[152]

It is important to underline that there are a number of diverse streams that comprise the emerging church movement.[153] Some pastors of these churches, such as Jonny Baker, are comfortable with the term "emerging church" in articulating a desire for church that is relevant to the emerging culture.[154] Others such as Ben Edson see the term as somehow implying that such churches are not quite a church yet, rather than pointing to a discontinuity with what has gone before.[155] Gibbs outlines some of the attempts to define particular aspects of emerging churches,[156] with one example being Mark Scandrette:

> The emerging church is a quest for a more integrated and whole life of faith. There is a bit of theological questioning going on, focusing more on kingdom theology, the inner life, friendship/ community, justice, earth keeping, inclusivity, and inspirational leadership. In addition, the arts are in a renaissance, as are the

---

150. Murray, *Post-Christendom*, 3.
151. Driscoll, "A Pastoral Perspective on the Emergent Church," 89–90.
152. Frost and Hirsch, *The Shaping of Things to Come*.
153. Gibbs, *ChurchMorph*, 58–62.
154. Gibbs and Bolger, *Emerging Churches*, 41.
155. Gibbs and Bolger, *Emerging Churches*, 41–42.
156. Gibbs, *ChurchMorph*, 57–62.

classical spiritual disciplines. Overall, it is a quest for a wholistic spirituality.[157]

Since Gibbs lists mission engagement as the key criterion, many have used the term "emerging missional churches" (EMC) to describe this movement.[158] The key implication of the culture shift towards postmodernity is that how Christians do church must change paradigmatically. Different parts of the EMC movement see that change in different ways, with some examples as follows.

Woods outlines seven congregational megatrends or shifts; from mass evangelism to relational evangelism, from tribal education to immigrant education, from surrogate missions to hands-on missions, from reasonable spirituality to mysterious spirituality, from official leadership to gifted leadership, from segmented programming to holographic programming, and from secondary planning to primary planning.[159] Similarly, Brian McLaren asserts that "Opposing postmodernism is as futile as opposing the English language. It's here. It's reality. It's the future,"[160] and he outlines thirteen strategies for a "reinvented church":[161] maximize discontinuity, redefine your mission, practice systems thinking, trade up your traditions for tradition, resurrect theology as art and science, design a new apologetic, learn a new rhetoric, abandon structures as they are outgrown, save the leaders, subsume missions in mission, look ahead—farther ahead, enter the postmodern world—understand and engage it, and add to this list.[162] While some see EMCs as focused on how Christians do church, Frost looks beyond that context to living missionally in a post-Christian culture through authenticity, serving a cause greater than ourselves, creating missional community, generosity, hospitality, working righteously, confronting injustice and oppression, and caring for creation.[163] Accordingly, the key issue for many of these authors and practitioners is not doing church in a different or more biblical way than other churches, but about connecting with our changing culture in relevant ways, so that Christians may engage with it missionally.

157. Gibbs and Bolger, *Emerging Churches*, 41–42.
158. Gibbs, *ChurchMorph*, 62.
159. Woods, *Congregational Megatrends*.
160. McLaren, *Reinventing Your Church*, 69.
161. McLaren, *Reinventing Your Church*, 21.
162. McLaren, *Reinventing Your Church*.
163. Frost, *Exiles*, 81–274.

It is outside the scope of this study to present an exhaustive analysis of EMCs. The question in the context of this research is whether congregational vitality is more strongly related to factors internal to a church, or whether external factors such as local demographic, denominational, national, or cultural trends exert the stronger influence. That is, whether cultural shifts such as postmodernity must radically transform how churches and individuals interact with the surrounding culture in order to remain relevant and missionally effective. The corollary question is whether EMCs will exist alongside other churches, or whether EMCs will come to the fore over time as the only expression of church that is engaging in an appropriate way with the culture. If the latter is true, the implication for church consultancy may be that it is irrelevant to seek to bring health to existing churches when a new way of doing church and the Christian life is needed.

However it appears that, "Generation X is turning away from the Church at an alarming rate . . . [and] the emergence of these [EMC] movements has not at this point made a sufficiently large impact to arrest the decline in Church attendance."[164] While care should be taken with self-reported attendance figures, research in the US revealed that 3 percent of the adult population had attended a meeting of a house church but had not attended a conventional church during the past month, and a further 3 percent had "attended both a conventional church and a house church during the past month."[165]

While EMCs are part of the Australian church landscape, it is difficult to make a definitive call on their contribution or "success." Firstly, because the vast majority, especially in the Australian context, are smaller[166] and they have eschewed buying into the church growth agenda so popular amongst evangelical modernist churches: "The focus of emerging churches is on incarnating the gospel, not numerical or economic success."[167] Secondly, because of their organic nature, attendance and survey results may be harder to track. For example, "The other two churches did not complete NCLS; the postmodern leadership at Solace did not want to measure themselves in traditional Sunday-service-focused ways,

---

164. Gibbs, "The Emerging Church," 1.
165. Barna, *New Statistics on Church Attendance and Avoidance*.
166. Powell, *NOVUS: Innovations in Australian Church Life*, 5–36.
167. Gibbs and Bolger, *Emerging Churches*, 94.

and the young adult leadership at Eastern Hills did not get around to it."[168] And lastly, because there is, at least from some quarters, a questioning of the postmodern premise on which the EMC movement is founded. This arises in three ways. One way this questioning arises is whether "the postmodern moment has passed"[169] or even whether it was real; "for people like Terry Eagleton and Christopher Norris, postmodernism is certainly finished, even passé; indeed, for them it's a failure, an illusion":[170]

> The strongest announcements of the end of postmodernism have come from within the universities, where the end of postmodernism has been a topic of discussion since the late nineteen eighties. One irony is that these announcements of the end of postmodernism have come from within the field of theory, and that the end of postmodernism is defined as a speculative theoretical project (a situation which tends to add to the impression that postmodernism has been an invention of the age of academic theory)."[171]

While this is a minor voice, it is not insignificant, and both within and outside of mainstream evangelicalism there are those that have not announced the death of modernity with such fervor. The second way this questioning arises is through the attribution of other cultural forces, apart from or in addition to postmodernity, to the shifting context for the Western church:

> The cultural shifting we speak of relates not so much to the overhyped rise of postmodernism alone but rather to the emergence of various large scale cultural forces in the twenty-first century: globalization, climate change, technological breakthroughs, international terrorism, geopolitical shifts, economic crises, the digitalization of information, social networks, the rise of bottom-up people-movements, the rise of new religious movements, even the New Atheism, and others. These all conspire together to further accelerate the marginalization of the church as we know it, forcing us to rethink our previously privileged relationship to the broader culture around us.[172]

168. Cronshaw, "Fresh Forms of Church for Today," 16.

169. Hutcheon, "Postmodern Afterthoughts," 11; Rudaityte, *Postmodernism and After: Visions and Revisions*; Stierstorfer, *Beyond Postmodernism*; Adam and Allan, *Theorizing Culture*; Simons and Billig, *After Postmodernism*.

170. Hutcheon, "Postmodern Afterthoughts," 5.

171. Kruse, "After Postmodernism."

172. Hirsch and Ferguson, *On the Verge*, 26.

The third way this questioning arises is from the recognition that throughout the church's history there have *always* been those calling the church back to greater purity, relevance, and effectiveness. Some examples are Luther, Calvin, and Zwingli in the Magisterial Reformation, with the English Dissenters and the Radical Reformation building on those foundations. From the 1800s, the "Christian Radicalism" or "Radical Discipleship" movement has sought to take transformation of self and subversion of the social order further, and this diverse movement has been given voice by those such as Søren Kierkegaard, Dietrich Bonhoeffer, Gustavo Gutiérrez, Jacques Ellul, Ched Myers, and Shane Claiborne.[173]

While applied Christology (i.e. discipleship) and missiology have been at the forefront of this disparate movement, this has often taken shape in a more "organic" and less "institutional" ecclesiology. In other words, the "this time it is different" proponents of the postmodern moment are merely prophets in the stream of all who have gone before them, calling the church to be the faithful bride of Christ.

The central place in society the church once held in the Christendom or modernist paradigm has been eroded by increasing secularization and a multiplication of other worldviews, with the result that many churches have increasingly struggled to be effective in outreach and church planting. The question is whether this will ultimately result in a variety of churches existing in parallel, or whether EMCs will gradually become the normal expression of church because they are aware of and operating effectively within this postmodern shift. Only time will tell, but we can assert that context broadly, whether local, national, or wider cultural, does have a significant, but not central, impact on a church's vitality.

2.8 Conclusion

Church health or vitality is an important subject in the New Testament. For example, Christ evaluates the seven churches of Asia Minor (Rev 2–3), and Paul spends the bulk of his first letter to the church at Corinth appraising their vitality. While there are also many biblical passages such as Eph 5:25–30 and Rev 19:7 that convey a lofty view of the church, the apostles were often dealing with the other polarity in their dealings with

---

173. Kierkegaard, "Training in Christianity"; Kierkegaard, "Attack Upon Christendom"; Bonhoeffer, *The Cost of Discipleship*; Gutiérrez, *A Theology of Liberation*; Ellul, *The Subversion of Christianity*; Myers, *Binding the Strong Man*; Claiborne, *The Irresistible Revolution*.

churches; areas of theology that bear on church health include the nature of human sin and how that impacts relationships, the process of sanctification, an understanding of the nature and purposes of the church (ecclesiology), and the mission of the church (missiology). Nevertheless, as the foregoing discussion in this chapter shows, it is extraordinarily difficult to effectively define and capture the essence of church health. There are many complex and interrelated variables that contribute to that health. This is compounded by the variety of foci of church health. Should church health be seen as in systems theory: broadly speaking, the healthy functioning of an organism or system? There are churches which have the spiritual equivalent of a blocked artery, and no amount of new programs or revisioning is going to move the church from being terminal without addressing the root causes of disease. Whether it is a church-wide trauma that needs to be worked through, dealing openly and gently with conflict, heightened anxiety in a church, or tacit roles of various people within a church (e.g. a patriarch who gives or withholds permission for every decision taken), a systems perspective brings strength in uncovering and working through these and similar subsurface health issues that may be frustrating a church in achieving its goals. Therefore, a more comprehensive picture of church health is gained through adding the aspects that seek to measure that health through instruments, and define the purposes of the church, particularly in the area of mission (i.e. health is not just about an organism or church, but implies reproduction and an outward focus).

A sense of convergence by a number of authors around the purposes of the church has led to the emergence of some core qualities of church health or vitality. These core qualities of church health or vitality can, to some extent, be measured, and this has led to the emergence of two church health instruments that are based on significant research in churches across a number of countries. These instruments are NCD, which incorporates eight indicators of church vitality, and NCLS/ICLS which incorporates twelve indicators. Various concerns, primarily methodological, expressed by a number of authors above regarding NCD suggests that NCLS is the preferred measure of church vitality.

The theology of church health, outlined in this chapter, and which informs the evaluations, conclusions, and recommendations of this thesis can be summarized in the following assertions:

A theology of systems theory in that the biblical understanding of the interdependence of persons means that issues in a church are often system wide and frequently below the surface and must be addressed as such. The positive aspect of a theology of systems theory means that a healthy church will facilitate an environment for individual attenders' spiritual growth and wholeness. Systems theory must therefore inform and shape our theology of church health, as well as our practice of health intervention.

A theology of ecclesiological purpose in that balance across the five biblical purposes of a church (worship, fellowship, discipleship, ministry, and mission) is key.[174] This is discussed particularly in the literature regarding faithfulness to the purposes of the church. A focus on the biblical purposes of the church, and balance across them, is foundational for church health. It is at this juncture that many churches lose their way, with for example, an overfocus on fellowship at the expense of local mission. Yoder helpfully comments that "Peoplehood and mission, fellowship and witness, are not two desiderata, each capable of existing or of being missed independently of one another; each is the condition of the genuineness of the other."[175] Therefore the reverse is also true: growth at any price, church growth without attending to discipleship, worship, church health, and sustainability, does not adequately reflect the theology of ecclesiological purpose outlined in the Bible, expanded on by church health literature, and developed in this research.

A theology of sin and sanctification, in that sin disrupts not only a Christian's relationship with God and their sense of self but also impacts their interpersonal relationships, and therefore the health of the church they attend. Whether this is outworked in such examples as a broken or strained relationship, a desire for power in leadership, a battle over a church's vision and direction, or competition between various ministries for scarce people or financial resources, sin negatively impacts church health. This is not to say that every aspect of unhealth in churches is the result of sin, but it can be a significant factor. Furthermore, sin can become entrenched in a particular church as it is overlooked (e.g. bullying by leaders, lack of compassion for the poor in the local community) and forms a pattern for the church and the discipleship of those who join the church. Therefore, sanctification, the process of becoming like Christ, begins to break down individual or communal patterns of relating and acting that do not foster church health and replaces them with patterns

---

174. Warren, *The Purpose Driven Church*, 103–7.
175. Yoder, "A People in the World," 66–101.

that promote Christlikeness and restoration in every dimension. Furthermore, sanctification includes the concept of being set apart for God's purposes, and so contains within it the seeds for ministry and mission to others that reflect church health. That is, sanctification results in local church attenders' discipling others, so that they increasingly embrace the way of Christ, and also results in mission to those in the surrounding community.

A theology of the church, particularly an ecclesiology that reflects the Free Church tradition. In this sense, the emphasis in Baptist churches on a fellowship of regenerate believers is counterpoised with churches being comprised of imperfect sinners, and this is a locus on which issues of church health often turn. As has been discussed, the Baptist understanding of the "priesthood of believers" calls forth a picture of mutual ministry to one another reflective of the Trinity[176] and of impactful mission on behalf of God to mankind as significant markers of the health of a church. The sense that a church is autonomous in Free Church ecclesiology means that the object of any consultancy or health intervention is a process to *build the capacity* of the church and its leaders for its own health and growth, rather than providing a fix or encouraging any dependence on consultants or denomination. The central place in Free Church ecclesiology of the Bible means that a strong component of health includes calling churches to the biblical mandate for their life and mission.

A theology of the church's mission, at its ultimate, is the proclamation that Jesus is Lord over all of life and the world. This mission includes the church as God's instrument, but also transcends the church, because it is rooted in the nature of God.[177] There are many aspects to that mission, and it cannot be captured by mere slogan-words such as "words" and "deeds." A missional vision of church health includes Christians sharing their faith with others, speaking up for justice, ministering to the poor, and much more that is consistent with the inbreaking of God's "now-and-not-yet" kingdom. Here is an intersection with Free Church ecclesiology, as the lordship of Christ, which is fundamental for Baptist Christians, is firstly lived out in the public square, then secondly calls for individuals and institutions to also live under Christ's lordship.

A theology of church and culture firstly recognizes that the ecclesiological response to culture at various times in church history may

---

176. Volf, *After Our Likeness*, 217.
177. Frost and Hirsch, *The Shaping of Things to Come*, 18.

move between the polarities of "organic movement" and "organized institution."[178] However, church health is metacultural; a response to culture only on the level of ecclesiology is not sufficient, nor does it recognize the importance of internal drivers of a church's health. For example, EMCs can still have undealt with interpersonal conflict. Secondly, it affirms the strong relationship of a church's health or vitality to its internal factors, rather than those external to a church. That is, while local demographic, denominational, national, or cultural trends such as increasing secularism or postmodernity may influence a church's health, they are not determinative of a church's health. NCLS highlights the importance of internal health factors for local churches when it found that "While context can have a significant impact, it is not determinative of the likely fortunes of a church."[179] These issues are explored in more detail in the subsequent chapter, *Church Growth*.

There are many spheres and theologies that intersect with church health, which have been discussed at length in the body of this chapter and outlined above. In particular, for church health to converse with church growth and church consultancy has in some cases affirmed, in others critiqued, and in still others nuanced our understanding of church health. This has in turn integrated and made more explicit the overarching theology presented in this thesis.

These theologies sketched above will shape a response by a church, and the consultants working with that church, to issues of unhealth, or opportunities for greater health and vitality, where God's way forward is discerned together and then lived out. A church's shared understanding of their biblical purposes, and their understanding and practice regarding sin, sanctification, ecclesiology, and missiology will be crucial drivers of health or unhealth. Health will be fostered as the biblical purposes of a church are lived out in a balanced way by the congregation and regularly measured, as conflict is dealt with openly by individuals and the church, as meaningful connections are made with people in the church's local area, and as a willingness to address areas of blockage in the systemic life of the church is exhibited.

---

178. Stackhouse, "The Marks of Evangelical Ecclesiology," 87–88.
179. Kaldor et al., *Shaping a Future*, 199.

3

Church Growth

3.1 Definition

"Church growth is that discipline which investigates the nature, expansion, planting, multiplication, function, and health of Christian churches as they relate to the effective implementation of God's commission to 'make disciples of all peoples' (Matt 28:18–20)."[1] It includes a process of spiritual reproduction whereby leaders are trained, sent out (Acts 9:31; 13:1–3; 14:21–23) and new congregations are formed and planted (1 Thess 1:8).

Church growth seeks to integrate the principles of God's word concerning the growth of the church with the insights of contemporary social and behavioral sciences. Specifically, foundational principles of church growth include: "people movements, pragmatic research, scientific research, social networks, receptivity, priority of evangelism, and the central purpose of disciplemaking."[2]

3.2 History and Theology of Church Growth

The roots of the Church Growth Movement were formed through the missionary experience, field research, and reflection of J. Waskom Pickett[3] and Donald McGavran, especially through his classic work *Bridges*

---

1. Wagner, *Strategies for Church Growth*, 114.
2. McIntosh, *Evaluating the Church Growth Movement*, 27.
3. Pickett, *Christian Mass Movements in India*; Pickett et al., *Christian Missions*

of God.⁴ Working with castes in India, McGavran observed the spread of the gospel through, but not across, castes, with people remaining in their castes after conversion. McGavran further honed his ideas through field research in other parts of the world such as the Philippines, Jamaica, and Mexico.⁵

McGavran became more convinced that while his and other missionaries' involvement in health, relief, and education were good, that the essential task of mission was "discipling the peoples of earth" with the result that churches should grow.⁶

Returning to the United States from serving as a missionary, McGavran established the Institute of Church Growth in Eugene, Oregon, in 1961, where missionaries studied while on furlough. Fuller Theological Seminary invited McGavran to establish the School of World Mission in 1965.⁷

McGavran identified four questions that drove his research overseas and in the US as follows: 1) What are the causes of church growth? 2) What are the barriers to church growth? 3) What are the factors that can make the Christian faith a movement among some populations? 4) What principles of church growth are reproducible?⁸ From these questions, in addition to reflection on the power of group influence in eliciting a people movement towards faith in Christ, and observations that faith spread fastest where people had some commonality such as caste ("men like to become Christians without crossing racial, linguistic, or class barriers"⁹), the Homogenous Unit Principle was birthed¹⁰ and developed.¹¹ Nevertheless, McGavran clearly states that "The homogenous unit principle is

---

in *Mid India*; Pickett, *Christ's Way to India's Heart*; Pickett, *Present Day Mass Movements to Christianity*; Pickett et al., *Church Growth and Group Conversion*; Pickett, *The Dynamics of Church Growth*.

4. McGavran, *The Bridges of God*; McGavran, *Church Growth in West Utkal*; McGavran, *How Churches Grow*.

5. McGavran, *Multiplying Churches in the Philippines*; McGavran, *Church Growth and Mission in Jamaica (1958)*; McGavran et al., *Church Growth in Mexico*.

6. McGavran, "Wrong Strategy: The Real Crisis in Missions"; McGavran, "My Pilgrimage in Mission," 54.

7. McGavran, "My Pilgrimage in Mission," 54.

8. Hunter, "The Legacy of Donald A. McGavran," 158.

9. McGavran, *Understanding Church Growth*, 223.

10. Pickett et al., *Christian Missions in Mid India*.

11. McGavran, *The Bridges of God*.

certainly not the heart of church growth."[12] Gibbs and Coffey maintain that the homogenous unit principle contains within it the possibility of overresponding to one culture. Since no culture has a monopoly on the truth, that culture can lose the corrective of others' perspectives where one group is targeted for evangelism.[13] Van Rheenen goes even further in seeing the Church Growth Movement as anthropocentric rather than theocentric:[14] "The seeds of syncretism, however, were rooted in the very principles of cultural analysis and strategy formation employed by this movement."[15] Van Rheenen overstates the case in two ways. Firstly, the Church Growth Movement is a movement. Like any movement it is not uniform, contains a number of perspectives,[16] and any generalization does not hold true at every point. Secondly, it is possible, though not straightforward, for the gospel to be transforming culture in a way that is relevant to and respectful of that culture, without acceding to it. Nevertheless, MacArthur critiques the focus within the Church Growth Movement on accommodating "seekers": "The notion that church meetings should be used to . . . attract non-Christians is a relatively recent development. Nothing like it is found in scripture . . . "[17] Van Rheenen is not a lone voice in identifying an overfocus by the Church Growth Movement on techniques and pragmatics at the expense of theological rigor: "The danger is replacing theology with pragmatism."[18]

Research in US churches questions the efficacy of the homogenous unit principle when 61 percent of multiracial churches, versus just 31 percent of principally Anglo-Celtic congregations, had experienced

---

12. McGavran, *Understanding Church Growth*, 178.
13. Gibbs and Coffey, *Church Next*, 185.
14. Van Rheenen, "Contrasting Missional and Church Growth Perspectives," 28.
15. Van Rheenen, "Contrasting Missional and Church Growth Perspectives," 26.
16. McIntosh, *Evaluating the Church Growth Movement*. Five views are expressed in the book to which Van Rheenen contributes: 1) Effective evangelism view—church growth effectively confronts and penetrates the culture/Elmer Towns; 2) Gospel and our culture view—church growth lacks a sufficient view of the church, which hinders it from effectively engaging the culture/Craig Van Gelder; 3) Centrist view—church growth is based on an evangelistically focused and missiologically applied theology/Charles Van Engen; 4) Reformist view—church growth assumes theology but ineffectively employs it to analyze culture, determine strategy, and perceive history/Gailyn Van Rheenen; 5) Renewal view—church growth must be based on a biblical vision of the church as the vital community of the kingdom of God/Howard Snyder.
17. MacArthur, *Ashamed of the Gospel*, 83.
18. Rainer, *The Book of Church Growth*, 319.

growth.[19] Similarly within Australia, NCLS research: "does not provide support for general statements about homogeneity as a key characteristic of vital congregations. Indeed, socially diverse congregations appear more effective on a range of fronts."[20]

The Homogeneous Unit Principle is not only to be understood culturally/ethnically. Its roots in cross-cultural mission were in the study of castes, and homogeneity is a much wider concept than culture and ethnicity. Scripture records occasions when the gospel spreads through families (Matt 4:18–19), households (which may include servants and extended family; Acts 16:31; 18:8), friendship groups (Matt 11:19), and regions (Mark 5:20). Churches may target a particular demographic (e.g. Generation X or Baby Busters: those born from mid-1960s to early 1980s), socioeconomic (e.g. middle class), or social grouping (e.g. motorcyclists) in their outreach.

An initial reading of Scripture may seem to support the Homogeneous Unit Principle through examples such as God affirming his covenant with Abraham (Gen 15) and promising to work through Abraham's descendants (i.e. a particular culture/ethnicity) to bring salvation to the nations (Isa 2:1–4; Jonah). Similarly, Jesus' mission is to Israel (Matt 10:5–6), although glimpses of God's concern for all peoples are seen as Jesus' ministry progresses (Matt 8:5–10; 15:24–28; 25:31–32; Mark 7:24–30; 11:15–17; Luke 17:16–18; John 4:9). Jesus' focus widens dramatically as he commissions his followers to make disciples of all nations (Matt 28:18–19). The New Testament letters enlarge this theme further (Rom 1:16; Gal 3:28; Eph 2:14; Col 3:11). And there are compelling accounts in the New Testament of the gospel transcending and crossing barriers of ethnicity and religion (John 4:39–42), class and culture (Acts 8:27–39), and a deepening recognition that non-Jews were also part of God's plan of salvation (Acts 10:1–11:26).

C. Peter Wagner, who lectured with McGavran at Fuller Theological Seminary, and Win Arn, who founded The Institute for American Church Growth, were significant architects and popularizers of the Church Growth Movement in North American churches, and beyond, through their writings individually and collaboratively.[21]

---

19. Hadaway and Marler, "Growth and Decline in the Mainline," 14.

20. Kaldor et al., *Shaping a Future*, 234.

21. McGavran, *Understanding Church Growth*; McGavran and Arn, *How to Grow a Church*; McGavran and Arn, *Ten Steps for Church Growth*; Arn, *The Pastor's Church Growth Handbook*; Arn and McGavran, *Back to Basics in Church Growth*; Wagner et

The Church Growth Movement gathered pace, particularly in the United States. In its popular form it seemed to maximize "how-to" strategies[22] and minimize the cultural analysis in which it was birthed on the mission field in India. Similarly, research into church growth focused on pragmatics to the detriment of theology: "For a movement that has shown capacity to grow and refine its scientific theoretical framework, there has been a corresponding lag in development in its theological foundations,"[23] and in particular missiology, ecclesiology, and Christology, and their relation to culture, history, and the kingdom of God.[24]

However, proponents of the Church Growth Movement argue that: "The Great Commission of Jesus . . . is at the core of planning strategy for evangelism and missions. It is the key commandment for the Church Growth Movement . . . obeying this particular commandment—without detracting from the others—is the specialization of the Church Growth Movement."[25] In other words, if the "Great Commission" of Jesus (outlined in Matt 28:16–20; Mark 16:14–18; Luke 24:44–49; John 20:19–23; and Acts 1:4–8) is the *raison d'être* of each local church, a lack of conversion growth, or even decline, means that a local church has ceased to carry out its main function as mandated by Jesus. Paul Borden emphasizes this centrality of the process of conversion and disciple-making by a church in its community, and of reproduction or multiplication of churches:

> The purpose of focusing on health and growth is to see reproduction occur. Not all growing congregations are healthy ones. However, all healthy congregations are growing. They grow by making new disciples for Jesus Christ and they grow by creating new congregations that grow and then reproduce. A judicatory is doing its job well when it is seeing both transformation and reproduction happen regularly and consistently in a majority of its congregations.[26]

Matthew 16:18 does not necessarily mean that Jesus will build and grow *each* local church. As early as the New Testament, where Jesus

---

al., *Church Growth: State of the Art*; Arn, *The Church Growth Ratio Book*.

22. McGavran and Arn, *How to Grow a Church*; Searcy and Henson, *Ignite*.

23. Shenk et al., *The Challenge of Church Growth*, 21.

24. Frost and Hirsch, *The Shaping of Things to Come*; Stetzer, "The Evolution of Church Growth, Church Health, and the Missional Church"; Gary L. McIntosh, *Evaluating the Church Growth Movement*.

25. Wagner, *Strategies for Church Growth*, 49.

26. Borden, *Direct Hit*, 16.

threatened to close the church at Ephesus (Rev 2:5) and certainly down through the history of the church, such an assertion cannot be maintained as individual churches have been birthed, matured, and died. McIntosh explores this phenomenon of the life cycle of congregations.[27] Rather, the focus in Matthew 16:18 appears to be Peter's role as leader of the apostles, rather than as some claim, his confession.[28] Peter's leadership will be the instrument through which Jesus will build his new community so that, "the church as God's eschatological community will never die or come to end—this despite the eventual martyrdom of the apostles [such as Peter] and even, more imminently, the death of its founder . . . The church—conceived of as the community of saints at any particular time, or as the saints of every age who cumulatively make up the church in toto—can never be destroyed."[29] Therefore, in the face of such threats to individual leaders, the identification of Peter as the "rock" (Gk πέτρα)[30] is not a narrow endorsement of the Catholic papacy, but a wider conferring of authority on those who are leaders of this indestructible church.

This truth is seen even in the face of persecution (e.g. Acts 4:5–21), as the early church expands in the book of Acts through Peter and the other apostles. "The risen Lord's mandate to mission begins to be fulfilled in Acts. Acts 1:8 is a kind of 'Table of Contents' for the book."[31]

In conclusion, the Church Growth Movement represented a recovery of a vision for local and global mission which had become diffuse. The Church Growth Movement helps to refocus local churches on that mission, and calls individual Christians and churches to live out Christ's Great Commission. While some glimpses of the effectiveness of the Homogeneous Unit Principle can be seen in contemporary society, other church-based sociological research and Scripture (e.g. Eph 2:14–18, along with passages cited above) do not appear to give such a definite warrant for the principle.

Mark Olson, following Guinness,[32] sees the Church Growth Movement as tightly linked to modernity, and therefore in his book *Moving*

---

27. McIntosh, *Taking Your Church to the Next Level*, 20–113.
28. Caragounis, *Peter and the Rock*, 104.
29. Hagner, *Matthew 14–28*, 472.
30. Blomberg, *Matthew*, 251–2; Carson, "Matthew, Mark, Luke," 368.
31. Stott, *The Spirit, the Church and the World*, 43.
32. Guinness, *Dining with the Devil*.

Beyond Church Growth questions its effectiveness into the future.[33] In it he posits an alternative vision for a postmodern milieu: in contrast with McGavran's blunt "Church growth is faithfulness,"[34] Olsen ventures that praise, righteousness, and compassion are a truer measure of a congregation's life than the numerical growth that modernity is so obsessed with.[35]

A lack of theological underpinnings in the Church Growth Movement can result in Christians viewing mission as a technique, as something that they do. McGavran was right to emphasize mission as including the growth of churches, but theologically and practically mission is far broader and more expansive than that.[36] Rather, mission is something that proceeds from the nature of God,[37] that is enlivened and directed by the God[38] who birthed the church as his instrument for mission.[39] In other words, missiology precedes ecclesiology, lest mission become a subset of what the church does, rather than its *raison d'être*[40]: "It is not the Church of God that has a mission in the world—it is the God of mission who has a Church in the world."[41] Frost and Hirsch rightly remind us of the vastness of that mission, as the lordship of Jesus is proclaimed and enacted in all of life:

> And what is mission? It is the outward impulse of God's people. Above and beyond evangelism or social justice, it is the irresistible propulsion of the Spirit that sends his people out to declare the lordship of Jesus in all and over all. This can be manifest in sharing the gospel, planting churches, feeding the hungry, agitating against injustice, and more. These are missional activities. But mission itself is the overarching sentness of God's people as

---

33. Olson, *Moving Beyond Church Growth*.
34. McGavran, *Understanding Church Growth*, 6.
35. See also section 2.7 above which explores these issues further; Olson, *Moving Beyond Church Growth*, 46–48.
36. McGavran, "Wrong Strategy: The Real Crisis in Missions"; McGavran, "My Pilgrimage in Mission," 54.
37. Frost and Hirsch, *The Shaping of Things to Come*, 18.
38. Bosch, *Transforming Mission*, 390.
39. Bell, *Velvet Elvis*, 165.
40. McLaren, *A New Kind of Christian*, 157; Wright, *Simply Christian*, 204.
41. Dearborn, *Beyond Duty Leader's Guide*, 2.

they infiltrate all of society and stake a claim for the unending rule of Jesus in every sphere of life.[42]

3.3 Relationships Between Congregational Growth and Other Factors

The growth and decline of congregations is a complex subject, with many interrelated contributing factors. Four areas of research have emerged in seeking to establish relationships with church growth: local context (such as changes in surrounding community demographics and economic trends), local church characteristics (such as leadership, programming, and levels of conflict), national context and trends (such as church attendance rates, birth rates, or changing values) and national institutional characteristics (such as denominational emphases).[43]

In addition to evaluating these four areas and their relationship with church growth, an examination will be undertaken of some of the literature that lists factors believed to be related to growth.

Although Thom Rainer identified only thirteen churches out of around fifty thousand US churches that fit the criteria of being "breakout churches"[44] he sought to distill "eight keys to Acts 6/7 leadership" as essential to growth from these churches: fierce biblical faithfulness, tenure,[45] confident humility, acceptance of responsibility, unconditional love of the people, persistence, an outwardly focused vision, and a desire for a lasting legacy.[46]

Hadaway's research suggests that prayer is a significant factor in church growth: 71 percent of previously declining or plateaued churches now experiencing growth reported an increased emphasis on prayer over

---

42. Frost and Hirsch, *ReJesus*, 181.

43. Hoge and Roozen, *Understanding Church Growth and Decline*; Roozen and Carroll, "Recent Trends in Church Membership and Participation"; Roozen and Hadaway, "Do Church Growth Consultations Really Work?".

44. "Declining or plateaued churches that have broken out of that to sustain significant growth through conversions over several years under the same senior pastor"; Rainer, *Breakout Churches*, 20–21.

45. Average tenure of these pastors is 21.6 years.

46. Rainer, *Breakout Churches*, 53–67.

the past several years as compared to only 40 percent of churches which continued on the plateau.[47]

Thom Rainer explores the history and theology of church growth and then outlines thirteen principles for growing a church: prayer, leadership, laity ministry, church planting, evangelism, worship, finding the people, receptivity, planning and goal setting, physical facilities, assimilation and reclamation, small groups, and signs and wonders evidencing spiritual power.[48] Gary McIntosh sketches ten church growth principles: the right premise—God's word; the right priority—glorifying God; the right process—discipleship; the right power—the Holy Spirit; the right pastor—a faithful shepherd; the right people—effective ministers; the right philosophy—cultural relevance; the right plan—target focused; the right procedure—simple structure; and mix it right.[49]

Geoff Surratt comes from the opposite perspective when he identifies, through interviews with pastors, common mistakes that impede church growth.[50] These mistakes include: promoting talent over integrity, copying another successful church, and mixing ministry and business.[51] Copying another successful church has been a significant problem in popularized church growth, with mission statements, strategies, and programs being copied by pastors from other churches with little regard to the varying cultural context of their own church, or of effectively engaging their church's attenders in the process.

Macintosh identifies the importance of having sufficient staff for growth, which staff positions to add first, and he gives comprehensive guidelines for building and nurturing a healthy staff team.[52]

Easum and Cornelius deal at length with internal barriers to church growth within the pastor,[53] as well as how to break specific growth barriers, a focus shared by a number of authors, particularly regarding transitioning the two hundred or pastoral to program size barrier.[54]

47. Hadaway, *Church Growth Principles*, 164.
48. Rainer, *The Book of Church Growth*, 171–316.
49. McIntosh, *Biblical Church Growth*.
50. Surratt, *Ten Stupid Things That Keep Churches from Growing*.
51. Surratt, *Ten Stupid Things That Keep Churches from Growing*, 93–112, 133–52, 169–82.
52. McIntosh, *Staff Your Church for Growth*.
53. Easum and Cornelius, *Go Big*, 33–66.
54. Mann, *Raising the Roof*; Gaede, *Size Transitions in Congregations*; Fletcher, *Overcoming Barriers to Growth*.

3.3.1 Local Context

The question of the relationship between local context or community factors and church growth has been debated over a number of years.[55] More recently, US research appears to demonstrate that growth can occur in all contexts, including inner city and rural areas.[56] However, "congregations located in newer suburbs are more likely to experience growth than congregations in any other type of location. Congregations are least likely to grow in rural areas and small towns. Newer suburbs are where the greatest population growth is occurring."[57] NCLS research of Australian churches and their contexts shows that church attendance as a percentage of the population is significantly higher in communities with higher proportions of professionals than in blue-collar areas, and in stable commuting suburbs compared to inner-city or multicultural areas.[58] Young adults are underrepresented among church attenders, probably because they are shifting away from church involvement generally.[59] However, NCLS research in Australia indicates that "the demographic characteristics of communities, such as their age profile and socioeconomic and ethnic make-up, account for about 4% in the variation of the patterns of growth of Anglican and Protestant congregations and 11% of the variation in the levels of newcomers."[60] So while the local context is significant, it is not determinative; internal factors have a higher statistical significance[61] with congregational vitality than local contextual factors.[62] Because context is influential, a church's ministry and local mission must recognize the importance of understanding and being responsive to its local community context.[63] A church must perceive and adapt to any changes that

---

55. Hadaway, "The Demographic Environment and Church Membership Change," 77; Iannaccone, "Reassessing Church Growth"; Sturgis, "Institutional Versus Contextual Explanations for the Growth of the Jehovah's Witnesses in the United States, 1945–2002"; Thomas and Olson, "Testing the Strictness Thesis and Competing Theories of Congregational Growth."

56. Hadaway and Marler, "Growth and Decline in the Mainline," 20.

57. Hadaway, *FACTs on Growth*, 2.

58. Kaldor et al., *Shaping a Future*, 193–5.

59. Bellamy et al., *Why People Don't Go to Church*, 24.

60. Kaldor et al., *Build My Church*, 66–67.

61. Internal factors percent of variance (adjusted R^2) with levels of newcomers (33, 12) and numerical growth (24, 8).

62. Kaldor et al., *Shaping a Future*, 196–9.

63. Kaldor et al., *Shaping a Future*, 200.

are taking place in their community early on. For example, being aware of an influx of young families, or a particular cultural group, into their local area, and seeking to react to that in their outreach and programming. This responsiveness and adaptability lie within the power of a congregation, no matter what their local context. Therefore, it is unfortunate that many long-established congregations become rigid and unresponsive to such demographic changes, feeling that they are at the mercy of their area. Instead, as explored below, local church characteristics have a much stronger relationship than context with congregational vitality, levels of newcomers, and numerical growth.

3.3.2 *Local Church Characteristics*

Church health is a significant correlate of church growth. Though growth sometimes occurs when a church is not healthy, church dysfunction such as ongoing, intense conflict is a good predictor of decline: "Lingering conflict is strongly associated with declining vitality and declining membership. Conflict tends to cast a shadow across the activities and ethos of the congregation as a whole, even the capacity to enlist volunteers."[64] Conflict as a normal part of life cannot be avoided, and sometimes precipitates healthy change. So it may be more accurate to say that where minor conflict is not addressed at an early stage and worked through, such that it escalates to become serious, debilitating conflict involving a large portion of the congregation, then congregational decline becomes more probable.[65] Results from the US Faith Communities Today survey indicated that 80 percent of congregations that dealt very openly with conflict reported high vitality.[66] Conversely, one of the strongest correlates of growth is the absence of serious conflict: of those congregations who had not had a serious conflict within the last three years, 72 percent claimed high vitality, whereas for those who had a serious conflict within the last three years, 51 percent of congregations claimed high vitality.[67] In a similar way, "congregations that have experienced major conflict are quite likely to have declined in attendance. Congregations with no conflict during the previous two years are least likely to decline and most

---

64. Dudley and Roozen, *A Report on Religion in the United States Today*, 61.
65. Kaldor et al., *Shaping a Future*, 130-1.
66. Dudley et al., *Insights Into: Congregational Conflict*, 3-4.
67. Hadaway and Marler, "Growth and Decline in the Mainline," 13.

likely to grow . . . whether . . . a congregation finds itself mired in serious conflict is the number one predictor of congregational decline."[68] Given this, it is not surprising that Hadaway believes this identifies a training need in conflict resolution skills amongst clergy.[69] It also reveals a need for skilled interventionists such as mediators, church consultancy teams, and intentional interim ministers to be available to churches.

However, growth is much more than the absence of decline or dysfunction. A survey of the research literature identifies factors or characteristics that are correlates of growth in local churches.

The US Congregational Life Survey, built on the work of the NCLS team in Australia,[70] surveyed many denominations. Data was used to compare the four hundred fastest-growing Presbyterian (US) churches with a random sample of 523 Presbyterian (US) churches that also took part in the survey. Results reveal that "churches are more likely to be growing churches when: (1) larger percentages of worshippers are growing spiritually; (2) the percentage of worshippers who started attending in the previous five years is larger; and (3) larger percentages of worshippers see their leaders as empowering."[71]

Using a resource mobilization framework, Iannaccone, Olson, and Stark[72] hypothesize that church growth is a function of the inputs of labor and capital. They seek to demonstrate that levels of involvement (i.e. labor) and giving are some of the most significant correlates of growth.[73] The authors acknowledge inaccuracies in attendance data, and the inadequacy of this data as a proxy for levels of attender involvement, but their initial findings warrant further research, perhaps using data supplied directly by attenders (rather than denominations or church leaders).

Hadaway's study of factors related to the revitalization of Southern Baptist congregations concluded that "the keys to renewed growth apparently are evangelism and goal setting."[74] Similarly, Roozen identified a higher correlation with growth for factors over which churches have control such as "the breadth of internal programming" and "the use of

---

68. Hadaway, *FACTs on Growth*, 8, 16.
69. Hadaway, *FACTs on Growth*, 16.
70. Bruce et al., "An International Survey of Congregations and Worshipers."
71. Bruce et al., "Fast-Growing Churches," 111.
72. Iannaccone et al., "Religious Resources and Church Growth."
73. Iannaccone et al., "Religious Resources and Church Growth," 707.
74. Hadaway, "From Stability to Growth," 191.

electric guitars in worship," with lower correlations for population change in the local community.[75] Similarly, NCLS research finds "contemporary styles of worship have a positive relationship with numerical growth and other aspects of vitality"[76] and Hadaway's US research indicates a significant correlation between worship style and growth.[77]

Research into Australian churches finds no consistent correlation emerging between church vitality/growth and leadership models or how congregations are structured.[78] However, Schwarz's research in the area of functional leadership structures revealed that 85 percent of churches that were both high quality and growing had departmental leaders for the individual areas of ministry in their churches.[79] It also revealed that "leaders of growing churches concentrate on empowering other Christians for ministry."[80] The primary function of pastors/ministers is to develop volunteer leaders and ministers, rather than performing ministry.[81] NCLS research identifies leadership that "is inspiring and directive, yet puts a priority on listening to attenders' ideas and encouraging them to use their gifts and skills" as a key contributor to congregational vitality.[82] Therefore the importance of a strong sense of vision and direction, along with a permission-giving, empowering, equipping stance that releases people towards mission/ministry, will be crucial towards realizing that vision. NCLS research reveals that "vital congregations tend to have a higher proportion of attenders who believe that the most important role of their minister is that of an equipper or an evangelist" and that "an outward focus by the senior minister is very important in relation to . . . numerical growth."[83] The critical importance of effective leadership is shown by the high correlation between growth, and leadership style and emphasis.[84]

75. Roozen, "Oldline Protestantism," 16–17.
76. Kaldor et al., *Shaping a Future*, 215.
77. Hadaway, *FACTs on Growth*, 10.
78. Kaldor et al., *Shaping a Future*, 234.
79. Schwarz, *Natural Church Development*, 28.
80. Schwarz, *Natural Church Development*, 28.
81. Mallory, *The Equipping Church*, 15.
82. Kaldor et al., *Shaping a Future*, 231.
83. Kaldor et al., *Shaping a Future*, 154.
84. The percent of variance explained by each factor after accounting for the effects of context and faith type (change in adjusted R^2) is 5.2%; Kaldor et al., *Shaping a Future*, 15, 155.

3.3.3 National Context and Trends

In 1960, 41 percent of Australians attended church at least monthly, but by 1980 this figure had declined to 25 percent.[85] "The 1998 Australian Community Survey found that 20.0% of the population claimed to attend religious services at least monthly or more often. The 2002 Well-being and Security Survey found that this figure had dropped to 18.6% of the population,"[86] which then diminished further to 17 percent by 2007.[87]

This downward trend in regular church attendance will, generally speaking, have a negative impact on the growth and vitality of local churches. However, this is not uniform, so while some local churches are static or declining, others are growing strongly, and congregations from Charismatic or Pentecostal streams are most likely to be growing.[88]

The rise of EMCs and alternative forms of church has coincided with a decline in attendance at conventional church services. George Barna asserts: "measures such as the percentage of people who are 'unchurched'—based on attendance at a conventional church service—are out of date. Various new forms of faith community and experience, such as house churches, marketplace ministries and cyber-churches, must be figured into the mix . . ."[89] Barna's US research revealed that 56 percent of the adult population have attended a conventional church (but had not attended a house church) during the past month. A further 15 percent of the adult population have participated in either a conventional church or an organic faith community (e.g. house church, simple church, intentional community) within the past year, but not during the past month. And 6 percent had attended either a meeting of a house church (3%) or both a conventional church and a house church (3%) during the past month.[90] If these trends are replicated in Australia, the percentage of the adult population attending a Christian spiritual community of some form may be higher than those indicating that they are attending conventional churches at least monthly through regular channels of reporting such as NCLS surveys and denominational statistics.

---

85. Kaldor et al., *Build My Church*, 22.
86. Bellamy and Castle, *2001 Church Attendance Estimates*, 9.
87. Powell, *Why Innovation Is Needed in Church Life*, 1.
88. Kaldor et al., *Build My Church*, 68.
89. Barna, *New Statistics on Church Attendance and Avoidance*, 1.
90. Barna, *New Statistics on Church Attendance and Avoidance*, 1.

However, the increasing secularization of Australian society is underlined by the proportion of those self-reporting a Christian affiliation, dropping from 73 percent in 1986, to 70.9 percent in 1996, then to 63.9 percent in 2006.[91] While this is still much greater than the 17 percent who attend a church service at least monthly,[92] this large decrease means that local churches, drawing from a smaller pool of people identifying as Christian, are generally struggling to grow in this increasingly secular milieu. While this is a significant factor regarding the growth of churches, local church characteristics have a stronger correlation to growth than local context and national trends and context.

3.3.4 National Institutional Characteristics

Some researchers, most notably Dean Kelley, have sought to evidence a link between "strictness" or conservatism and patterns of growth.[93] Others have come to the research conclusion that "liberal churches are slightly more likely to be growing," and underscore the complexity of multiple variables that impact growth: "no single factor explains why some churches grow and others decline."[94] Yet authors such as Iannaccone continue to agree with Kelley regarding the importance of strictness.[95]

NCLS research in Australia indicates that "congregations identifying with Charismatic or Pentecostal traditions are most likely to be growing or drawing in newcomers" whether or not those churches are from Pentecostal denominations or charismatic congregations within non-Pentecostal denominations.[96] In contrast, "the Traditional and Liberal Protestant sectors of the church are less likely to be growing."[97] NCLS tends not to support Kelley's thesis,[98] instead seeing internal factors (24 % of variance [adjusted R^2]) as far more significant to numerical growth

---

91. ABS Census of Population and Housing 1986, 1996, and 2006.
92. Powell, *Why Innovation Is Needed in Church Life*, 1.
93. Kelley, *Why Conservative Churches Are Growing*; Kelley, "Why Conservative Churches Are Still Growing," 165.
94. Thompson et al., "Growth or Decline in Presbyterian Congregations," 205–6.
95. Iannaccone, "Why Strict Churches Are Strong."
96. Kaldor et al., *Build My Church*, 68.
97. Kaldor et al., *Build My Church*, 68.
98. Kaldor et al., *Shaping a Future*, 215.

than either faith type (6%) or local context (8%).[99] Evangelism and an outward focus has a greater strength of relationship to numerical growth, growth in faith, and sense of belonging than does faith type.[100] Hadaway's summation of his research into the causes of growth and decline concluded: "Evangelism may be the most important one thing church leaders can do if they want their church to grow."[101]

3.4 Measurement of Church Growth

NSW and ACT Baptist churches measure attendance at morning and evening services, membership gains (by baptism, visitation, or transfer), membership losses (by death, transfer out, or roll revision), and total baptisms (which also includes baptisms not resulting in membership gains).[102]

When an individual local church comes to assess their growth, it is helpful to measure growth against growth or decline in the surrounding community. For example, stable church attendance in an area where population is declining markedly would be considered a better outcome than slight church growth in a community experiencing a rapid influx of residents. Community profiles are generally published by the Australian Bureau of Statistics, local councils, or can be obtained through NCLS.

While growth is important, to say that it is the only measure of the health or success of a church would be reductionist. Churches are vastly different from each other, so to seek to measure effectiveness or vitality in a way that enables some sense of comparison between churches means that a wide number of measures must be used around various tasks such as worship, fellowship, discipleship, ministry, evangelism, community compassion, and justice. NCLS research sought to measure the numerical growth of each local church in three ways: attracting and integrating newcomers, retaining young adults, and numerical growth in attendance.[103]

---

99. Kaldor et al., *Shaping a Future*, 212.
100. Kaldor et al., *Shaping a Future*, 218.
101. Hadaway, "Is Evangelistic Activity Related to Church Growth?," 187.
102. Soden, *NSW and ACT Baptist Churches Handbook 2009–2010*, 254–63.
103. Kaldor et al., *Shaping a Future*, 245–8; Bellamy et al., *Enriching Church Life*, 5.

3.5 Conclusion

Church growth is concerned about the conversion of non-believers and drawing them into the life of each local church so that it increases in number. To achieve this, a church must be functioning in healthy ways. The development of new churches is also a key commitment of church growth. The rise of the Church Growth Movement in the 1960s was helpful in refocusing churches on this primary task of local and worldwide evangelism. However, there have been critics of the Church Growth Movement's pragmatic focus in areas such as the Homogeneous Unit Principle and its lack of theological depth, noting that it would benefit from some further theological work in the future.

The theology of church growth, delineated in this chapter and which informs the assessments, deductions, and recommendations of this thesis can be summarized in the following theological assertions.

A theology of growth and reproduction. Intrinsic in the commission of Jesus to make disciples (Matt 28:19) is the growth of churches and the multiplication of reproducing church planting movements. McGavran asserted that such movements may be facilitated by (though are not limited to) a shared commonality that enhances the power of group influence amongst a people.[104] The Church Growth Movement's contribution was to remind the church that the normative experience of a healthy church is growth and reproduction through planting.

A theology of growth with health. Foundational to this is the research-based critique made of the Church Growth Movement by Schwarz: the health of a church is a good predictor of its growth.[105] However, the reverse does not hold true: a growing church is not necessarily a healthy church.[106] Therefore, as has been clearly demonstrated from the Bible and literature, attention to both church growth *and* church health is essential.

A theology of growth with real missional expression. Mission includes the growth of a local church but goes beyond it in three ways. Firstly, as discussed in "a theology of growth with health" above, for growth to have real missional expression, it must focus on a high level of newcomers to church life, rather than merely attracting those from other churches.[107]

---

104. McGavran, *Understanding Church Growth*, 223.
105. Schwarz, *Natural Church Development*, 46–48.
106. Borden, *Direct Hit*, 16.
107. One of the critiques levelled against NCD is that it does not measure conversion growth, while NCLS divides newcomers into those new to church and "switchers"

This may also result in the planting of new churches in an effort to continue to connect meaningfully with those in the community outside of Christ. Secondly, growth with real missional expression includes those aspects of mission that may not necessarily result in increased numbers at a church: examples include acts of mercy toward the hurting, poor and marginalized, and working for justice in society. Thirdly, such a theology of growth with real missional expression finds its locus in the missionality of God and his lordship over all creation: "Above and beyond evangelism or social justice, it is the irresistible propulsion of the Spirit that sends his people out to declare the lordship of Jesus in all and over all."[108]

The doctrine of God and the gospel. A vision for church growth, evangelism, and church planting is rooted in an accurate understanding of the nature of God and of the gospel. That is, mission proceeds from the nature of God as a missionary God,[109] and is enlivened and directed by God.[110] The gospel is an expression both of the love of God for a lost and sin-scarred humanity and of the holiness of God. God demonstrates in Christ's incarnation a suffering with and for people in their predicament of sin, and also pays the horrific price for that sin, allowing the restoration of relationship with people. However, the gospel is no mere "ticket to heaven" for those who put their faith in Christ, but a discipleship call to proclaim and live out the "now-and-not-yet" kingdom of God:

> But if he was an eschatological prophet/Messiah, announcing the kingdom and dying in order to bring it about, the resurrection would declare that he had in principle succeeded in his task, and that his earlier redefinitions of the coming kingdom had pointed to a further task awaiting his followers, that of implementing what he had achieved.[111]

That is, bound up in the embracing of the gospel by people is a living out of the sentness or missionality of God.

Theological anthropology and soteriology. Implicit in the previous point, "the doctrine of God and the gospel," is the biblical understanding of man as a creation of God, made in the image of God for relationship

---

from other denominations.

108. Frost and Hirsch, *ReJesus*, 181.
109. Frost and Hirsch, *The Shaping of Things to Come*, 18.
110. Bosch, *Transforming Mission*, 390.
111. Wright, *Jesus and the Victory of God*, 660.

(e.g. know, love, worship, and obey) with God.[112] The potential for such relationship is realized through evangelism, church growth, and church planting. Soteriology includes but is not limited to concepts of reconciliation with God, forgiveness of sin, eternal life, redemption, and participation in the victory of God through Christ. Such benefits are made available to people through the incarnation, life, death, resurrection, and ascension of Christ, and are realized by grace through faith in Christ. In 2 Cor 5:18–20, Paul makes it clear that evangelism, church growth, and church planting are birthed out of our desire to see people reconciled with God:

> All this is from God, who reconciled us to himself through Christ, and has given us the ministry of reconciliation; that is, in Christ God was reconciling the world to himself, not counting their trespasses against them, and entrusting the message of reconciliation to us. So we are ambassadors for Christ, since God is making his appeal through us; we entreat you on behalf of Christ, be reconciled to God.

A theology of the church, including the church as the agent of God's mission in the establishment of his kingdom.[113] This has been covered at length in this chapter and is recapped in the above four points. What Christians believe about the church affects the kind of growth they strive for, and this is one area where authors have critiqued the Church Growth Movement for overfocusing on growth sometimes to the detriment of other important and biblical areas of church life:

> Healthy, lasting church growth is multidimensional. My definition of genuine church growth has five facets. Every church needs to grow warmer through fellowship, deeper through discipleship, stronger through worship, broader through ministry, and larger through evangelism.[114]

Such a statement affirms the priority of growing people if one is to grow a church. It also underlines the massive potential within churches for attenders to minister effectively to one another, and to advance the mission of God in their communities, nation, and world.

A theology of systems theory as it intersects with church growth. Church growth is much more complex than using *x* technique to gain

112. Erickson, *Christian Theology*, 470–1.
113. Dearborn, *Beyond Duty Leader's Guide*, 2.
114. Warren, *The Purpose Driven Church*, 48.

y growth. The formalized rules, roles, rituals, and goals, that determine how a congregation functions, and particularly those that are informal and tacit, must be determined. For example, a tacit goal of "let's grow old together" may trump formal goals regarding church vision, mission, and values that include effective outreach to the community. The system must firstly be uncovered, its points of interconnection determined, and then patiently changed to reflect biblical rules, roles, rituals, and goals. The ability of a pastor to do this may be hampered if he/she is new to the church, or has joined the system so completely that he/she cannot see these implicit rules, roles, rituals, and goals. In such cases an outside church consultant may bring an objective viewpoint and systemic discernment that helps to "unstick" a church and so free it to grow.

A theology of church and culture. There are four broad areas that have emerged from research into possible correlates of church growth. Local community context, local church internal characteristics, national context and trends, and national denominational characteristics. These have been examined in this and the preceding chapter. While some of these factors are beyond the control of local churches, the most significant determinants for growth lie within the power and characteristics of each local church:

> The life of a congregation, defined in terms of its leadership style, direction setting, mission involvement, communal processes, demographic make-up and religious practices, accounts for 33% of the variation in the numerical growth of congregations and for more than 47% of the variation in the level of newcomers in congregations.[115]

Local, national and denominational contexts do exert some influence, even if that negatively impacts growth. However, because a local congregation's internal characteristics are central to vitality, it still has the potential or possibility of growth. Research data gathered by the NCLS Team over many years, not only in Australia, but also in New Zealand, United Kingdom, and United States[116] has helped to clarify which of these four factors influence the growth of a local congregation, and to what extent. Some of the characteristics of vital congregations identified

---

115. Kaldor et al., *Build My Church*, 70.
116. Bruce et al., "An International Survey of Congregations and Worshipers"; Sterland et al., "Attracting and Integrating Newcomers into Church Life"; Bellamy et al., *Enriching Church Life*, 9.

by NCLS in their research are: having an outward focus, high levels of involvement in congregational activities, a strong sense of community within the congregation, a clear sense of direction and purpose, effective leadership, a lively faith among attenders, and the age profile of the congregation.[117]

There are many areas and theologies that interconnect with church growth which have been delineated above. In particular, church growth dialoguing with church health and church consultancy has in some cases confirmed, in others critiqued, and in still others nuanced our understanding of church growth. This has in turn unified and made more explicit the overarching theology presented in this thesis.

---

117. Kaldor et al., *Shaping a Future*, 226–32.

4

Church Consultancy

Church consultancy is one strategy for church health and church growth. A literature survey of consultancy generally, and church consultancy more specifically, reveals three approaches to consultancy, and various academic disciplines that inform consultancy. The approach taken in Baptist churches in NSW/ACT tends to be towards the Process Facilitator-Participant/Learner model. This proven model of church consultancy is being used by churches across Australia from a wide variety of denominations.[1] The theological underpinning for church consultancy is examined, showing a biblical intersection with other types of ministry. Recognizing that there are other types of health interventions in churches, a rationale for when church consultancy may be an appropriate tool to use for fostering church health will be explored. A detailed examination of various types of church consultancy which are used in this model then follows. A brief look at another particular model of church consultancy, and the context in which it is used, concludes the chapter.

4.1 Definition

Church consultancy is a process of working together with a church and its leadership aimed at serving and supporting the local church, with a view to improving the health of congregations so that they may have a greater impact for the kingdom of God.[2] It seeks to build the capacity of a church

1. Dyer, "Church Consultancy Training," 1.
2. Scarborough et al., *Church Consultancy Manual*, 1.

to clarify and fulfill its mission and goals in a way that is sustainable. While church consultancy may involve giving specialist advice to a church, that will generally not be the main focus, and in this sense it is differentiated from management consultancy. The International Labor Organization (ILO) defines management consulting as: "an independent professional advisory service assisting managers and organizations in achieving organizational purposes and objectives by solving management and business problems, identifying and seizing new opportunities, enhancing learning and implementing changes."[3] Church consultants are most often from outside a church, giving them the advantage of an "external perspective."[4]

4.2 Literature Survey/Approaches to Church Consultancy

Maula and Poulfelt differentiate between two generally opposed styles of consulting: "directive" or "content-based" consulting that is distinguished by knowledge flowing "from the consultant to the client," and "non-directive" or "process-based" consulting involving bidirectional knowledge flows characterized by "interaction and feedback between the consultant and the client."[5] Adding a middle way, Schein differentiates between three broad types of consultancy in any context, according to the level of client involvement: *the purchase of expertise*, where the responsibility for fixing the problem that the client has identified lies principally with the consultant, *the doctor-patient relationship*, where the consultant identifies the problem and offers a remedy for the client to act on, and the *Process Facilitator-Participant/Learner*, where the client takes responsibility for the problem and engages the consultant in a process of helping and training them in assessing the difficulty and implementing organizational change.[6]

There may be occasions, such as an assessment by an acoustic specialist of a worship space (sometimes referred to as a consultancy), when a more content-based consultancy approach will be appropriate. However, a process-based approach offers the greatest potential for client

---

3. Kubr, *Management Consulting*, 10.
4. Burtonshaw-Gunn, *Essential Tools for Management Consulting*, 11–12.
5. Maula and Poulfelt, *Knowledge Transfer, Consulting Modes and Learning*, 7–8.
6. Schein, *Process Consultation*, 22–35.

ownership of the problem, buy-in, action, and lasting organizational transformation in a church context:

> A congregation may carry the delusional hope that something outside itself will save it. In fact, I have seen many congregations place their well-being in the hands of a magical helper, an instant solution, or a sure-fire programmatic cure. Looking outside for help may be a forfeiture of responsibility. Wanting to be taken care of simply compounds the illness. Helplessness is a disease in itself. Congregations need to see themselves as the source of their own healing . . . An effective outside source of help will not support dependency. Rather it will help the congregation to build the inner resources that can stabilize life together and produce a more adequate organization for the future.[7]

So, particularly in a Baptist context that affirms the autonomy of a local church, church consultancy that is process-based respects that independence and places the responsibility for a church's life, health, and mission back onto the church. Such an approach is contextualized: that is, rather than a standard "off the shelf" consultancy program, it will use different approaches for different types of church consultancies. That contextualization also extends to recognizing and affirming the particular local community context in which a church does mission, and the importance of demographic analysis to recognize needs. It also emphasizes partnership, since the local church invites the consultants and sets the objectives for the consultancy. While trained and accredited consultants bring their skills they also seek to uncover and utilize skills in the church, and together seek to discern God's call for the church.[8]

Therefore, provided that the church actually carries out the recommendations of the change agent/consultant for "sustainable transformation,"[9] process-based church consultancy is one of the more efficient uses of outside resources, as churches are walked through a process whereby their capacity is built to increasingly solve their own problems and further develop their health and growth.[10]

---

7. Steinke, *Healthy Congregations*, 17–18.

8. Seeking to discern God's call together, and in so doing advancing God's kingdom within and beyond the church, is one of the significant differences of church consultancy from business consultancy.

9. Buono and Kerber, "Intervention and Organizational Change: Building Organizational Change Capacity," 58–59.

10. Buono and Kerber, "Intervention and Organizational Change: Building

Church consultancy has developed from a number of academic disciplines. While there are some similarities with the field of organizational development[11] and the various academic disciplines it draws from, church consultancy has some unique characteristics in that its goal is the effective ministry and mission of a local church in its community context. This indicates the importance of a number of areas of theology in informing the work of church consultancy, such as ecclesiology and missiology. Some consultants tend to favor drawing on one or two of these foundational academic disciplines in their approach, while others such as Schaller tend to favor a more eclectic method.[12] Those essential disciplines are psychology, especially organizational psychology,[13] sociology, which includes scientific sampling research (exemplified by the NCLS Team) and group dynamics,[14] ethnography,[15] which applies cultural anthropology to the local church situation,[16] and literary symbolism, or the narrative dimension of a church's corporate life.[17]

Theology, or identifying what is happening between the church and God, is a crucial component of church consultancy, for which ecclesiology[18] will be one important part along with the practical application of

---

Organizational Change Capacity," 82–83.

11. Lewin, *The Complete Social Scientist: A Kurt Lewin Reader*; Bennis and Townsend, *Reinventing Leadership*; Bennis, *Beyond Bureaucracy*; Carter et al., *Best Practices in Leadership Development and Organization Change*; Senge, *The Fifth Discipline*; Rothwell and Sullivan, *Practicing Organization Development*; Malony, *Church Organization Development*; Lovell, *Consultancy Modes and Models*.

12. Browning, "Integrating the Approaches: A Practical Theology," 236–7.

13. Savage, "Psychology Serving the Church in the United Kingdom: Church Consultancy and Pastoral Care," 338–42; Savage and Boyd-MacMillan, *The Human Face of Church*; McMinn and Dominguez, *Psychology and the Church*.

14. Bruce et al., "Fast-Growing Churches: What Distinguishes Them from Others?," 111–26; Woolever and Bruce, *A Field Guide to U.S. Congregations*; Woolever and Bruce, *Places of Promise*; Woolever and Bruce, *Beyond the Ordinary*; Dudley et al., *Insights Into: Congregational Conflict*, 1–8; Dudley and Roozen, *A Report on Religion in the United States Today*, 1–69.

15. Robson, *Real World Research*.

16. Stringer, "Putting Congregational Studies to Work: Ethnography, Consultancy and Change," 203–14.

17. Hopewell, *Congregation: Stories and Structures*; Branson, *Memories, Hopes, and Conversations*; Whitney and Trosten-Bloom, *The Power of Appreciative Inquiry*; Yust, "Playing with Mirrors: Narrative Inquiry and Congregational Consultation," 84–93.

18. Hough, "Theologian at Work: Theological Ethics," 112–32.

that theology.[19] These areas will be developed in more depth in section 4.3.

Some church consultants specialize in one area of consultancy (e.g. Speed Leas in conflict consulting[20]), while others have a broader focus.

Many church consultancies have revolved around issues of evangelism and church growth. In the US, C. Kirk Hadaway analyzed 208 Disciples of Christ churches that participated in church consultations from 1983 to 1986.[21] These consultations were either a visit by a consultant seeking to inspire the church with a prepackaged evangelism/growth program, or an open-ended planning consultation focused around the needs of the church.[22] The average church experienced a decline of 1 percent in participating membership in the year prior to the consultation and an increase of 1.7 percent in the year of the consultation.[23] Few churches saw long-term growth with only 12 percent growing during the consultation year and during the two subsequent years.[24] Hadaway recognizes the lack of deep buy-in by many congregations when he writes, "In order for a church to see long-term benefits from a consultation, however, profound changes must be made in the identity and structure of a congregation."[25] The limitations of a prepackaged consultation in obtaining that deep buy-in and effecting sustainable change, in contrast to one where the church's felt needs are being addressed, may be a factor in these results. Also, encouraging the congregation to do evangelism and teaching them how may not address other blockages to growth (e.g. "I am reluctant to bring my unsaved friends to this church because of the conflict here"). Measuring vitality indicators and attendance (rather than membership) four to five years after the consultancy may give a truer picture of the

---

19. Dudley, "Integrating the Approaches: A Practical Theology," 230–7; Dudley, *Building Effective Ministry*, 38–153.

20. Leas, *Moving Your Church Through Conflict*; Dobson et al., *Mastering Conflict and Controversy*; Leas, *Discover Your Conflict Management Style*; Leas, *Leadership and Conflict*.

21. It is recognized that this study is quite dated; the paucity of research on the effectiveness of church consultancy is one factor that led to the author embarking on this project.

22. Roozen and Hadaway, "Do Church Growth Consultations Really Work?," 149–50.

23. Roozen and Hadaway, "Do Church Growth Consultations Really Work?," 150.

24. Roozen and Hadaway, "Do Church Growth Consultations Really Work?," 153.

25. Roozen and Hadaway, "Do Church Growth Consultations Really Work?," 154.

value of that consultancy for a church. This approach will be taken with our cohort of consultancy churches in chapter 5.

Why do otherwise gifted and accomplished pastors feel the need to invite a church consultancy? And what are the foremost issues that cause them to do so? Two e-mail surveys were conducted in the US, one of church leaders and one of church consultants, with responses received from 320 consultants and 515 pastors. Those responses included the dominant motivations to seek a consultant:

- Need for a new church vision—49%
- Irresolvable conflict within the congregation—25%
- Decline in attendance—24%
- Decline in overall perceived spiritual health/growth of members—23%
- Want help launching new ministries—22%
- Constructing new space—22%.[26]

It should be noted that more than one response could be given, meaning that percentages exceed 100 percent. The positive contribution of the consultancy is indicated in that "almost two-thirds of church leaders were satisfied or very satisfied with the results of their consultants' work."[27]

The prevalence of vision and conflict figuring in the need for church consultancy in this survey may indicate a training need for pastors and church leaders in these areas. The consultancy objectives set by the ten churches that form our study are analyzed in chapter 5 and reproduced in the appendices. While these are a small sample, "constructing new space" does not figure highly in the needs expressed by the leadership of these NSW/ACT Baptist churches. Some recommendations are made in chapter 6 concerning training needs that arise from our research in this local context.

4.3 Theology of Church Consultancy

An exploration of the theological and biblical considerations of church consultancy.

---

26. Mancini, *The 2010 Church Consulting Future Trends Report*, 7–8.
27. Mancini, *The 2010 Church Consulting Future Trends Report*, 8.

4.3.1 Church Consultancy in the New Testament Epistles

Many of the letters in the New Testament can be understood as Paul, Peter, John, and James consulting with individual local churches, coaching church leaders, evaluating and developing a theology of leadership, and making recommendations about leadership appointments and ministries. For example, 1 Corinthians is a letter to the church at Corinth responding to issues that visitors from the church had raised (1 Cor 7:1; 8:1; 12:1; 16:1) or that had come to Paul's attention (1 Cor 1:11). In it Paul addressed such issues as divisions in the church (1 Cor 1:10-17; 3:1-9), immorality (1 Cor 5:1-13; 6:12-20), conflict, lawsuits and love (1 Cor 6:1-11; 13:1-13), marriage and singleness (1 Cor 7), exercising spiritual gifts appropriately (1 Cor 12), and worship (1 Cor 11; 14).[28]

In a similar way, 2 Corinthians is a response to false teachers within the Corinthian church who were challenging Paul's authority over the church and his apostleship (1 Cor 6:1–13; 10:1–12:23). He addresses this issue along with concerns about appropriate church discipline (1 Cor 2:5–11) and giving to the poor (1 Cor 8:1–9:15).[29]

The importance of having a solid theological framework when consulting with churches is underscored by these examples of correcting doctrinal error and the resultant behavior that accompanied it. Paul's letter to the Galatians is written in the context of converted Jews seeking to navigate the transition from Judaism to Christianity and sought to refute the teaching of those who insisted on adherence to the laws of Moses.[30] Similarly, the author of Hebrews wrote to Jewish Christians grappling with this same paradigm shift to affirm the superiority of Christ's sacrifice on the cross over the Jewish sacrificial system (see especially Heb 4:1–13, 16).[31] Paul also countered a mix of extreme Judaism and incipient Gnosticism in the church at Colossae which was resulting in both an unhealthy asceticism (Col 2:16-23) and licentiousness (Col 3:1-25). So, Paul emphasizes the full deity of Christ, rather than any inferior system of angelic mediators and secret knowledge (Col 1:13-23; 2:9-10, 18).[32]

---

28. Fee, *The First Epistle to the Corinthians*, 1–880.

29. Martin, *2 Corinthians*, 1–527.

30. For example, circumcision (Gal 2:11–16; 5:1–12); Longenecker, *Galatians*, 1–323.

31. Lane, *Hebrews 1–8*, 1–211; Lane, *Hebrews 9–13*, 213–617.

32. O'Brien, *Colossians, Philemon*, 1–328.

Correcting false teaching was a significant focus of many of the New Testament epistles.

The use of letters to coach church leaders is exemplified by Paul. Paul had left Timothy in charge of the church at Ephesus while he travelled to Macedonia. Some people in the church were teaching false doctrines (1 Tim 1:3–4), and Paul gave Timothy instructions about worship (1 Tim 2:1–15) and the appropriate setting apart of church leaders (1 Tim 3:1–13), as well as personal encouragement for his leadership role (1 Tim 1:18–20; 4:11–16). Paul's concern for the Ephesian church during Nero's persecution dominates his charge to Timothy to endure through difficult times, and to faithfully preach the gospel even in the face of suffering (2 Tim 2:1–4:8).[33]

These are just some examples of various New Testament authors addressing particular concerns in churches, whether they were in need of encouragement in the face of persecution, correction regarding false teaching, addressing sensitive moral issues, encouragement to live faithful Christian lives, or some other matter. The issues of persecution and false teaching do not figure as highly in our Australian contemporary context as they do in the New Testament epistles. However, leadership matters, encouragement of churches and leaders, divisions and conflicts, moral issues, and living faithful Christian lives are still as relevant to the modern Christian and church setting as they were then, and are therefore the concern of pastors and church consultants today.

4.3.2 Evaluating Churches

Theologically and biblically, why should churches be evaluated?

Firstly, God is an evaluator.[34] God is often portrayed as judging (κρίνω, ἀνακρίνω, and διακρίνω) nations (1 Chr 16:33; Pss 7:8; 9:8; 96:10, 13) and individuals (Rom 2:6, 16), or kings with an evaluation of their reign as good (e.g. 1 Kgs 22:43; 2 Chr 24:16) or evil (e.g. 1 Kgs 16:25, 30; 2 Kgs 8:18, 27).[35] In a similar way, Jesus is one who evaluates the nations (Matt 25:31–32), churches (Rev 2:1–3:22), and individuals (2 Thess 1:8; 2 Tim 4:1). In passages such as Matthew 25:1–46, Jesus as the "Son of Man" (Matt 25:31) is depicted as the one supervising the process of sift-

---

33. Mounce, *Pastoral Epistles*, 1–641.
34. Dyer, "Biblical and Theological Basis for Consulting," 1.
35. Louw and Nida, *Vol 1: Greek-English Lexicon of the New Testament*, 363.

ing and evaluation, or separation (Matt 25:32) to "eternal punishment" or "eternal life" (Matt 25:46).

Part of the church consultancy process is evaluative, as churches and issues are assessed. However, the aim of this evaluation process is to be grace-filled and redemptive: that is, for the purpose of those individuals or churches being strengthened or repenting (Rev 3:19–21). This may occur, for example, as those with broken or strained relationships with others in the church are challenged to take steps towards reconciling those frayed relationships.

Secondly, this assessment is something that is often delegated to God's appointed leaders such as prophets (Hos 6:5), priests (Deut 17:9, 17), judges (Judg 4:4), and kings (2 Sam 14:17).

Thirdly, every person should assess themselves spiritually (Judg 5:15–16; Psalm 139; Prov 4:23; Rom 7:14–25; 2 Cor 13:5; Phil 3:12–14; Gal 6:4–5), and Christians are regarded as more competent to evaluate or judge than secular people (1 Cor 2:12–16), with some Christians having special gifts in the area of discernment (1 Cor 12:10) to assist in this process. However, because of our tendency towards self-deception (Jer 17:9; Prov 12:15; 16:2; 21:2) as individuals and churches, it is vitally important for the evaluation of others to be done with a view to encouragement towards spiritual health and growth (Eccl 4:10, 12; Gal 6:1–3; Rev 2:1–3:22).

Fourth, as indicated above, many of the New Testament letters to churches are concerned with the evaluation of churches and individuals in terms of such things as Christ-like living (e.g. 1 Cor 5:1–13), conflict (1 Cor 6:1–11), and correct doctrine (e.g. Col 2:8–23), so that these issues may be addressed. In church consultancies such matters may be addressed from time to time, either to the whole church, or in a private discussion with an individual as appropriate.

Biblically, God has entrusted the church generally with specific purposes. Some authors have attempted to outline these purposes (see section 2.4), with Rick Warren listing them as worship (Matt 4:10), fellowship (Eph 2:19), discipleship (Col 1:28), ministry (Eph 4:12), and mission (Matt 28:19–20).[36] Additionally, each local church has a specific vision and mission that reflects their unique identity and their specific local context. Whether that focus is on the general purposes of the church, or the specific vision and mission of a local church, part of this sacred

---

36. Warren, *The Purpose Driven Church*, 103–7.

responsibility is asking, "How is this church succeeding with what God has entrusted us to do?" This is one area of evaluation, and in the context of church consultancy is effected firstly by a church's leadership in assessing their need of a consultancy, and secondly by inviting the church consultant(s) to partner with them further in that process of church evaluation.

Evaluation is an important theme in Scripture. It is carried out by God, God's leaders, authors of letters to churches in the New Testament, and every Christian in different degrees and contexts. The purpose of such evaluation is to ensure that the ministry of churches is effective and God-honoring, reflects biblical purposes such as that people are coming to faith in Christ and growing in Christian maturity, and that improvements are regularly made as a result of that feedback.

4.3.3 A Multifaceted Christian Ministry

However, to frame church consultancy as merely a tool to evaluate churches would not give the whole picture. At its base it is a Christian ministry that seeks to minister both to churches and to the individual attenders within a church. In this it shares many of the characteristics of other Christian ministries. That is, it seeks to encourage towards growth and health, individually and corporately (Acts 14:22; 15:31–32; 16:40; 20:1–2; Rom 1:12; 1 Cor 14:3, 31; 2 Cor 7:4–7; Eph 6:22; Col 2:2; 4:8; 1 Thess 2:12; 3:2; 1 Pet 5:1).[37]

It can encompass a ministry of comfort or consolation to those who have experienced a church-wide trauma, including but not limited to, extensive bullying by a leader, or a breach of ethical boundaries by a leader impacting the trust of those in their care (2 Cor 1:3–7).

Church consultancy can be a ministry of exhortation for times when a church needs to be urged to return to its scriptural mission, or when individual attenders need to be called back to Christ-like living (1 Thess 4:1; 5:14; 1 Tim 4:13; 2 Tim 4:2; Titus 2:15; Heb 12:5; 13:22).[38]

It can incorporate a ministry of equipping (Eph 4:11–12), as consultants assist a church and its leaders with the processes, tools, and strategies they need to grow in health and strength. Equipping can also include

---

37. Dyer, "Biblical and Theological Basis for Consulting," 1.
38. Dyer, "Biblical and Theological Basis for Consulting," 1.

consultants facilitating or recommending skilled people to run specific workshops in areas needing to be addressed.

Church consultancy can be a ministry of reconciliation in situations of conflict or strained relationships (Matt 5:24; Acts 7:26; Col 1:20; Eph 2:14–22; Phil 4:1–3), as is appropriate for those who have been firstly reconciled to God (1 Cor 5:18–20).[39]

Church consultancy can be a ministry of evangelism (Matt 5:14–16; 9:9–13; 10:33; 28:18–20; Acts 1:8) insofar as it facilitates a greater missional focus on the surrounding community by a local church. The aim is that those outside a church increasingly come to faith in Christ. This may involve a church dealing with any internal blockages, such as conflict, that mar its witness in the community.

Church consultancy is a multifaceted ministry grounded in the Bible that shares many of the characteristics of other ministries, seeking to bring God's wholeness into situations of stress or stagnation, or realize potential. While not specifically termed "church consultancy," in the New Testament, there are many examples where apostles consulted with and encouraged churches and church leaders regarding effective ministry, identification of emerging leaders, doctrinal error, appropriate behavior, and many other issues. Working with church leaders in evaluating the effectiveness of that church's ministry, outreach, and growth in Christian maturity, and recommending ways to increasingly honor God and expand his kingdom have been, and continue to be, the agenda of God and his servants.

4.4 A Rationale of, and Indicators for Using, Church Consultancy

In cases of systemic dysfunction, church consultancy can be used. Simple conflict between a limited numbers of people may be best handled through mediation, leadership dysfunctions through external or internal recommendations for improvement, and victimization through contacting authorities.[40] But systemic dysfunctions can be addressed through a church consultancy intervention across the whole church/system.[41] Another possibility for a system-wide intervention would be to use an

---

39. Dyer, "Biblical and Theological Basis for Consulting," 1.
40. See Appendix F.
41. Brubaker, "Diagnostic Flow Chart for Intragroup Intervention," 257.

intentional interim pastor over twelve to eighteen months, particularly to assist a congregation to navigate critical developmental tasks upon the ending of a pastorate.[42] So church consultancy may be suggested when a church needs outside expertise or specialized skills, independent assessment or judgment, to deal with sensitive matters within the church, or when a church does not have the capacity, ability, or will to deal with a matter internally.[43] Loren Mead adds "offering . . . a process by which the client can reach a resolution of the problem" and "someone who agrees to work on the client's agenda, not simply install the agenda of the consultant, bishop, or other outside authority."[44] For a church consultant seeking God's agenda together with their client church, the importance of prayerful dependence on God, and a solid grounding in the Bible and theology cannot be underestimated.

However, it is critical to note that church consultancy is not only for situations of dysfunction or conflict. Many healthy, growing churches are gaining from having an objective, outside appraisal every two to three years. They may gain much more from a consultancy or other intervention than a church that is struggling with dysfunction. Schwarz's survey of one thousand churches in thirty-two countries revealed that among the key variables related to leadership, the factor with the highest correlation to the overall quality and growth of a church, is leadership's regular use of an outside consultant or advisor (used by 58 percent of growing, high quality churches, but only by 12 percent of declining, low quality churches).[45] Some of the "problems of growth" such as navigating size transitions[46] may benefit from a church consultancy. This is especially the case if the pastor and other leaders have not experienced that transition, along with the associated changes in role/function of the minister and leadership structures to accommodate that growth.

Any church consultancy, whether for issues surrounding growth or focused around a problem, is only as effective as a church's implementation of consultancy recommendations. A consultant should seek to identify any factors that may lead to "poor implementation" before the

---

42. Nicholson, *Temporary Shepherds*, v. Such a process can also be achieved through a transitional consultancy (see section 4.5.4).

43. Koehn, "Considerations for the Consultant," 2.

44. Mead, "Seeking Significant Intervention," 157.

45. Schwarz, *Natural Church Development*, 23.

46. Gaede, *Size Transitions in Congregations*; Mann, *Raising the Roof*.

consultancy commences.[47] Otherwise, church and consultant will be frustrated with the outcome, and this may negatively impact the take-up of consultancy by other churches. Such factors may include a lack of buy-in on the part of a church, its pastor, or its leadership, or a lack of consensus surrounding the request for a consultancy. The identification of people in the church (and particularly outside of the busy leadership group) who have the requisite skills to lead an implementation of the consultancy recommendations will also be an important consideration. It is possible that such an initial assessment may lead the consultant to the conclusion that this will not be a productive health intervention. Perhaps it is not the right time in the life of a church for a consultancy, or a meeting with the leadership team to raise concerns is warranted, or a workshop outlining the consultancy process to the church is appropriate. It is possible that instead of a consultancy, other health tools such as coaching of the pastor, or an intentional interim pastor, may be more suitable.

4.5 A Model of Church Consultancy

The process for a church consultancy in this model is: setting objectives for the consultancy with the appointed leadership of the church, assessment and data gathering, and making recommendations through a report.[48] Assessment and data gathering may include obtaining demographics of the area, surveys of the church, interviews, comment groups, or combinations of these.[49] Because this model is process-oriented, the focus of assessment and data gathering will largely depend on the type of consultancy and the particular objectives in that instance.

The key steps in the consultancy process in this model are:

a. Local church requests consultancy through co-coordinator

b. Type of consultancy is agreed upon

c. Consultancy team (two consultants) appointed to local church

d. Consultancy agreement is established with local church through the elected leadership or appointed group

47. Mancini, *The 2010 Church Consulting Future Trends Report*, 8.
48. Koehn, "Considerations for the Consultant," 2.
49. Gales, *Diagnostic Review-Training Teams to Assess the Ministry of Local Churches*. This model was further developed in Australia by Rev. Les Scarborough and is used in a number of denominations.

e. Consultancy process undertaken

f. Consultation report is prepared and presented to the elected leadership or appointed group of the local church

g. Supervision and evaluation throughout the consultancy process.[50]

Experienced church consultant Lyle Schaller expands on this list[51] by encouraging a prior step—"respond affirmatively only to invitations that suggest this will be a good client who is committed to making it a productive intervention."[52]

This church consultancy model has a range of types of consultancies and various processes that are commonly used within them, which are detailed below.

4.5.1 Standard or Proactive Consultancies

The standard consultancy process is used for most proactive consultancies. It covers the engagement process with a church, the establishment of objectives (which are quite open and determined by the church leadership in the standard process), the gathering of data and research, analyzing collected information, and writing and presenting the report with recommendations for growth and development. In certain situations, some assistance with implementation may be required but this is not presumed in the standard process.

Standard or proactive consultancies are usually of three broad types.

4.5.1.1 THE PROBLEM OR ISSUE-BASED CONSULTANCY

In this type of consultancy, the church has a clear sense of identity, mission, and direction. Consultants are usually engaged short term to assist the church in reaching a particular goal, or in solving a specific problem.[53] The issues relating to processes, pathways, procedures, and policies are easily identified and clarified, and there is a high level of agreement around them. The focus in this type of consultancy is on exploring issues, generating options, and determining the criteria or process for decision-

---

50. Scarborough et al., *Church Consultancy Manual*, 4.
51. Schaller, *The Interventionist*, 64–67.
52. Schaller, *The Interventionist*, 64.
53. Dyer, "Standard and Specialist Consultancies," 1.

making. Implementation is key to a sense of moving through the issue towards their vision of the future.[54]

4.5.1.2 Developmental Consultancy

Within a developmental consultancy there is still a clear sense of identity, however the church is less clear about the next stages of vision and direction. A significant part of the consultancy process is to assist the church to articulate its next stage of growth or change.[55] There may be a sense of being authentic and faithful, but questions such as how the church should be growing and outreaching are eliciting "holy conversations" about a fresh and deeper sense of vision and mission.[56] It will be critical to revisit mission, paint a bigger vision, and then clarify the pathway to get there.[57]

4.5.1.3 Reframing Consultancy

Reframing needs to occur where a church has lost clarity on its identity and it may have become disconnected from, and essentially irrelevant to, its community and locality. This type of consultancy may require longer term involvement and may result in significant transition for the congregation.[58] A new future needs to be envisioned, and then a pathway towards that worked out and usually supported over a period of time. However, a heightened anxiety and typically greater resistance may mean a lower likelihood of success even in the face of careful consultancy and coaching over twelve to eighteen months.[59] Because everything must be reinvented: the core identity of a church, its sense of mission and to whom, and the pathway for achieving this, it may be worth considering replanting the church, since these new paradigms may be out of the reach of existing leaders, and discontinuity with the past is needed to move into God's new future for the church.

---

54. Dyer, "Types of Proactive Consulting," 4–5.
55. Dyer, "Standard and Specialist Consultancies," 1.
56. Rendle and Mann, *Holy Conversations*.
57. Dyer, "Types of Proactive Consulting," 7–9.
58. Dyer, "Standard and Specialist Consultancies," 1.
59. Dyer, "Types of Proactive Consulting," 10–12.

4.5.2 Specialist Consultancies

The six specialist areas in church consultancy include working with churches in major transitions, assisting with staff and leadership team reviews, helping to shape governance development, advising on strategic planning processes, working with churches through times of conflict, and recovery from critical and traumatic situations.

While all aspects of the standard process are used and kept in mind, specialist areas have several unique features. Some of these have elements of the three types above but the unique elements mean they have been allocated specialty areas.

In specialist consultancies, the objectives are usually given by the nature of the situation that the church is dealing with. While terms of reference still need to be clarified, there is not usually the need for an evening exploring objectives as is common in the standard process.

There are usually unique dynamics which need to be understood to consult effectively in the situation (e.g. recovery from a betrayal of trust by a church leader, the specific dynamics of power and leadership within Christian communities, team relationships in a ministry context). Consultants will need to receive specialist training in these areas to be effective. These dynamics will have a critical impact on the type and process of data gathering that is used in assessing the situation.[60]

The standard process assumes broad consulting with the church as a whole and maximal participation by all. Specialist consultancies may need by their nature to work at different levels of the church and may not necessarily involve all parishioners or members of all congregations.

There is usually an assumed involvement in the implementation process following assessment of the situation. This often involves consultants giving some input including the potential of training, equipping, or running workshops on specific issues. This is not normally the case in proactive consultancies where consultants are more cautious about direct involvement within the church system.

Due to the higher level of involvement in implementation, it is customary in each of the specialist consultancies to use an equipped and supported small group of local church members and leaders as an implementation team. These have different names in the different types

---

60. Dyer, "Standard and Specialist Consultancies," 1.

of consultancies but are common to all (e.g. Transition Team, Recovery Oversight Group, Mediation Team, Review Group, or Planning Group).[61]

4.5.2.1 Transition

These consultancies usually focus on assisting churches process pastoral transitions, particularly after long pastorates, difficult endings, or other complicating factors. They may also include major changes in size through growth or decline, and may involve assisting churches process closures, mergers, or new developments.[62]

The consultants will work with the church and leadership to ensure that steps are taken to help people respectfully let go of the past. This may include special celebrations, and/or church services that seek to bring a sense of closure and acknowledge the change that has taken place, as well as to anticipate a future in which God will continue to reveal his faithfulness. The important tasks of the consultants will be: facilitating effective grieving, reiterating the big picture, and outlining the reasons for change and the steps to navigate it. Most transitional consultancies help the church process the leaving of a pastor, especially if the pastor has resigned due to conflict, was terminated due to incompetence, became burned out, or on the departure of a long-serving pastor, even under good circumstances. It will be important that there is a carefully facilitated transition period, so that any emotions and issues are addressed, and there is a clear sense of the church's identity and mission before requesting a new pastor. This type of transition can be carried out by an intentional interim pastor[63] or by church consultants. Research led by Loren Mead has identified five tasks of churches in transition.

Coming to terms with history through healing of any wounds and unhelpful patterns. Some churches look back to see repeated conflict with previous clergy, and this time can be a time of examination, taking responsibility, and repentance. Celebrating and letting go of the former pastor and his/her ministry will be an important part of this time, for only when the congregation has let go of the former pastor/minister can a new pastor be fully accepted.

---

61. Dyer, "Standard and Specialist Consultancies," 1.
62. Dyer, "Standard and Specialist Consultancies," 2.
63. Nicholson, *Temporary Shepherds*; Oswald et al., *Beginning Ministry Together*; Phillips, *Pastoral Transitions*; Bridges, *Managing Transitions*.

Examining leadership and organizational needs through reexamining leadership structure and decision-making structures. Transition can be a great opportunity to develop and deploy new leadership from the congregation.

Rethinking denominational linkage will occur as a congregation reflects on its identity without its former pastor; its values, theology, and missional focus. This will assist a church in linking with a new pastor who is an appropriate match for the congregation. This will be facilitated through forging a closer and more direct link with the denomination, rather than a connection that may have been mediated through the previous pastor.

Deepening a sense of identity and developing fresh vision, as a church reflects on changes in its membership and in its local community. The periodic task of clarifying and deepening a sense of its vision, mission, values, and goals is an ideal task for the interim interval.

Preparation to welcome new pastoral leadership. After a congregation has completed the preceding four tasks, it can move on to searching for a pastor who will be an appropriate match for this congregation. The congregation then prepares practically and emotionally to welcome a new pastor.[64]

If the congregation engages widely and deeply in these tasks, the probability of a fruitful, long-lasting ministry partnership is greatly increased.

4.5.2.2 Leadership, Staff, and Team Reviews

Churches often benefit from external assistance when conducting reviews of senior pastoral staff and whole leadership teams. These can often be difficult situations in churches and are commonly avoided or put off due to fear of the process and its outcomes. A healthy process facilitated by trained external consultants working with a church-based review team often produces a healthy pathway forward.[65] Roy Oswald suggests that a church should evaluate its own ministry every four years, and that carrying out a pastoral review in this context is more beneficial than a review

---

64. Mead, *A Change of Pastors.*
65. Dyer, "Standard and Specialist Consultancies," 2.

done in isolation.[66] This recognizes the partnership in ministry between the pastor and the church.

4.5.2.3 Governance Development

Many church issues are traced to governance processes which are inadequate for the size and complexity of a congregation. Governance is being rediscovered in many churches and a number of models are being explored (e.g. the Carver model[67] with varying degrees of success, as denominational traditions and multiple roles of board members make implementation of this model in a church setting more difficult than in the context of a non-profit one).[68] Assistance with establishing a healthy working understanding of the spiritual and organizational dynamics of governance is a common consultancy agenda. Work takes place with staff and lay governing elders or board members around establishing healthy processes, accountabilities, and empowerment to lead.[69]

There are a number of different models of governance used in churches such as a board-centered model, a committee-centered model, and a staff-centered model.[70] Each of these models have their advantages and disadvantages, and each will be more suited to various sizes of church and specific contexts. It is vitally important to have a suitable governance structure in place to navigate the next size transition for the church.[71]

Some churches have adjunct ministries such as a preschool or school. In some of those situations, the board of the adjunct ministry is completely or partially separate from the governance of the church. In other settings the ancillary ministry is run by the leadership body of the church. In this latter case, an adjunct ministry may outgrow the size of the church that commenced it and/or the level of competence of the church's governance. These scenarios can complicate a church's governance picture, and they may benefit from a governance development consultancy.

---

66. Oswald, "Getting Feedback on Your Ministry: Three Ways to Do Evaluation Without Risking a Public Flogging," 3.

67. Carver, *Boards That Make a Difference*; Carver and Carver, *The Policy Governance Model and the Role of the Board Member*; Borden, *Direct Hit*.

68. Hotchkiss, "Borrowing from Business: How Church Boards Can Benefit from Secular Practices," 31.

69. Dyer, "Standard and Specialist Consultancies," 2.

70. Hotchkiss, *Governance and Ministry: Rethinking Board Leadership*.

71. Gaede, *Size Transitions in Congregations*; Mann, *Raising the Roof*.

Three modes or types of governance—fiduciary,[72] strategic,[73] and generative[74]—are suggested as a means to effective non-profit leadership.[75] The authors assert that generative governance is underutilized in many organizations, and as has been noted in 4.5.1.2 above and 4.5.2.4 below, some churches need to strengthen this mode of governance to enable them to move ahead.[76] Governing bodies in churches often lack adequate time and focus being given to strategic governance, leading to a reactive stance.

4.5.2.4 Strategic Planning

Many churches have vision and direction but are unable to translate this to the next level of a strategic plan, implemented over a specific time frame. Consultants assist a planning and implementation group to develop this and establish the process so that the church is empowered to move forward.[77]

4.5.2.5 Conflicted Congregations

It is inescapable that at some point in a church's life, conflict will arise. Conflict is a critical situation in churches and many find themselves unprepared to deal with it wisely and well. Conflict trained consultants seek to negotiate peace, to equip churches to deal with their disagreements with care and integrity, and to resolve or manage their situations appropriately.[78]

The extent of conflict in terms of how many people it touches, and its intensity (e.g. Leas' five levels of conflict) will be impacted by a number of things.[79] In a church environment there is often a widespread failure to anticipate and normalize conflict. This failure also results in a lack of process and will to deal with conflict when it inevitably arises. This is

---

72. Financial/legal.
73. Achieving the plan.
74. Framing problems and clarifying values, which in turn shape the strategic.
75. Chait et al., *Governance as Leadership*, 6–7.
76. Chait et al., *Governance as Leadership*, 10.
77. Dyer, "Standard and Specialist Consultancies," 1.
78. Dyer, "Standard and Specialist Consultancies," 2.
79. Dobson et al., *Mastering Conflict and Controversy*, 84–93.

quite paradoxical given that a central task of those who follow Jesus is to reconcile others to God (2 Cor 5:16–20), to take the initiative in seeking reconciliation with others in their own relationships (Matt 5:21–24), and to exercise the role of peacemaker in others' conflicts (Matt 5:9). Consequently, many churches have a pattern of extreme responses of "flight" or "fight": denying, avoiding, and minimizing conflict, which often leads to a later eruption of conflict with greater intensity, overreactions on the part of people, and the need for outside intervention such as consultancy. The tasks of a consultancy in this context are: where possible bring reconciliation in relationships, when emotions have dissipated to deal with the issues surrounding the conflict, and to build the capacity of the church to deal more effectively with conflict in the future, through workshops and policy adoption.

4.5.2.6 Recovery from Crisis

Churches can face traumatic incidents including serious accidents, crime, natural disasters, the death of an incumbent pastor, and also moral and ethical misconduct in leadership. These events can have a profound impact on a spiritual family and leave people deeply wounded and hurt. Consultancy teams assist churches to work through the processes of restoration and recovery.[80]

While the consultancy team will seek to deal with the presenting issue (and referral to authorities if warranted), this type of consultancy will necessitate a high level of pastoral care, or possibly referral of some people for individual counselling.

4.6 Other Consultancy Models

There are many individual consultants and many models of church consultancy, all falling into one of the three categories proposed by Schein and noted above.[81]

A catalogue of each and every method of church consultancy used worldwide is outside the scope of this study, but attempts to replicate one model in a number of places such as Western Australian Baptist

---

80. Dyer, "Standard and Specialist Consultancies," 2.
81. Schein, *Process Consultation*, 22–35.

churches and New Zealand Baptist churches have been made.[82] That is, Paul Borden's Great Commission Network integration of consultancy, intentional interim ministry, training and coaching of pastors, accountability for growth, and the Carver governance model.[83] Borden was a middle judicatory leader of the American Baptist Churches of the West, and through this integrated approach they were able to improve from 16 percent of churches growing to 72 percent of churches growing in five years.[84] Church consultancy was an important part of this growth, but it is important to recognize the other aspects of this model which "incorporates all of what we see as essential for growth to take place over a region."[85] It is also vital to recognize that church consultancy in the context of this model is used in a different way to some other church consultancies.

> A second action we stopped was conducting conflict mediation. We really believed that conflict mediation in congregations for the most part does not work, only produces more conflict mediation, never produces organizational health or growth, and communicates that most of the region's resources need to be focused on the islands of sickness rather than on islands of health.[86]

Rather, each area consultant was to select seven to ten congregations "they believed have the best chance of turning around" in that consultant's area "to work with intensively for a year."[87] The criteria used as a basis to select churches varied, but included "current history," "intense desire for change," and a few churches that were both growing and healthy.[88] Of course, churches and pastors that were resistant to change or did not see the need for change were not targeted and of course would not invite a consultancy.[89]

82. Bryant, "Do Church Health Consultancies Assist Local Churches to Become Healthier? Two Western Australian Case Studies," 31–48.
83. Borden, *Direct Hit*; Carver, *Boards That Make a Difference*.
84. Easum, "Transformation and Reproduction Across Denominational Lines," 12.
85. Easum, "Transformation and Reproduction Across Denominational Lines, 12.
86. Borden, *Direct Hit*, 72.
87. Borden, *Direct Hit*, 82.
88. Borden, *Direct Hit*, 82.
89. Borden, *Direct Hit*, 82.

While this emphasis on a "productive intervention" may be something that good freelance consultants practice,[90] in a denominational setting the pressure to avoid churches failing may mean that marginally viable churches undergo multiple consultancies without any apparent improvement. Church consultancy is not a sure-fire remedy, but if used in an appropriate way with the right church at the right time, can make a significant difference to the health and growth of a church. Accordingly, church consultancy can never be seen as an isolated strategy, but to have the greatest success must be part of an overall leadership paradigm for church health and growth.

4.7 Conclusion

Church consultancy is one significant strategy for the growth and health of churches. Church consultancy draws particularly on the field of organizational development, as well as other academic disciplines. However, church consultancy is markedly unique from other types of organizational consultancy through its connection with various branches of theology, such as ecclesiology and missiology, which are used in shaping a Godward and missional response for a local church. In fact, church consultancy has many of the characteristics of other forms of Christian ministry.

There are many other health strategies, and they may be more appropriate to use at particular times than a church consultancy. For example, conflict between two to four families that has not spread church-wide may be best handled by mediation. And a difficult, conflicted leave by the outgoing pastor may be best approached through an intentional interim pastorate.[91] The effectiveness enjoyed by Paul Borden in using church consultancy as part of an integrated health strategy is again noted.[92]

Nevertheless, there are many opportunities for church consultancy alone to make a significant difference, whether through a specific problem or issue to solve or at some other point on the standard or proactive consultancy process. At other times, churches may need to call in specialist teams to deal with transition, leadership reviews, recovery from crisis, governance development, or conflict.

---

90. Schaller, *The Interventionist*, 64.
91. See Appendix F.
92. Borden, *Direct Hit*.

The type of church consultancy used in Baptist churches tends towards the Process Facilitator-Participant/Learner model of consultancy, and in many cases a small team from the church is formed not only to assist with the process and contextualize it to that particular church, but also to receive training so that the church is further equipped and strengthened for the future, having less need of outside assistance.

The theology of church consultancy outlined in the chapter, and which informs the evaluations, recommendations, and conclusions of this thesis, can be summarized in the following theological assertions.

A theology of church and kingdom, that sees the church generally, and a local church specifically, as an instrument of God's missional purposes in the world for the establishment of his kingdom. Local churches can be more or less effective as such agents; both in their local outreach and in their common life together (e.g. the quality of their relationships). Church consultancy can therefore be one way in which local churches can be released to greater levels of effectiveness as agents of God's kingdom advance, and the proclamation of his lordship over all of creation.

A theology of process and capacity-building affirms the relational nature of a consultancy, with bi-directional knowledge flows acknowledging the dignity and contributions of both consultant and church, and reflecting the mutuality of the body of Christ. This mutuality is further underscored as consultants and church *together* seek to discern God's call for the church, and contextualize that to the local church and local community through the involvement of local church leaders and a local consultancy oversight/implementation group. The responsibility of a church for its own life and health, particularly in the context of Free Church ecclesiology, is upheld, and further strengthened as individuals within a church are mentored, coached, and equipped by consultants. A process-based approach offers the greatest potential for ownership by a church of the issues, buy-in, action, and lasting organizational transformation as the capacity of a church and its leadership is built towards being a "learning organization."[93]

A theology of interdisciplinary insight acknowledges that all truth is God's truth, and rather than rejecting such insights, asks what they may contribute to our understanding and practice of church. Care needs to be taken where interdisciplinary insights are accepted uncritically or are inconsistent with Scripture. However, the insights of the social sciences

---

93. Senge, *The Fifth Discipline*.

regarding such examples as systems theory and church consultancy have been examined over many decades and used to great effect in fostering church health and facilitating church growth. The importance of developing a theological framework around interdisciplinary insights cannot be underestimated. For church consultancy, developing ecclesiological, missiological, and other theological frameworks recognizes that church consultancy is much more than "organizational development for churches."[94] Rather, it has unique characteristics and goals regarding the practice of effective ministry and mission of a local church in its community context.[95]

A theology of the church, as it intersects with church consultancy, will include the New Testament patterns of addressing issues through consulting with individual local churches and coaching church leaders. It also centers on the theology and practice of evaluation, in a redemptive context, to maximize church health and church growth consistent with the biblical purposes of the church. And church consultancy can be a means of ministry to a church and/or individuals within the church, in a specific and contextualized way; including consolation, reconciliation, equipping, and exhortation.

A theology of change and transition recognizes both the dynamic leading of God, and the God-opportunities that are often present in change. Transition involves navigating the emotional and spiritual processes that accompany change. The motif of journey is one that is evident in Scripture (e.g. Israel's exodus) and involves an ending, neutral zone/wilderness/transition, and a new beginning.[96] In churches this can include pastoral transitions but is broadly centered on God's dynamic call to new arenas of effectiveness and maturity, while letting go of past experiences or patterns that have been less helpful. Some churches are more adept at navigating changes, while others, especially if a massive change is involved (e.g. retirement of the founding pastor after twenty years),

---

94. Lewin, *The Complete Social Scientist: A Kurt Lewin Reader*; Bennis and Townsend, *Reinventing Leadership: Strategies to Empower the Organization*; Bennis, *Beyond Bureaucracy: Essays on the Development and Evolution of Human Organization*; Carter et al., *Best Practices in Leadership Development and Organization Change*; Senge, *The Fifth Discipline*; Rothwell and Sullivan, *Practicing Organization Development: A Guide for Consultants*; Malony, *Church Organization Development: Perspectives and Processes*; Lovell, *Consultancy Modes and Models*.

95. Dudley, "Integrating the Approaches: A Practical Theology," 230–7; Dudley, *Building Effective Ministry: Theory and Practice in the Local Church*, 38–153.

96. Bridges, *Managing Transitions: Making the Most of Change*.

respond well to a church consultancy or intentional interim ministry to lead them through the five developmental tasks outlined above.[97]

A *theology of leadership*, as it intersects with church consultancy, firstly recognizes both the importance and the difficulty of accountability. Pastors will often engage in relational accountability with a mentor or a renewal retreat group, but churches are often concerned with job accountability and performance reviews. Best practice ministry reviews in a church context are mutual: that is, since biblically the pastor is not responsible for carrying out all the ministries of the church, it is valuable to review the church at the same time.[98] Best practice ministry reviews in a church context are developmental, just as God seeks to develop and mature us: that is, they don't carry the threat of job loss or salary cuts, but are concerned with the personhood of the pastor, and maximizing his/her effectiveness through such initiatives as identifying training needs. Best practice ministry reviews are delegated to a small church-based review team to carry out, rather than the whole church. Best practice reviews are regular and ongoing, and this reduces the anxiety felt by pastors and churches that avoid reviews for many years. Nevertheless, such reviews can be very helpful, so churches often benefit from the objectivity of external church consultants when conducting reviews of senior pastoral staff and whole leadership teams.

Secondly, while cognizant of the variety of church governance models within Free Church or Baptist settings, and the plethora of models in other ecclesiologies, a *theology of leadership* is contextual as it transects with church consultancy.[99] That is, it is related to that particular church, in its specific local community, and to its size.[100]

---

97. Mead, *A Change of Pastors*.

98. Oswald, "Getting Feedback on Your Ministry: Three Ways to Do Evaluation Without Risking a Public Flogging," 3.

99. In stating this, a case for the importance of a worked through ecclesiology as it touches leadership and governance has already been made elsewhere in this research. While a contextual approach may seem overly pragmatic, it does not dismiss other aspects. It does honor the uniqueness of each local church, and how leadership *functions* in a particular church at a particular time (rather than how it is structured) is a primary concern of church consultancy.

100. Mann, *Raising the Roof*; Gaede, *Size Transitions in Congregations*; Fletcher, *Overcoming Barriers to Growth*. For example, a church comprised mainly of a lower socioeconomic may have a more consultative and participatory approach to leadership; a church that is growing through a size transition may need to add to the leadership team and review roles.

And thirdly, a *theology of leadership* recognizes the centrality of the equipping function (Eph 4:11–12) for releasing health and growth in a church. That is, how leadership *functions*; through facilitating a clear and owned vision, through inspiring and empowering attenders to use their gifts in ministry, and through creative, open, and flexible innovation.

There are many fields and theologies that intersect with church consultancy, which have been discussed at length in the body of this chapter and outlined above. In particular, a conversation connecting church consultancy with church health and church growth has in some cases affirmed, in others critiqued, and in still others nuanced our understanding of church consultancy. This has in turn integrated and made more explicit the overarching theology presented in this thesis.

5

Data Analysis

5.1 Church Consultancy Case Studies

MANY CHURCHES, AT SOME point or points in their history, go through periods of crisis, difficulty, or are plateaued in their growth. The leadership of some churches may deny that a problem exists or attempt to solve it on their own. However, increasingly, Baptist churches in NSW/ACT are inviting outside assistance, with over one third of those 303 churches having invited a church consultancy team since 1999.[1] For some, it is to deal with a specific issue, for others to envision the future, or perhaps to get some insights about breaking through a growth barrier.[2] These ten churches were designated on the basis of having completed both NCLS-2001 and NCLS-2006, and having commenced a church consultancy in 2001 or 2002, giving a four-to-five-year time span to seek to assess the impact of the church consultancy on the health and growth of the church. They are a broad mixture of churches, large and small, multi-pastor and sole pastor, rural and urban. They have also entered into consultancies for a variety of reasons. What follows is background regarding each church, consultancy objectives set by each church's leadership, and indications towards the impact of the church consultancy over the period to 2006 on each church's health and growth.[3]

   1. Davies, "Consultancy Master List Numerical 070919 (Version 2).xls," 1.
   2. Mann, *The In-Between Church*; Mann, *Raising the Roof*.
   3. Summaries of the church consultancy reports incorporating objectives that

5.1.1 Church A[4]

5.1.1.1 Background

Church A is located in the northern beaches area of Sydney and had an attendance of 135 at the time of the church consultancy.

In this suburb, 69 percent of residents were born in Australia, above the Sydney average (61%). Children and youth are strongly represented, with 19 percent of residents aged 5 to 19 years (Sydney 14%). Sixty-four percent of residents are married (Sydney 51%). The largest occupational grouping is professionals at 12 percent (Sydney 9%), indicating a higher socioeconomic.[5]

An awareness of "a degree of people being unsettled relationally," unhealed hurts from a major church split ten years before, and a sense of frustration surrounding a united, owned sense of vision and mission were some of the catalysts for this church consultancy.[6] These tensions were unpacked further during the church consultancy as "historical research and input during the consultancy process highlighted some historical, systemic patterns relating to periods of stability and instability and feelings towards pastoral leadership in the life of the Church."[7]

5.1.1.2 Church Consultancy Objectives

The following objectives were agreed upon and established by the church leadership for the consultancy:

1. To assist the church in the development of a vision for the future.

---

were set by the various leadership groups of those churches and recommendations made by the consultants regarding each objective are contained in appendices AA to JJ.

4. The terms "Church A," "Church B," and so forth used in this thesis are used to protect the identity of the churches, pastors, and attenders. Where confidentiality is an issue, pseudonyms are used, gender is disguised, and the word "date" or similar is used instead of specific dates. Where such changes are made to an existing document, such as a consultancy report, these changes are contained in square brackets.

5. ABS Census of Population and Housing, "Suburb Profiles—Demographics."

6. Pastor of Church A, Interview Transcript, 1–4.

7. Baptist Churches of NSW and ACT Church Consultancy Team, "Church A Baptist Church Consultancy Report," 4.

2. To clarify the congregation's understanding and expectations of the present church leadership and any suggested improvements.

3. To identify both ministry priorities and potential resources to maximize opportunities in the life of the church.

4. To enable the church to implement a leadership development process, including training, support, and communication strategies.

5. To explore creative decision-making processes.[8]

5.1.1.3 Indications Towards the Impact of Consultancy on Church A Health and Growth

The leadership team and church accepted the report. An interview with the student associate (later pastor [2002–03], then pastoral leader [2003–08]) indicated that the consultancy recommendations were carried out, with a significant re-visioning process engaged in by the church.[9] This saw the NCLS core quality indicators increase for vision (by 100%) and leadership (by 97%).[10] Improvement in total core quality indicators from NCLS-2001 to NCLS-2006 was 47 percent.[11] Attendance rose to 180, an increase of 33 percent in the interval to 2006.[12]

5.1.2 Church B

5.1.2.1 Background

Church B is located in the inner south-west of Sydney and had an attendance of fifty at the time of the church consultancy.[13]

In this suburb, a below average 36 percent of residents were born in Australia (Sydney 61%), indicating the strong multicultural nature of this community. Correspondingly, 40 percent list their religion as Islam.[14]

---

8. Baptist Churches of NSW and ACT Church Consultancy Team, "Church A Baptist Church Consultancy Report," 4.

9. Pastor of Church A, Interview Transcript, 1.

10. NCLS Research, *Church Life Profile—Church A Baptist Church*, 6, 15–16.

11. NCLS Research, *Church Life Profile—Church A Baptist Church*, 6.

12. NCLS Research, *Church Life Profile—Church A Baptist Church*, 23.

13. NCLS Research, *Church Life Profile—Church B Baptist Church*, 24.

14. ABS Census of Population and Housing, *Suburb Profiles—Demographics*.

Youth and children are strongly represented in this community, with 21 percent aged 5 to 19 years (Sydney 14%) and 10 percent aged 0 to 4 years (Sydney 7%). Only 4 percent of residents in this area are professionals (Sydney 9%), indicating a lower socioeconomic.[15]

This consultancy was brought about through the church facing a plateau in attendance and seeking to increase its relevance and outreach to an increasingly multicultural community. The church was also struggling to resource and support present and projected ministries, with a small congregation, limited finances, and an ageing core.[16] Indications are that the church receives a small subsidy from the Baptist Union to assist with insurance, and "there is also recognition that the [part-time] pastor is working beyond the hours the Church pays him."[17]

5.1.2.2 Church Consultancy Objectives

Objectives set with the leadership group for the course of the consultancy were:

1. To clarify the church's vision for the future
2. To assist the congregation in encouraging greater personal spiritual maturity
3. To assist the church in motivating greater involvement in ministry
4. To identify appropriate community outreach strategies and ways of building people into the life of the church
5. To assist the leadership in developing effective ministry training strategies.[18]

---

15. ABS Census of Population and Housing, *Suburb Profiles—Demographics*.

16. Baptist Churches of NSW and ACT Church Consultancy Team, "Church B Baptist Church Consultancy Report," 3.

17. Baptist Churches of NSW and ACT Church Consultancy Team, "Church B Baptist Church Consultancy Report," 4.

18. Baptist Churches of NSW and ACT Church Consultancy Team, "Church B Baptist Church Consultancy Report," 3. See Appendix BB for recommendations.

5.1.2.3 Indications Towards the Impact of Consultancy on Church B Health and Growth

The leadership team and the church accepted the report. The church has committed to objective 4 recommendations regarding identifying appropriate community outreach strategies in this multicultural context. It is also engaging with families with young children (e.g. objective 5, recommendation 3) such that the average age of the congregation decreased by over five years between 2001 and NCLS-2006.[19] Accordingly, the proportion of attenders aged 30 to 39 years tripled to 30 percent.[20]

However, large increases in NCLS-2006 core quality indicators for worship (40%) and service (63%) could not offset decreases or small increases in other core qualities, leading to an overall decline of 5.6 percent.[21]

Attendance rose to sixty-eight, an increase of 36 percent.[22] It is encouraging that despite the church having considerable viability concerns in 2001, its smaller size, and operating in a challenging community environment, an intentional engagement by the church in the consultancy process has borne encouraging fruit in attendance over this five-year period.

5.1.3 Church C

5.1.3.1 Background

Church C is located on a coastal strip near a major regional center in NSW and had an attendance of seventy-five at the time of the church consultancy.[23]

In this locality, a high 84 percent of residents were born in Australia (regional center 73%). Age groupings were typical of the nearby regional center, with those aged 20 to 39 years and 40 to 59 years most strongly represented. Occupational groupings were mixed with professionals

---

19. NCLS Research, *Church Life Profile—Church B Baptist Church*, 24.
20. NCLS Research, *Church Life Profile—Church B Baptist Church*, 24.
21. NCLS Research, *Church Life Profile—Church B Baptist Church*, 6.
22. NCLS Research, *Church Life Profile—Church B Baptist Church*, 23.
23. NCLS Research, *Church Life Profile—Church C Baptist Church*, 23.

(7%), intermediate clerical/sales/service (7%), and tradespersons and related workers (6%) the top three.[24]

During the consultancy, 36 percent of those interviewed indicated that there were conflict issues from the past that the church may have to deal with, with a further 25 percent indicating they were "not sure."[25] The church had split five years before, after which the senior pastor at the time of the church consultancy was appointed.[26] The church was also grappling with the viability and direction of its youth ministry.[27]

5.1.3.2 Church Consultancy Objectives

The following objectives were established by the church leadership for the consultancy:

1. To examine the respective processes for communication and conflict management in the church.
2. To identify the unmet needs and aspirations of the church attenders.
3. To explore strategies to facilitate the growth of the youth ministry both spiritually and numerically.
4. To discover the attitude of the clients of the ministries of Church C toward the church and to explore strategies to more effectively incorporate them into the church.[28]

5.1.3.3 Indications Towards the Impact of Consultancy on Church C Health and Growth

The leadership team and the church accepted the report. The church consultancy sought to deal with the residual conflict issues and the

---

24. ABS Census of Population and Housing, *Suburb Profiles—Demographics*.

25. Baptist Churches of NSW and ACT Church Consultancy Team, "Church C Baptist Church Consultancy Report," 7.

26. Pastor of Church C, Interview Transcript, 1.

27. Baptist Churches of NSW and ACT Church Consultancy Team, "Church C Baptist Church Consultancy Report," 3.

28. Baptist Churches of NSW and ACT Church Consultancy Team, "Church C Baptist Church Consultancy Report," 3.

consultancy precipitated the implementation of a conflict policy.[29] Subsequent to the consultancy, the associate pastor left the church in 2002. The senior pastor concluded in 2004, and an interim pastor was appointed to the church. This may explain the considerable decrease for each inspirational core quality (vision, leadership, and innovation) in NCLS-2006. Total core quality indicators decreased 12 percent in the period between NCLS-2001 and NCLS-2006.[30] Attendance rose to seventy-six, an increase of 1 percent.[31]

5.1.4 Church D

5.1.4.1 BACKGROUND

Church D is located in the developing suburban ring in Western Sydney and had an attendance of ninety-one at the time of the church consultancy.[32]

In this suburb, the country of origin is Australian born for 68 percent of residents (Sydney 61%).[33] The largest age group is those aged 20 to 39 (34%; Sydney 33%), with a correspondingly high proportion of those aged 5 to 19 (25%; Sydney 14%) indicating that this is an area where young families settle, with many purchasing homes (46%; Sydney 23%).[34] Occupational groupings are mixed with intermediate clerical/sales/service (10%), professionals (8%), and tradespersons and related workers (6%) the top three.[35]

Rather than seeking to address a serious problem, this proactive consultancy is mainly focused around growth issues: how to inculcate vision to those who are joining the church, structures that will be effective for this stage of the church's growth, and enhancing communication in the context of the church's development.[36] While there will always be issues to address in any church, inviting outside assistance early to assist

---

29. Pastor of Church C, Interview Transcript, 2.
30. NCLS Research, *Church Life Profile—Church C Baptist Church*, 6.
31. NCLS Research, *Church Life Profile—Church C Baptist Church*, 23.
32. NCLS Research, *Church Life Profile—Church D Baptist Church*, 23.
33. ABS Census of Population and Housing, *Suburb Profiles—Demographics*.
34. ABS Census of Population and Housing, *Suburb Profiles—Demographics*.
35. ABS Census of Population and Housing, *Suburb Profiles—Demographics*.
36. Baptist Churches of NSW and ACT Church Consultancy Team, "Church D Baptist Church Consultancy Report," 4.

with navigating expansion issues is perhaps a more effective use of the church consultancy process, enabling such churches to take the step to the next level of growth.

5.1.4.2 Church Consultancy Objectives

The following objectives were established by the church leadership for the consultancy:

1. Develop and implement appropriate communication processes within the church.
2. Define and share a vision in a way that the church owns it.
3. Design the most effective structures and strategies to achieve the church's vision.[37]

5.1.4.3 Indications Towards the Impact of Consultancy on Church D Health and Growth

The leadership team and the church accepted the report. The church had already taken "significant steps . . . to address communication, vision and structure issues" addressed in the consultancy report at the time of its writing.[38] NCLS-2006 indicated that a clear and owned vision was the church's strongest core quality indicator, and this had increased 67 percent from NCLS-2001.[39] The core quality indicator of inspiring and empowering leadership increased 121 percent over this time, reflecting that effective structures and strategies (along with strong empowerment of attenders for ministry) to achieve the church's vision had progressed.[40] Considerable increases were recorded for each of the nine core quality indicators, leading to an overall increase of 63 percent.[41] The senior pastor

---

37. Baptist Churches of NSW and ACT Church Consultancy Team, "Church D Baptist Church Consultancy Report," 3.
38. Baptist Churches of NSW and ACT Church Consultancy Team, "Church D Baptist Church Consultancy Report," 6.
39. NCLS Research, *Church Life Profile—Church D Baptist Church*, 6.
40. NCLS Research, *Church Life Profile—Church D Baptist Church*, 6.
41. NCLS Research, *Church Life Profile—Church D Baptist Church*, 6.

serving the church in 2001 has continued to lead it to the present. Attendance grew to 150, an increase of 65 percent over the period to 2006.[42]

The benefits of using church consultancy proactively to address structures and strategies surrounding growth (rather than reacting to problems) is underscored in this case. This would be a worthwhile area for further research.

5.1.5 Church E

5.1.5.1 Background

Church E is located near a major coastal regional center in NSW and had an attendance of sixty-eight at the time of the church consultancy.[43]

In this locality, occupational groupings indicate a lower socioeconomic with tradespersons and related workers (7%), intermediate clerical/sales/service (7%), and intermediate production and transport (6%) the top three.[44]

This church applied in June 2002 to the Baptist Churches of NSW/ACT for admission to the Partnership Scheme. The application was successful. While this scheme involves some level of financial assistance over a two-year period, the purpose of the scheme is to foster a church's growth and health. To this end, successful applicant churches are strongly encouraged to enter into a church consultancy at the commencement and conclusion of their two-year Partnership Scheme.[45]

Some within the church were struggling with issues surrounding change, and this is against a backdrop where the local community is "moving through significant transition" and increasing ministry effectiveness will not occur through "incremental change."[46] One example of this is "the need to modify the morning worship service to incorporate young families and make it more relevant for unchurched people."[47]

---

42. NCLS Research, *Church Life Profile—Church D Baptist Church*, 23.
43. Soden, *NSW and ACT Baptist Churches Handbook 2001–2002*, 351.
44. ABS Census of Population and Housing, *Suburb Profiles—Demographics*.
45. Baptist Churches of NSW and ACT Church Consultancy Team, "Church E Baptist Church Consultancy Report," 3.
46. Baptist Churches of NSW and ACT Church Consultancy Team, "Church E Baptist Church Consultancy Report," 5.
47. Baptist Churches of NSW and ACT Church Consultancy Team, "Church E Baptist Church Consultancy Report," 7.

Sixty-five percent of church attenders interviewed during the consultancy were involved in ministry for six or more hours a week, yet this does not appear to be translated into effective outreach in the community and the growth of the church.[48] Rather, 67 percent of those interviewed reported that they "feel exhausted and tired."[49] This exhaustion is further compounded by the negative emotions that surround conflict: 80 percent of those interviewed were aware of unresolved conflict in the life of the church, and 62 percent believed that the church does not currently resolve conflict in a healthy way.[50] The overall result is an impairment of hope for the future of the church.

5.1.5.2 Church Consultancy Objectives

The following objectives were established by the church leadership for the consultancy:

1. To identify ministry strategies to take up the opportunities presented by existing and potential contacts in the light of current church activities and services.
2. To evaluate the level of fatigue amongst church workers and provide suggestions for the way forward.
3. To identify levels of conflict in the life of the church and develop a process to implement a biblical conflict resolution strategy.[51]

5.1.5.3 Indications Towards the Impact of Consultancy on Church E Health and Growth

The leadership team and the church received the report. There has been some progress made in implementing the recommendations of the report. The NCLS core quality indicators of faith, service, and inclusion

---

48. Baptist Churches of NSW and ACT Church Consultancy Team, "Church E Baptist Church Consultancy Report," 9.

49. Baptist Churches of NSW and ACT Church Consultancy Team, "Church E Baptist Church Consultancy Report," 9.

50. Baptist Churches of NSW and ACT Church Consultancy Team, "Church E Baptist Church Consultancy Report," 11.

51. Baptist Churches of NSW and ACT Church Consultancy Team, "Church E Baptist Church Consultancy Report," 3.

have grown considerably between 2001 and 2006.[52] However, over this interval the average age of the church has increased by over ten years to 53 years, 10 months, indicating a failure to connect strongly with young families in the community.[53] Furthermore, the fact that 20-to 29-year-olds in 2006 only comprise 4 percent (2001; 7%) and 30-to 39-year-olds make up 4 percent (2001; 20%) of the church shows a loss of those within the church in this crucial demographic over the period.[54] Church attendance has also decreased 41 percent to forty.[55] The percentage of church attenders who are employed has fallen from 61% to 38%, which may indicate some financial strain for the church. However, as the two-year Partnership Scheme concluded during this interval, those giving 10 percent or more of their income has climbed from 29% to 65%.[56] The pastor serving the church in 2001 has continued to the present, albeit in a part-time capacity.

In the light of the attendance decline, the increase of overall core quality indicators by 45 percent seems paradoxical.[57] It is possible that core long-term attenders who are resistant, both to change and to an influx of newcomers into the church, have maintained their influence, and they feel more comfortable as a result. The church had struggled with its financial viability as a prelude to it applying to the Partnership Scheme, and this struggle with viability may be reflected in other areas of outreach and ministry which are now more evident with the passing of time.

5.1. Church F

5.1.6.1 BACKGROUND

Church F is located in an isolated mining city in the far west of NSW and had an attendance of forty-five at the time of the church consultancy.[58,59] The average age of those attending the church in 2001 was 57 years, 5

---

52. NCLS Research, *Church Life Profile—Church E Baptist Church*, 6.
53. NCLS Research, *Church Life Profile—Church E Baptist Church*, 24.
54. NCLS Research, *Church Life Profile—Church E Baptist Church*, 24.
55. Soden, *NSW and ACT Baptist Churches Handbook 2001–2002*, 351.
56. NCLS Research, *Church Life Profile—Church E Baptist Church*, 25.
57. NCLS Research, *Church Life Profile—Church E Baptist Church*, 6.
58. NCLS Research, *Church Life Profile—Church G Baptist Church*, 23.
59. NCLS Research, *Church Life Profile—Church G Baptist Church*, 23.

months.⁶⁰ This is well above the average age of attenders in all NSW/ACT Baptist churches who completed NCLS-2006 (n=150) of 46 years, 8 months.⁶¹

In this city, a high 95 percent of residents were born in Australia. The community has a higher than average 22 percent of residents whose stated religion is "no religion" (NSW 13%). Occupational groupings indicate a lower socioeconomic with intermediate clerical/sales/service (5%; NSW 7%), and tradespersons and related workers (5%; NSW 5%) being the top two.⁶²

This church was at the time of the consultancy in receipt of a subsidy from the Baptist Churches of NSW/ACT, and as such was encouraged to consider a church consultancy to seek to address any issues of health and growth.

5.1.6.2 Consultancy Objectives

The following objectives were then established by the church leadership for this consultancy:

1. To explore ways of encouraging non-members to take the step into membership.
2. To encourage and support the Aboriginal leadership in the growth and development of their fellowship within the life of the church.
3. To develop the corporate prayer life of the church.
4. To develop mission strategies that will lead to effective church growth.
5. To enhance the overall music ministry of the church.
6. To become a financially [self] sufficient church under the guidance of God.⁶³

---

60. NCLS Research, *Church Life Profile—Church F Baptist Church*, 24.

61. NCLS Research, *Regional Church Life Profile—Baptist Churches NSW/ACT*, 24.

62. ABS Census of Population and Housing, *Suburb Profiles—Demographics*.

63. Baptist Churches of NSW and ACT Church Consultancy Team, "Church F Baptist Church Consultancy Report," 4.

5.1.6.3 Indications Towards the Impact of Consultancy on Church F Health and Growth

The leadership team and the church accepted the report. Many of the recommendations from the report have been implemented. There is a sense of energy, encouragement, and anticipation among the congregation, since "the consultancy in some way provided some hope; that it didn't necessarily mean that when the money ceased, life would cease."[64] The number of children from outside the church attending the Oasis ministry continues to grow.[65] The growth of the Aboriginal Fellowship continues, with involvement of Aboriginal young people in the music ministry of the church. This alleviated some of the concerns raised in objective 5 of the 2001 Consultancy Report regarding the ongoing viability of worship music in the church, as health concerns raised questions surrounding the future availability of the organist.[66] Finances continue to be an area of concern for the church. The lack of clarity regarding the church's vision, mission, and values did not appear to have been addressed when a review consultancy was conducted in 2003.[67] However, the focus beyond the church into the community grew over this time frame, and the church gained encouragement as they felt "maybe we're achieving something here... being more effective."[68]

NCLS-2006 reveals an increase in the proportion of church attenders who are employed (22% in 2001, to 36%), and a decrease in the proportion of church attenders who are retired (52% in 2001, to 36%).[69] Clear advancement in objective 6 is demonstrated in those not giving to the church declining from 14 percent (2001) of the congregation to 0 percent, and those who regularly give 10 percent or more of their net income increasing from 36 percent (2001) to 41 percent.[70] The work the church has put in to enhancing its life and outreach is reflected in the

---

64. Pastor of Church F, Interview Transcript, 1.

65. Pastor of Church F, Interview Transcript, 3.

66. Pastor of Church F, Interview Transcript, 2; Baptist Churches of NSW and ACT Church Consultancy Team, "Church F Baptist Church Consultancy Report," 13.

67. Baptist Churches of NSW and ACT Church Consultancy Team, "Church F Baptist Church Consultancy Report," 3.

68. Pastor of Church F, Interview Transcript, 2.

69. NCLS Research, Church Life Profile—Church F Baptist Church, 24.

70. NCLS Research, *Church Life Profile—Church F Baptist Church*, 25.

overall increase of core quality indicators of 52 percent.[71] The only core quality indicator to decrease is vision.[72] The effort put into an intentional welcoming strategy for newcomers is reflected in the core quality indicator for inclusion increasing by 150 percent.[73]

During the five years to 2006, the attendance increased by 11 percent to fifty, and the proportion of 30-to 49-year-olds attending the church increased.[74] It is encouraging that despite the church's smaller size, operating in an isolated community environment, and having some significant viability concerns in 2001, an intentional engagement by the church in the consultancy process has resulted in encouraging outcomes in both attendance and health indicators over this 5-year period.

5.1.7 Church G

5.1.7.1 Background

Church G is located in Western Sydney and had an attendance of 140 at the time of the church consultancy.

In this suburb, the country of origin is Australia for 78 percent of residents (Sydney 61%). The largest age group are those aged 20 to 39 (32%; Sydney 33%), with a correspondingly high proportion of those aged 5 to 19 (25%; Sydney 14%) indicating that this is an area where young families settle, with many purchasing (36%; Sydney 23%) or fully owning (32%; Sydney 41%) their homes. Occupational groupings tend to reflect a lower socioeconomic with intermediate clerical/sales/service (9%), tradespersons and related workers (7%), and intermediate production and transport (5%) the top three.[75]

There appear to be issues of conflict in the past and, while largely resolved, the apparent lack of a clear process for managing differences is hindering progress in this regard. In the absence of a peak ministry leadership group meeting regularly, particularly in a church of this size, it is not surprising that "there was widespread concern expressed about

---

71. NCLS Research, *Church Life Profile—Church F Baptist Church*, 6.
72. NCLS Research, *Church Life Profile—Church F Baptist Church*, 6.
73. NCLS Research, *Church Life Profile—Church F Baptist Church*, 6.
74. NCLS Research, *Church Life Profile—Church F Baptist Church*, 23–24.
75. ABS Census of Population and Housing, *Suburb Profiles—Demographics*.

the lack of communication and cooperation between ministries."[76] The lack of a cohesive vision for children's and youth ministry appears to be fragmenting effort and not maximizing outcomes in this area.[77]

5.1.7.2 Church Consultancy Objectives[78]

The following three objectives were established by the church leadership for the consultancy:

1. To develop and train present and potential leaders.
2. To explore the current practices and outcomes of the Children's and Youth Ministries.
3. To continue to develop ownership and commitment to Church G Baptist Church.[79]

5.1.7.3 Indications Towards the Impact of Consultancy on Church G Health and Growth

The leadership team and the church accepted the report. There has been some progress made in implementing the recommendations of the report, but the crucial area of youth identified in the consultancy report does not appear to have been sufficiently addressed. Attenders who are parents of children 15 years and over indicated in NCLS-2006 that only 34 percent still attend this church (down from 59% in 2001), while those who attend elsewhere has increased to 20 percent (13% in 2001), and those who do not attend any church has increased to 46 percent (28% in 2001).[80] The level of attenders who are satisfied with what is offered in

---

76. Baptist Churches of NSW and ACT Church Consultancy Team, "Church G Baptist Church Consultancy Report," 5.

77. Baptist Churches of NSW and ACT Church Consultancy Team, "Church G Baptist Church Consultancy Report," 3.

78. Baptist Churches of NSW and ACT Church Consultancy Team, "Church G Baptist Church Consultancy Report."

79. Baptist Churches of NSW and ACT Church Consultancy Team, "Church G Baptist Church Consultancy Report," 3.

80. NCLS Research, *Church Life Profile—Church G Baptist Church*, 21.

the church for 12-to 18-year-olds has decreased to 47 percent (72% in 2001).[81]

The senior pastor serving the church in 2001 has continued to the present. Slight increases in three core quality health indicators could not overcome decreases in the other six indicators, resulting in an overall minor decrease of 13 percent.[82] Attendance declined 14 percent to 120 over the five years to 2006.[83]

5.1.8 Church H

5.1.8.1 Background

Church H is located on the lower north shore of Sydney on a major transport node and had an attendance of eighty at the time of the church consultancy.[84]

In this locality, a high proportion of those aged 20 to 39 years (44%; Sydney 33%), as well as an above average percentage of those renting (42%; Sydney 30%) indicates strong mobility.[85] This mobility is reflected in objective 5 under section 5.1.8.2 below as the church seeks ways to "enhance integration into the congregation." The transitory nature of this community is underscored by the high proportion of residents who have never married (43%; Sydney 33%).[86] The percentage who claimed "no religion" in the Census is high (24%; Sydney 13%), demonstrating the challenge that lies before churches in this community.[87] The incidence of professionals is well above average (20%; Sydney 9%) and is indicative of a high socioeconomic.[88]

This consultation was initiated by the senior pastor, along with the deacons, as the church was grappling with issues surrounding clarity of vision, targeted and effective outreach into the community, and

---

81. NCLS Research, *Church Life Profile—Church G Baptist Church*, 21.
82. NCLS Research, *Church Life Profile—Church G Baptist Church*, 6.
83. NCLS Research, *Church Life Profile—Church G Baptist Church*, 23.
84. NCLS Research, *Church Life Profile—Church H Baptist Church*, 23.
85. ABS Census of Population and Housing, *Suburb Profiles—Demographics*.
86. ABS Census of Population and Housing, *Suburb Profiles—Demographics*.
87. ABS Census of Population and Housing, *Suburb Profiles—Demographics*.
88. ABS Census of Population and Housing, *Suburb Profiles—Demographics*.

integration of newcomers into the church.[89] "The state of the church was that for some years the numbers of people had been declining . . . the church needed to take a fresh approach."[90]

5.1.8.2 Church Consultancy Objectives[91]

At a meeting on [date] with the senior pastor and deacons, the following consultancy objectives were agreed upon.

1. To explore ways to sharpen the church's spiritual focus.
2. To suggest appropriate outreach strategies, including potential target groups within the community.
3. To identify ministry priorities that effectively utilize the church's present resources (people, facilities, finances, etc.).
4. To review present leadership roles, responsibilities and structures and recommend any changes that will enhance the effectiveness of leadership in the life of the church.
5. To identify any barriers to belonging in the life of the church and to recommend strategies to strengthen community and enhance integration into the congregation.

5.1.8.3 Indications Towards the Impact of Consultancy on Church H Health and Growth

The leadership team and the church accepted the report. There has been some progress made in implementing the recommendations of the report, but the crucial area of vision does not appear to have been sufficiently addressed, with NCLS-2006 indicating that each of the inspirational core qualities (vision, leadership, and innovation) has declined.[92] The senior pastor concluded his ministry at the church in 2003, and this may account for the decrease in inspirational core qualities. Only three

---

89. Baptist Churches of NSW and ACT Church Consultancy Team, "Church H Baptist Church Consultancy Report," 2.

90. Pastor of Church H, Interview Transcript, 1.

91. Baptist Churches of NSW and ACT Church Consultancy Team, "Church H Baptist Church Consultancy Report," 3.

92. NCLS Research, *Church Life Profile—Church H Baptist Church*, 6.

core quality indicators increased (worship, service, and inclusion) and only two indicators were above 4.4 out of 10 (inclusion [10] and service [6.8]).[93] According to NCLS-2006 results, it appears that good attention has been given to the issue of incorporating and welcoming newcomers.[94] However, the same cannot be said for faith-sharing/targeted and effective outreach into the community, or clarity of vision.[95] Overall there was a slight decrease in core quality indicators of 6 percent over the period to 2006.[96] The largest grouping in the community (20-to 49-year-olds) is now less represented in the church, decreasing from 31 percent to 26 percent over the five-year period to 2006.[97] This decrease in the church's connection into the community in this demographic tends to indicate a lack of effective outreach. It also underscores the finding of the church consultancy team that there was a "wide acknowledgement that the Church will struggle to attract and maintain young families with children to the current morning service."[98] During the period to 2006, attendance declined 43 percent to forty-six.[99]

5.1.9 Church I

5.1.9.1 BACKGROUND

Church I is located in a residential suburb in the Inner West of Sydney and had an attendance of seventy-five at the time of the church consultancy.[100] Fifty-three percent of residents in this suburb were born in Australia (Sydney 61%), indicating a greater level of multiculturalism than other areas, with strong representation from those born in Greece (4.5%) and United Kingdom (3.6%).[101] There are a high proportion of residents who have never married (43%; Sydney 33%).[102] When residents were

---

93. NCLS Research, *Church Life Profile—Church H Baptist Church*, 6.
94. NCLS Research, *Church Life Profile—Church H Baptist Church*, 6.
95. NCLS Research, *Church Life Profile—Church H Baptist Church*, 6.
96. NCLS Research, *Church Life Profile—Church H Baptist Church*, 6.
97. NCLS Research, *Church Life Profile—Church H Baptist Church*, 24.
98. NCLS Research, *Church Life Profile—Church H Baptist Church*, 9.
99. Baptist Churches of NSW and ACT Church Consultancy Team, "Church H Baptist Church Consultancy Report," 23.
100. Soden, *NSW and ACT Baptist Churches Handbook 2001–2002*, 351.
101. ABS Census of Population and Housing, *Suburb Profiles—Demographics*.
102. ABS Census of Population and Housing, *Suburb Profiles—Demographics*.

asked in the Census to state their religion, "no religion" was the highest response with 19 percent (Sydney 13%).[103] The proportion of those who are tertiary educated is well above average (17%; Sydney 9%), and indicates a high socioeconomic.[104] Many of these factors were perceived to be barriers to the growth of the church in interviews with attenders during the consultancy: "the cultural and religious diversity of the community, the lack of spiritual interest in the community, and the transient nature of the community."[105]

The church at the time of the consultancy was predominantly a regional church focused on a particular ethnicity, with the result that "probably 80% of the church members travel from anywhere between 20 to 50km to church."[106] As a consequence, the church was struggling to develop an owned vision and clear direction for its future ministry, and was conscious of its lack of missional impact in the local community.[107] The church was at that time in receipt of a subsidy from the Baptist Union of NSW/ACT. Due to a change in policy this subsidy ceased on 30 June, 2002.[108] Assistance with moving forward financially in the light of this change was sought as a part of the consultancy process.

5.1.9.2 Church Consultancy Objectives

The following objectives were set for the consultancy by the church leadership:

1. To review and assess the congregation's growth and any barriers to growth.
2. To review and assess the congregation's ownership of the church's vision and future ministry direction.
3. To review and assess the congregation's present and projected financial situation toward self-reliance.

---

103. ABS Census of Population and Housing, *Suburb Profiles—Demographics*.
104. ABS Census of Population and Housing, *Suburb Profiles—Demographics*.
105. Baptist Churches of NSW and ACT Church Consultancy Team, "Church I Baptist Church Consultancy Report," 5.
106. Pastor of Church I, Interview Transcript, 1.
107. Pastor of Church I, Interview Transcript, 1.
108. Baptist Churches of NSW and ACT Church Consultancy Team, "Church I Baptist Church Consultancy Report," 6–7.

4. To review and assess the church's leadership support structure.[109]

5.1.9.3 Indications Towards the Impact of Consultancy on Church I Health and Growth

The leadership team and the church accepted the report. The church has substantially addressed financial issues to become more self-sufficient.[110] More importantly, the church has become much more strongly focused on reaching those in the local community. This is reflected in the large increases in the core quality indicators for worship (61% increase) as the church seeks to engage seekers with an attractive and contemporary worship service, and faith-sharing (76% increase), as various tools and resources were introduced into the church to facilitate this.[111] The result was that "people were talking to them about their faith."[112] However, other core quality indicators decreased, or increased by small amounts, so that overall core quality indicators increased by 9 percent.[113]

It is also remarkable that in the five years to 2006, the percentage of newcomers increased from 0% to 16%.[114] Therefore it is not surprising that a 20 percent increase in church attendance to ninety was experienced over this period. The issues of distance and limiting involvement in the local community to the weekends are still present. However, gaining clarity through the consultancy process regarding future ministry direction and then taking action to merge an aging, declining Anglo-Celtic congregation with a strong ethnic congregation has resulted in a growth spurt.[115]

The pastor serving the church in 2001 has continued to the present.

---

109. Baptist Churches of NSW and ACT Church Consultancy Team, "Church I Baptist Church Consultancy Report," 3.
110. Soden, *NSW and ACT Baptist Churches Handbook 2006–2007*, 279.
111. NCLS Research, *Church Life Profile—Church I Baptist Church*, 6.
112. Pastor of Church I, Interview Transcript, 2.
113. NCLS Research, *Church Life Profile—Church I Baptist Church*, 6.
114. NCLS Research, *Church Life Profile—Church I Baptist Church*, 22.
115. Pastor of Church I, Interview Transcript, 3.

5.1.10 Church J

5.1.10.1 Background

Church J is located in a suburb of a regional center. It is dominated by a large industrial complex and a seaport. Accordingly, 18 percent of residents are engaged in manufacturing, along with 12 percent in retail, indicating a lower socioeconomic.[116] The church had an attendance of twenty at the time of the church consultancy.[117]

Sixty-one percent of residents in this suburb were born in Australia (Regional Local Government Area 72%), with strong representation from Macedonians (13%), which is reflected in the large proportion of those who identified their religion as Eastern Orthodox (25%).[118]

The place of the church in this community is a question before the church, with 85 percent of those interviewed as part of the consultancy travelling more than ten minutes to attend church.[119]

This consultancy has arisen out of the approval of a grant under the Baptist Churches of NSW and ACT Church Development Partnership Scheme, for developing a ministry to the disadvantaged people of [suburb 1] and [suburb 2] and funding a part-time pastor to facilitate this. The grant is conditional upon the current consultation and the adoption of a satisfactory Strategic Plan.[120] The church and the pastor are at a crossroads, with the recent passing of the wife of the pastor a devastating blow to both.[121]

5.1.10.2 Church Consultancy Objectives

The following objectives were established by the church leadership for the consultancy:

1. Identify ways to improve the spiritual life of the church.

---

116. ABS Census of Population and Housing, *Suburb Profiles—Demographics*.
117. NCLS Research, *Church Life Profile—Church J Baptist Church*, 23.
118. ABS Census of Population and Housing, *Suburb Profiles—Demographics*.
119. Baptist Churches of NSW and ACT Church Consultancy Team, "Church J Baptist Church Consultancy Report," 7.
120. Baptist Churches of NSW and ACT Church Consultancy Team, "Church J Baptist Church Consultancy Report," 3.
121. Baptist Churches of NSW and ACT Church Consultancy Team, "Church J Baptist Church Consultancy Report," 13.

2. Develop strategies for the church to own and implement the vision.
3. Identify ways whereby the church can support and assist our pastor through his loss.
4. Develop and implement a strategy for effective pastoral care.[122]

5.1.10.3 Indications Towards the Impact of Consultancy on Church J Health and Growth

The leadership team and the church accepted the report. Every core quality indicator has increased substantially over the five years to 2006, such that the overall increase is 128 percent.[123] This increase was particularly reflected in the internal core qualities of faith, worship, and belonging, and the outward core qualities of service, faith-sharing, and inclusion.[124] This indicates that the issues raised in the consultancy surrounding spiritual vitality and pastoral care were receiving attention, and that action was being undertaken in reaching out to the surrounding community in a variety of ways. Attendance increased 40 percent to twenty-eight over this time.[125] This is very encouraging for a church that was evaluating its viability to continue. The pastor serving the church in 2001 concluded the following year, and a new pastor commenced in 2004.

5.1.11 Conclusion

Many of the churches that form our study were struggling numerically and financially prior to inviting a church consultancy, evidenced by 80 percent of these churches having an attendance of less than 100.[126] This numerical and financial stress is also indicated by 50 percent of consultancy churches being in receipt of a ministry subsidy from the Baptist Union of NSW/ACT at the time of the consultancy. This numerical and financial struggle appears to be symptomatic of weaker health as indicated by NCLS-2001. That is, in 2001 before the consultancy: 40 percent of the

---

122. Baptist Churches of NSW and ACT Church Consultancy Team, "Church J Baptist Church Consultancy Report," 3.
123. NCLS Research, *Church Life Profile—Church J Baptist Church*, 6.
124. NCLS Research, *Church Life Profile—Church J Baptist Church*, 6.
125. NCLS Research, *Church Life Profile—Church J Baptist Church*, 23.
126. Refer Appendix F.

DATA ANALYSIS

consultancy churches had zero of their nine core quality indicator scores over six (out of ten), whereas 23 percent of non-consultancy churches had zero scores over six. Conversely, zero consultancy churches had six or more scores over six, while 10 percent of non-consultancy churches were in this category.[127]

Interviews with five of the pastors of these churches indicated a sense of feeling stuck or being unsure how to move forward in the church's health and growth. These interviews will be further analyzed in section 5.2.

Objective	Church A	Church B	Church C	Church D	Church E	Church F	Church G	Church H	Church I	Church J	Total
develop/clarify/own the church's vision	X	X		X				X	X		5
leadership care, functioning & structure	X		X				X	X	X		5
ascertain ministry priorities & ministry resources	X		X				X				3
ministry/leadership development, training & involvement	X	X	X		X	X	X				6
improve decision-making processes	X										1
develop personal spiritual maturity & prayer		X			X		X		X		4
develop local community outreach		X	X		X	X		X	X		6
conflict management & communication			X	X	X						3
youth/children's ministry development			X			X					2
encouraging inclusion & belonging, pastoral care					X	X	X		X		4
developing worship & music ministry						X					1
achieving financial self-sufficiency						X		X			2
											42

Table 1: Consultancy Objectives

Classification of consultancy objectives into broad categories (refer Table 1) reveals a strong cluster surrounding ministry and leadership. This includes identification of those with gifts in ministry and leadership, training and development, then deployment and involvement in a particular area. Such objectives recognize the importance of a church leadership process whereby ministry priorities are ascertained and sought to be matched with available people resources. There are nine such objectives, making this area the most important need in the churches that were part of the research. Leadership structure and functioning, along with strategies for the care of leaders also figured highly with six objectives in this category. Development and ownership of a vision for the church was a common theme in the churches consulted with, with five churches inviting the assistance of consultants in this regard. Development of

127. Refer Table 5 and Appendix E.

local community outreach also figured highly, with six such objectives. Conflict and communication were also issues that arose at three of the churches.

The connectedness between some of these objectives is clear. For a church to move forward, the centrality of a compelling and owned vision is paramount. This then needs a process for strategic deployment: the correct structuring and functioning of leadership to identify giftedness and equip others for ministry within the church and for outreach into the community, consistent with that vision. Sometimes conflict is diminished as attenders see clear forward progress in a church; at other times such vision and action disturbs "controllers" who prefer power instead of a church's growth and health, and conflict can increase.[128]

The churches that form this study have engaged in the consultancy process and have essentially actioned the recommendations of the consultants concerning the objectives each church leadership set for the consultancy. Post-consultancy, most of the churches have enjoyed substantial growth, and considerable increases in health. NCLS-2006 indicated that nine (90%) of the consultancy churches achieved one or more quality indicator scores over six, with 70 percent obtaining three or more scores over six (only 44% of the non-consultancy churches achieved this). Conversely, NCLS-2006 indicates that only 10 percent of consultancy churches had zero scores over six compared with 40 percent in this category prior to the consultancy.[129]

An exploration of the health and growth of consultancy churches will be undertaken in greater depth later in this chapter.

5.2 Analysis of Interviews

Interviews with those who were the pastors of five of the consultancy churches at the time of the church consultancy were undertaken. This was done to provide a method of confirming (or not) and interpreting the quantitative data that had been collected through each church's participation in NCLS-2001 and NCLS-2006. The questions asked (refer Appendix A) reflect the NCLS core quality indicators and NCLS quantitative measures such as attendance, newcomers, and young adult retention. As indicated in the methodology, indications were sought as to

---

128. Easum, *Sacred Cows Make Gourmet Burgers*.
129. Scores over six are highlighted on the table at Appendix E.

whether these had grown, declined, or remained about the same, subsequent to the consultancy, with results as follows:

Health Indicator	Church A	Church C	Church F	Church H	Church I	TOTAL
3a Faith	0	1	1	0	1	3
3b Worship	-1	1	1	0	1	2
3c Belonging	0	1	1	1	1	4
3d Inclusion	-1	-1	1	0	1	0
3e Care for young people	1	1	0	1	0	3
3f Community focus beyond church	0	1	1	0	-1	1
3g Service	0	0	0	1	0	1
3h Faith-sharing	0	0	1	1	0	2
3i Integrating newcomers	0	1	1	1	0	3
3j Vision	-1	1	1	1	1	3
3k Innovation	0	1	1	1	0	3
3l Leadership	0	1	1	1	0	3
4 Overall health since	0	1	1	1	1	4
7 Attendance since	1	0	1	1	1	4

Table 2: Coded Health Indicators from Interviews

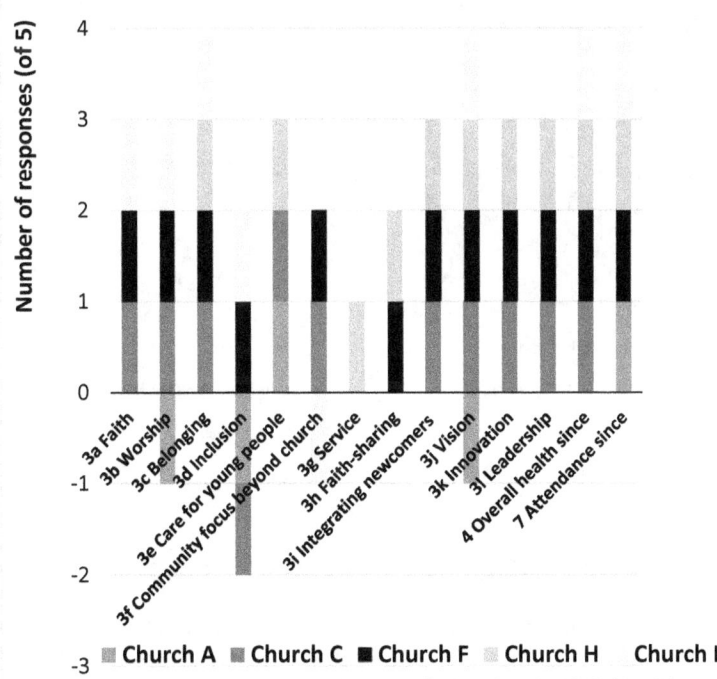

Figure 1: Interview Responses by Health & Growth Indicators

The number of responses were then graphed as stacked columns: firstly, by area of health or growth (Figure 1), and then by church (Figure 2). This was done to give some indication of each pastor's perception of what changes, if any, had occurred in the church they pastored subsequent to the consultancy. It is evident from the interview responses by health and growth indicators that they observed an increase across *almost all* health and growth indicators. Additionally, 80 percent of interviewees indicated growth in the *overall* health of the church since the consultancy.[130] And four of the five pastors interviewed indicated a growth in attendance since the church consultancy.

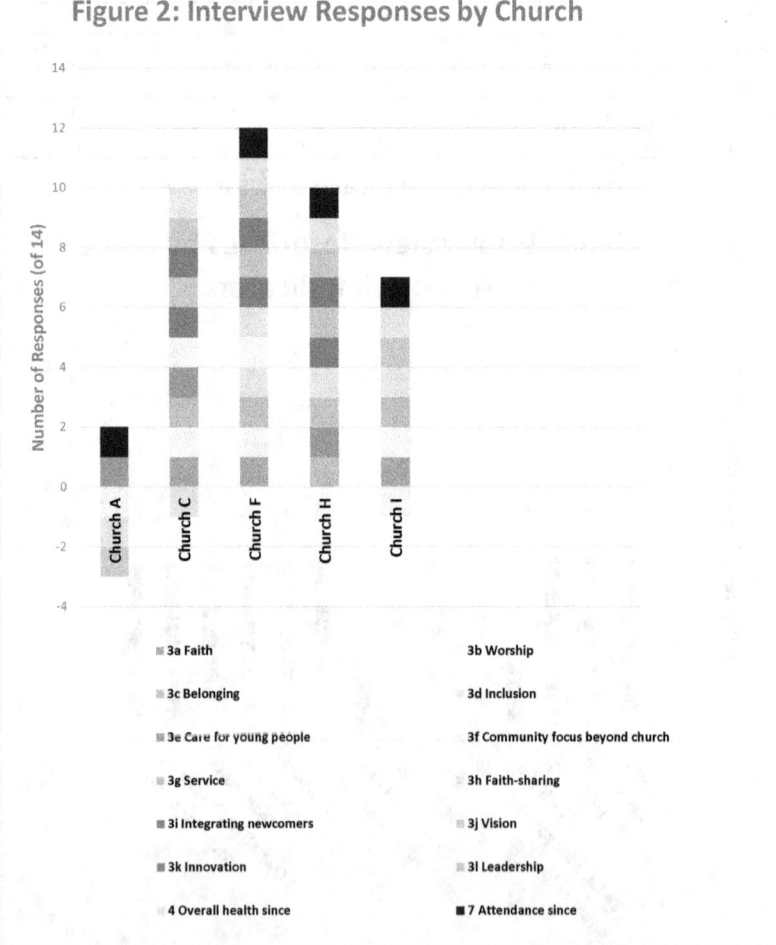

Figure 2: Interview Responses by Church

---

130. Pastor of Church C, Interview Transcript, 2; Pastor of Church F, Interview Transcript, 2; Pastor of Church H, Interview Transcript, 2; Pastor of Church I, Interview Transcript, 2.

It can be seen from the pastors' responses by church (Figure 2) that there were a variety of perceptions of the helpfulness of the church consultancy, with Church A markedly lower than the other four churches (in spite of recording strong growth in health and attendance in the period to 2006). The pastor of Church A indicated that in his opinion the church consultancy needed to reprioritize its objectives:

> There is little point addressing medium and long-term issues such as values, vision, mission, leadership and so on while there is this major [relational] issue we need to address, so let's put this other stuff on hold while we address this one."[131]

What did the pastors interviewed identify as the means used by the consultants to foster health and growth in the church?

Firstly, that in conjunction with the leadership of the church, they identified and addressed the issues facing the church.[132] This was further achieved through gathering information from those in the congregation through tools such as mapping exercises, listening groups, and interviews.[133] The consultants then made this collated information (with appropriate safeguards regarding confidentiality) available to each church, along with recommendations which sought to deal with each of these issues, or consultancy objectives.

Secondly, that it provides a pathway and suggests next steps for a church to follow.[134] That church consultancy provided part of the framework for moving a church forward.

---

131. Pastor of Church A, Interview Transcript, 5. As can be seen from objective 2, recommendations 8 and 9 in Appendix AA, there were steps taken to address this relational issue, but as indicated by the pastor interviewed, it became one of many objectives in the consultancy.

132. Pastor of Church C, Interview Transcript, 3; Pastor of Church F, Interview Transcript, 3; Pastor of Church I, Interview Transcript, 3.

133. Mapping exercises are group activities through which a consultant can quickly gather information (e.g. "How long have you known about this conflict?) and emotional temperature (e.g. "How hopeful are you about this church's future?") through people moving to a numbered piece of paper (e.g. scale of 1 to 10 [most hopeful]) or written priorities/alternatives (e.g. four issues facing the church in each corner of the hall; move to the one you consider most important: leadership, finances, music, or youth). These exercises can also be a helpful means of clarifying values and emotions for individuals participating, and a useful way of sharing information with one another (e.g. when people stood on a line indicating how long they had been at the church I realized that no one had been at the church for less than 10 years—new people aren't coming to the church. Why?).

134. Pastor of Church C, Interview Transcript, 3.

Thirdly, that church consultancy "encouraged people in their ministries in the church and the community" so that "worth is engendered in what they were doing and could do."[135] This is particularly important for churches that are struggling with their viability, and/or a loss of hope, so they are enabled to move into the future with a greater sense of confidence.

Fourth, church consultancy can put a church in touch with resources, either people or programs, which can assist them in addressing their objectives.[136] It can be difficult for church leaders and pastors to be cognizant of all the resources at their disposal, so the provision of expertise in this way is a helpful contribution to a church's health.

Fifth, church consultancy can bring an objective, realistic assessment of a church's health and assist a church in facing their situation and being "held accountable for what we are doing."[137]

Sixth, church consultancy can be used to bring hidden blockages to health, such as "systemic patterns of communicating and relating," out into the open, where they can be addressed.[138]

For some of the pastors interviewed, the consultancy was perceived as effective in dealing with a range of specific issues such as: dealing with conflict,[139] prompting inclusion of the Aboriginal community in the church's ministry,[140] or in instigating a strategic plan for growth.[141] Others identified areas for improvement in church consultancy such as "could bring stronger recommendations" and "further follow-up from consultants."[142]

---

135 Pastor of Church F, Interview Transcript, 3.
136. See Appendices AA to JJ.
137. Pastor of Church F, Interview Transcript, 3.
138. Pastor of Church C, Interview Transcript, 2.
139. Pastor of Church C, Interview Transcript, 3.
140. Pastor of Church F, Interview Transcript, 3.
141. Pastor of Church H, Interview Transcript, 1.
142. Pastor of Church C, Interview Transcript, 2.

5.3 Analysis of Core Vitality Indicators

5.3.1 Health

From their research of churches over many years, the NCLS Team have isolated nine core qualities of healthy and vital churches: an alive and growing *faith*, vital and nurturing *worship*, strong and growing *belonging*, a clear and owned *vision*, inspiring and empowering *leadership*, open and flexible *innovation*, practical and diverse *service*, willing and effective *faith-sharing*, and intentional and welcoming *inclusion*.[143]

5.3.1.1 Initial Analysis

The first analysis that was carried out compared core quality indicators of churches that had undertaken a consultancy (n=10) with churches that had not had a church consultancy in 2001 or 2002 but had participated in both NCLS 2001 and NCLS 2006 (n=88).[144]

		N	Mean	Std. Deviation	Std. Error	95% Confidence Interval for Mean		Minimum	Maximum
						Lower Bound	Upper Bound		
CQ1CHANGE	No consult	88	.68	1.824	.194	.29	1.06	-5	6
	Consult	10	1.67	2.911	.921	-.41	3.75	-2	8
	Total	98	.78	1.965	.199	.38	1.17	-5	8
CQ2CHANGE	No consult	88	.47	1.946	.207	.06	.88	-4	6
	Consult	10	1.90	1.330	.421	.95	2.85	0	4
	Total	98	.61	1.936	.196	.23	1.00	-4	6
CQ3CHANGE	No consult	88	.05	1.251	.133	-.22	.31	-3	4
	Consult	10	.77	1.961	.620	-.63	2.17	-2	4
	Total	98	.12	1.345	.136	-.15	.39	-3	4

---

143. Bellamy et al., *Enriching Church Life*, 10–29.
144. Davies, "Consultancy Master List Numerical 070919 (Version 2).xls," 1.

CQ4CHANGE	No consult	88	-.39	1.547	.165	-.71	-.06	-4	4
	Consult	10	.45	2.201	.696	-1.12	2.02	-2	4
	Total	98	-.30	1.632	.165	-.63	.03	-4	4
CQ5CHANGE	No consult	88	-.88	1.741	.186	-1.25	-.51	-5	4
	Consult	10	.35	2.829	.894	-1.67	2.37	-4	4
	Total	98	-.75	1.897	.192	-1.13	-.37	-5	4
CQ6CHANGE	No consult	88	.43	1.777	.189	.05	.80	-4	5
	Consult	10	.48	1.891	.598	-.87	1.83	-2	3
	Total	98	.43	1.779	.180	.08	.79	-4	5
CQ7CHANGE	No consult	88	.28	1.117	.119	.04	.51	-3	3
	Consult	10	1.19	2.017	.638	-.25	2.63	-2	5
	Total	98	.37	1.255	.127	.12	.62	-3	5
CQ8CHANGE	No consult	88	-.31	1.286	.137	-.58	-.04	-4	2
	Consult	10	.77	1.407	.445	-.24	1.78	-1	3
	Total	98	-.20	1.332	.135	-.47	.07	-4	3
CQ9CHANGE	No consult	88	1.54	2.256	.241	1.06	2.01	-6	6
	Consult	10	1.56	2.787	.881	-.43	3.55	-4	5
	Total	98	1.54	2.299	.232	1.08	2.00	-6	6
dy040601NEW	No consult	80	18.030	39.659	4.434	9.204	26.855	-55.00	143.0
	Consult	9	11.399	35.640	11.880	-15.996	38.795	-43.75	65.93
Attendance	Total	89	17.359	39.135	4.148	9.115	25.603	-55.00	143.0
NEWC-CHANGE	No consult	88	-.86	5.895	.628	-2.11	.39	-23	14
	Consult	10	-2.92	7.440	2.353	-8.24	2.41	-12	16
Newcomers	Total	98	-1.07	6.058	.612	-2.28	.15	-23	16
YAR02CHANGE	No consult	68	2.76	23.383	2.836	-2.90	8.42	-54	67
	Consult	4	-20.73	19.270	9.635	-51.40	9.93	-46	-2
Young Adult Retention	Total	72	1.45	23.686	2.791	-4.11	7.02	-54	67

Table 3: Initial Analysis Descriptives[145]

---

145. Sam Sterland, email message to author, 5 December, 2008.

DATA ANALYSIS

		Sum of Squares	df	Mean Square	F	Sig.
CQ1CHANGE	Between Groups	8.870	1	8.870	2.328	.130
	Within Groups	365.781	96	3.810		
	Total	374.651	97			
CQ2CHANGE	Between Groups	18.409	1	18.409	5.119	.026*
	Within Groups	345.231	96	3.596		
	Total	363.640	97			
CQ3CHANGE	Between Groups	4.670	1	4.670	2.624	.109
	Within Groups	170.861	96	1.780		
	Total	175.531	97			
CQ4CHANGE	Between Groups	6.281	1	6.281	2.394	.125
	Within Groups	251.929	96	2.624		
	Total	258.210	97			
CQ5CHANGE	Between Groups	13.525	1	13.525	3.869	.052
	Within Groups	335.560	96	3.495		
	Total	349.085	97			
CQ6CHANGE	Between Groups	.025	1	.025	.008	.930
	Within Groups	307.011	96	3.198		
	Total	307.036	97			
CQ7CHANGE	Between Groups	7.481	1	7.481	4.945	.029*
	Within Groups	145.224	96	1.513		
	Total	152.704	97			
CQ8CHANGE	Between Groups	10.434	1	10.434	6.194	.015*
	Within Groups	161.705	96	1.684		
	Total	172.140	97			
CQ9CHANGE	Between Groups	.006	1	.006	.001	.974
	Within Groups	512.725	96	5.341		
	Total	512.730	97			
dy040601NEW Attendance	Between Groups	355.652	1	355.652	.230	.633
	Within Groups	134417.536	87	1545.029		
	Total	134773.188	88			
NEWCCHANGE	Between Groups	38.060	1	38.060	1.037	.311

Newcomers	Within Groups	3521.794	96	36.685		
	Total	3559.853	97			
YAR02CHANGE	Between Groups	2084.994	1	2084.994	3.867	.053
Young Adult Retention	Within Groups	37746.766	70	539.240		
	Total	39831.760	71			

Table 4: Initial Analysis ANOVA[146]

*significant at p<0.05

Results of this analysis are recorded at Table 3 and Table 4, and church health components of analysis are represented graphically at Figure 3. It is evident from Figure 3 that there was an increase in each of the nine core quality scores post-consultancy, indicating a greater level of health subsequent to the church consultancy. Five of the churches had increases in their total core quality indicators of over 44 percent (refer Appendix E). The greater increase in core qualities for churches that have undergone a church consultancy compared with non-consultancy churches is remarkable.

The change in core qualities highlighted by the labelled bars (that is, worship, leadership, service, and faith-sharing) are statistically significant at p<0.1, with a further three qualities falling just outside this significance range. Worship, service, and faith-sharing are statistically significant at p<0.05. These are encouraging results concerning the correlation between church consultancy and these church health indicators. However, it is acknowledged that in such research other variables cannot be kept constant, nor can an unequivocal causal relationship be demonstrated.

146. Sam Sterland, email message to author, 5 December, 2008.

DATA ANALYSIS

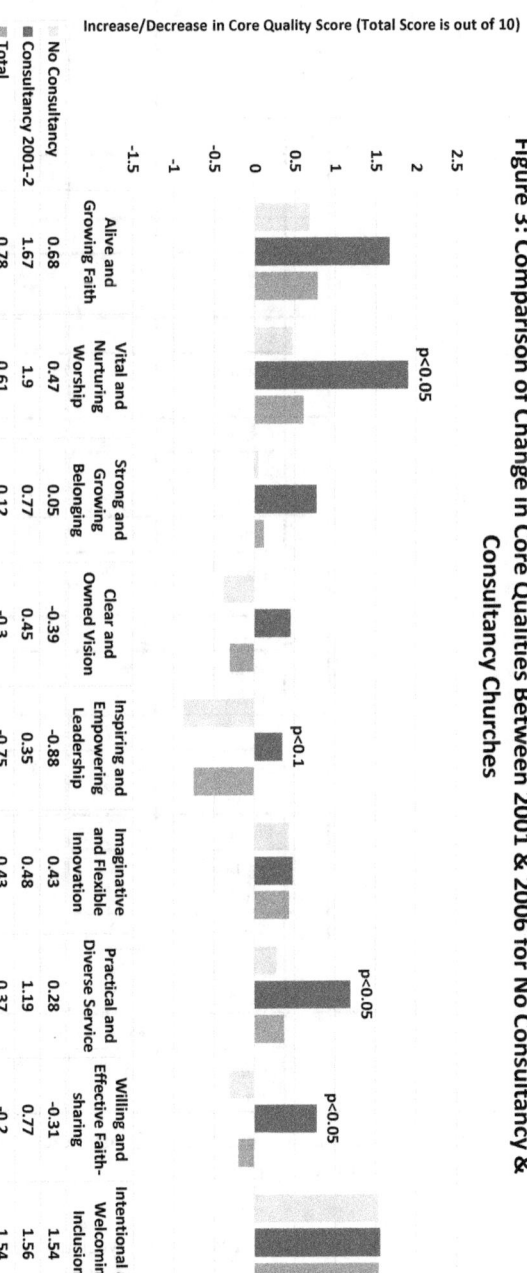

Figure 3: Comparison of Change in Core Qualities Between 2001 & 2006 for No Consultancy & Consultancy Churches

5.3.1.2 Weaker Churches Analysis

			2 groups		Total
			No consultancy	Consultancy	
NUMOVER6 Number of nine core quality indicator scores over 6 (out of 10)	0	Count	20	4	24
		% within 2 groups	22.7%	40.0%	24.5%
	1	Count	21	2	23
		% within 2 groups	23.9%	20.0%	23.5%
	2	Count	8	1	9
		% within 2 groups	9.1%	10.0%	9.2%
	3	Count	9	0	9
		% within 2 groups	10.2%	.0%	9.2%
	4	Count	16	2	18
		% within 2 groups	18.2%	20.0%	18.4%
	5	Count	5	1	6
		% within 2 groups	5.7%	10.0%	6.1%
	6	Count	4	0	4
		% within 2 groups	4.5%	.0%	4.1%
	7	Count	4	0	4
		% within 2 groups	4.5%	.0%	4.1%
	8	Count	1	0	1
		% within 2 groups	1.1%	.0%	1.0%
Total		Count	88	10	98
		% within 2 groups	100.0%	100.0%	100.0%

Table 5: Scores Over Six Consultancy and Non-Consultancy Groups Cross-Tabulation[147]

A second analysis was performed where only churches with lower core quality indicators in NCLS-2001 were included. This was done

---

147. Sam Sterland, email message to author, 5 December, 2008.

because the churches requiring a consultancy would most probably all be of lower health, whereas the "no consultancy" group would be mixed; some with strong health and higher NCLS core quality indicators, and others with weaker health and lower NCLS core quality indicators.[148] To achieve this, churches with five or more (out of the nine core quality indicators) scores over six (out of a maximum ten) were removed from both groups, leaving nine churches remaining in the consultancy group and seventy-four churches in the non-consultancy group.

Using this analysis on the original data sets (n=10, n=88) it was clearly demonstrated (Table 5) that the consultancy group of churches were less healthy in 2001 than the non-consultancy group of churches. In the consultancy group of churches, Church C had the highest NCLS-2001 core quality scores with five scores over six, whereas in the no consultancy group there were numerous churches with higher results. In the consultancy group 40 percent (four churches) had zero scores over six, compared to only 23 percent in the no consultancy group.

Therefore, by limiting the churches being compared to those which are weaker in terms of their core quality indicators, a more reasonable comparison might be made. Specifically, churches with stronger health (indicated by having five or more core quality indicator scores over six in NCLS-2001) were removed from both sets of data. That is, consultancy churches doing less well in their core quality indicators in NCLS-2001 (n=9, a loss of 1 from the initial analysis) are compared to other churches doing less well in their core quality indicators that did not enter into a consultancy (n=74, a loss of 14 from the initial analysis).

---

148. This is underlined by the concerns regarding numerical and financial viability demonstrated in five of the ten churches receiving a ministry subsidy at the time of the consultancies.

		N	Mean	Std. Deviation	Std. Error	95% Confidence Interval for Mean		Minimum	Maximum
						Lower Bound	Upper Bound		
CQ1CHANGE	Non-Consult	74	.61	1.808	.210	.19	1.03	-5	6
	Consult	9	1.71	3.085	1.028	-.66	4.08	-2	8
	Total	83	.73	1.989	.218	.30	1.17	-5	8
CQ2CHANGE	Non-Consult	74	.51	1.817	.211	.08	.93	-4	5
	Consult	9	1.93	1.406	.469	.85	3.01	0	4
	Total	83	.66	1.825	.200	.26	1.06	-4	5
CQ3CHANGE	Non-Consult	74	.16	1.230	.143	-.13	.44	-3	4
	Consult	9	.98	1.959	.653	-.53	2.48	-2	4
	Total	83	.24	1.337	.147	-.05	.54	-3	4
CQ4CHANGE	Non-Consult	74	-.34	1.618	.188	-.72	.03	-4	4
	Consult	9	.68	2.206	.735	-1.02	2.37	-2	4
	Total	83	-.23	1.705	.187	-.61	.14	-4	4
CQ5CHANGE	Non-Consult	74	-.64	1.699	.198	-1.03	-.24	-5	4
	Consult	9	.80	2.593	.864	-1.19	2.79	-3	4
	Total	83	-.48	1.851	.203	-.89	-.08	-5	4
CQ6CHANGE	Non-Consult	74	.71	1.705	.198	.32	1.11	-3	5
	Consult	9	.73	1.817	.606	-.66	2.13	-2	3
	Total	83	.72	1.706	.187	.34	1.09	-3	5
CQ7CHANGE	Non-Consult	74	.24	1.069	.124	-.01	.49	-3	3
	Consult	9	1.48	1.910	.637	.01	2.95	-2	5
	Total	83	.37	1.234	.136	.10	.64	-3	5
CQ8CHANGE	Non-Consult	74	-.27	1.250	.145	-.56	.02	-3	2
	Consult	9	.96	1.357	.452	-.09	2.00	-1	3

	Total	83	−.13	1.310	.144	−.42	.15	−3	3
CQ9CHANGE	Non-Consult	74	1.76	2.050	.238	1.29	2.24	−3	6
	Consult	9	1.62	2.948	.983	−.64	3.89	−4	5
	Total	83	1.75	2.142	.235	1.28	2.21	−4	6
dyo40601NEW	Non-Consult	67	12.172	33.297	4.068	4.051	20.294	−55.00	115.69
Attendance	Consult	8	12.657	37.887	13.395	−19.017	44.332	−43.75	65.93
	Total	75	12.224	33.536	3.872	4.508	19.940	−55	115.69
NEWC-CHANGE	Non-Consult	74	−.76	5.199	.604	−1.96	.45	−19	9
Newcomers	Consult	9	−1.85	7.037	2.346	−7.26	3.56	−8	16
	Total	83	−.88	5.386	.591	−2.05	.30	−19	16
YAR02-CHANGE	Non-Consult	59	.72	23.130	3.011	−5.31	6.74	−54	64
Young Adults	Consult	3	−12.30	11.419	6.592	−40.67	16.06	−25	−2
	Total	62	.09	22.823	2.899	−5.71	5.88	−54	64

Table 6: "Weaker Churches" Descriptives[149]

		Sum of Squares	df	Mean Square	F	Sig.
CQ1CHANGE	Between Groups	9.691	1	9.691	2.494	.118
	Within Groups	314.708	81	3.885		
	Total	324.399	82			
CQ2CHANGE	Between Groups	16.361	1	16.361	5.163	.026*
	Within Groups	256.698	81	3.169		
	Total	273.059	82			
CQ3CHANGE	Between Groups	5.427	1	5.427	3.112	.081^
	Within Groups	141.238	81	1.744		
	Total	146.665	82			
CQ4CHANGE	Between Groups	8.387	1	8.387	2.953	.090^

---

149. Sam Sterland, email message to author, 5 December, 2008.

	Within Groups	230.018	81	2.840		
	Total	238.406	82			
CQ5CHANGE	Between Groups	16.558	1	16.558	5.070	.027*
	Within Groups	264.531	81	3.266		
	Total	281.089	82			
CQ6CHANGE	Between Groups	.003	1	.003	.001	.976
	Within Groups	238.694	81	2.947		
	Total	238.696	82			
CQ7CHANGE	Between Groups	12.337	1	12.337	8.872	.004**
	Within Groups	112.630	81	1.390		
	Total	124.966	82			
CQ8CHANGE	Between Groups	12.004	1	12.004	7.553	.007**
	Within Groups	128.744	81	1.589		
	Total	140.749	82			
CQ9CHANGE	Between Groups	.154	1	.154	.033	.856
	Within Groups	376.172	81	4.644		
	Total	376.326	82			
dyo40601NEW Attendance	Between Groups	1.682	1	1.682	.001	.969
	Within Groups	83221.721	73	1140.024		
	Total	83223.402	74			
NEWCCHANGE Newcomers	Between Groups	9.604	1	9.604	.328	.568
	Within Groups	2369.263	81	29.250		
	Total	2378.867	82			
YAR02-CHANGE Young Adults	Between Groups	483.818	1	483.818	.928	.339
	Within Groups	31291.820	60	521.530		
	Total	31775.639	61			

Table 7: "Weaker Churches" ANOVA

^significant at p<0.10

*significant at p<0.05

**significant at p<0.01 (highly significant)[150]

---

150. Sam Sterland, email message to author, 5 December, 2008. NCLS data has kindly been made available for this project by NCLS Team and is the subject of a fair use agreement with the author.

DATA ANALYSIS

Results of this analysis are recorded at Table 6 and Table 7, and church health components of analysis are represented graphically at Figure 4.

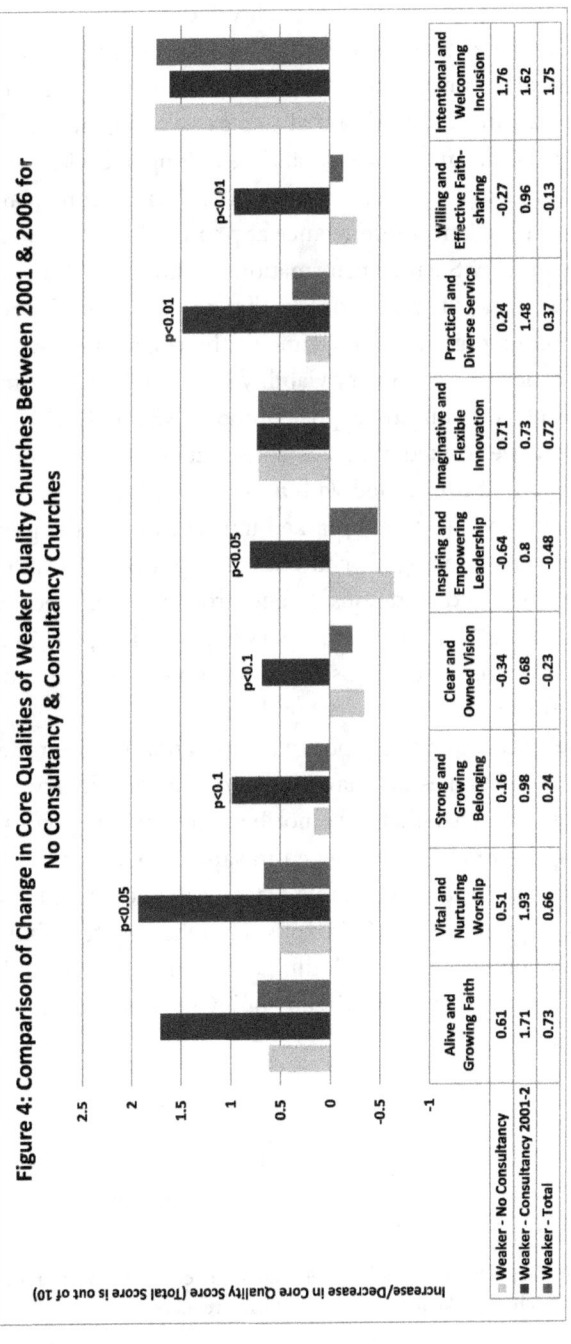

Figure 4: Comparison of Change in Core Qualities of Weaker Quality Churches Between 2001 & 2006 for No Consultancy & Consultancy Churches

	Alive and Growing Faith	Vital and Nurturing Worship	Strong and Growing Belonging	Clear and Owned Vision	Inspiring and Empowering Leadership	Imaginative and Flexible Innovation	Practical and Diverse Service	Willing and Effective Faith-sharing	Intentional and Welcoming Inclusion
Weaker - No Consultancy	0.61	0.51	0.16	-0.34	-0.64	0.71	0.24	-0.27	1.76
Weaker - Consultancy 2001-2	1.71	1.93	0.98	0.68	0.8	0.73	1.48	0.96	1.62
Weaker - Total	0.73	0.66	0.24	-0.23	-0.48	0.72	0.37	-0.13	1.75

It is evident from the graph at Figure 4 that overall there was an increase in eight of the nine core quality indicator scores post-consultancy. Results for this second analysis showed similar trends to the initial analysis. However, differences in core quality indicators were more marked for several qualities than in the initial analysis. As shown by the labeled bars on Figure 4 above, in this second analysis service and faith-sharing are highly statistically significant at $p<0.01$. Worship and leadership are statistically significant at $p<0.05$, and belonging and vision are statistically significant at $p<0.1$. In summary, six of the nine core quality indicators had some statistical significance at $p<0.1$, with one more, faith, just outside this range. Such transformation in church health is even more remarkable when put in the context that 50 percent of the consultancy churches were struggling at the time of the consultancy with their numerical, financial, and ministry viability such that they were in receipt of a ministry subsidy from the Baptist Union of NSW/ACT.

It could be argued that the consultancy churches in the initial analysis (n=10) above started with a lower health base (particularly the "subsidy churches") so that a marked improvement was a greater possibility. However, removing the churches having stronger health from both the consultancy and non-consultancy groups in this second "weaker churches analysis" minimizes this possibility, making any improvement in health indicators in the consultancy group of churches more comparable with the non-consultancy churches.

These results indicate a positive correlation between the health of churches, and churches that have engaged in a consultancy, in comparison to those churches that have not been involved in a consultancy. A larger sample size may have helped towards a higher level of statistical significance and the ability to draw a stronger conclusion. However, only a small number of NSW/ACT Baptist churches invite a church consultancy in any one year and excluding those churches that did not satisfactorily complete either NCLS-2001 or NCLS-2006 further narrows the data sample.[151]

---

151. "Satisfactorily complete" means that sufficient forms were returned for the size of the church to make the results statistically reliable.

5.3.2 Growth

NCLS has identified three quantitative measures of the missional impact of churches: the percentage of people in a church aged 15–19 years old who were also attending the same denomination five years ago, new attenders who have arrived in the last five years and who previously did not attend another church, and net change of attendance over five years.[152] These growth measures will be explored below for the churches in this research project.

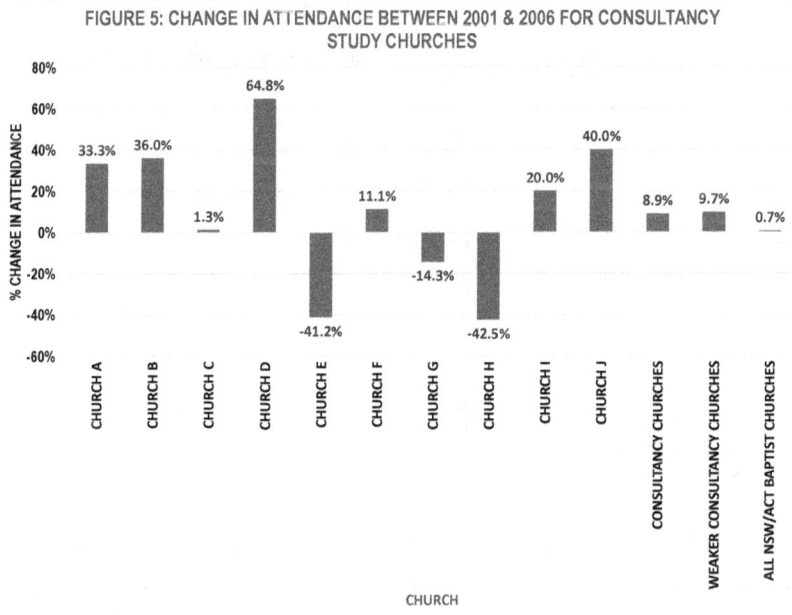

FIGURE 5: CHANGE IN ATTENDANCE BETWEEN 2001 & 2006 FOR CONSULTANCY STUDY CHURCHES

5.3.2.1 Initial Analysis

There are many factors that may contribute to a church's vitality and growth. However, as is evident from Figure 5, seven of the ten churches that form this study grew. Five of these grew by 20 percent or more over the five-year interval between NCLS-2001 and 2006, including one church that grew by 65 percent. Average growth over this period across the ten consultancy churches was 8.9 percent. Using the second analysis (weaker churches, n=9) aggregate growth of the consultancy churches was 9.7 percent. Given that average growth of all NSW/ACT Baptist

---

152. Bellamy et al., *Enriching Church Life*, 10–29.

Churches over this five-year interval to 2006 was 0.7 percent, the growth of churches that participated in a church consultancy is significant and warrants further research.[153] Such growth is even more remarkable when it is put in this context: 50 percent of the consultancy churches were struggling at the time of the consultancy with their numerical, financial, and ministry viability such that they were in receipt of a ministry subsidy from the Baptist Union of NSW/ACT.

5.3.2.2 WEAKER CHURCHES ANALYSIS

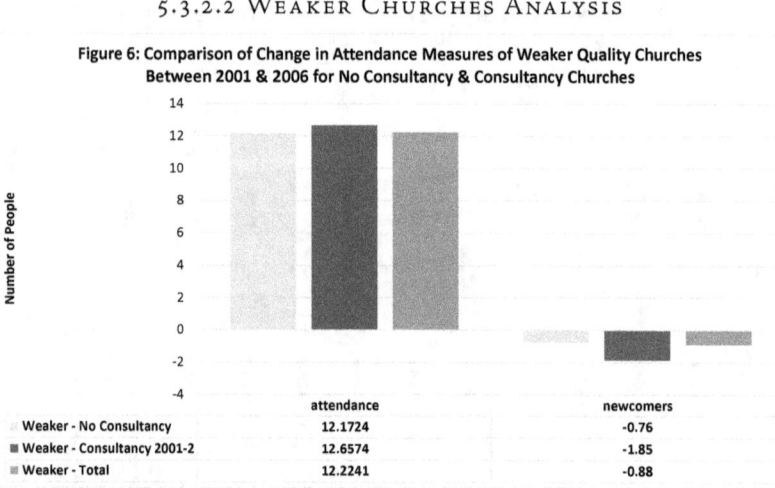

Figure 6: Comparison of Change in Attendance Measures of Weaker Quality Churches Between 2001 & 2006 for No Consultancy & Consultancy Churches

	attendance	newcomers
Weaker - No Consultancy	12.1724	-0.76
Weaker - Consultancy 2001-2	12.6574	-1.85
Weaker - Total	12.2241	-0.88

NCLS change in attendance measures (that is, attendance, newcomers and young adult retention) for both the initial (n=10) and second analyses (churches with weaker core quality indicators, n=9) were not statistically significant. In the weaker churches analysis, the increase in attendance between churches that entered into a consultancy and churches that did not enter into a consultancy is shown in the graph at Figure 6 above as being comparable.

---

153. There are some missing values in attendance data for all churches. However, membership data, which is more robust, confirms the small change in attendance patterns of all churches over this time period: membership in all NSW/ACT Baptist churches increased from 20705 in 2001 to 20776 in 2006, an increase of 0.3 percent. Again, in this instance, research is hampered by the small number of consultancy churches in gaining statistical significance of p<0.05; Soden, *NSW and ACT Baptist Churches Handbook 2001–2002*, 217; Soden, *NSW and ACT Baptist Churches Handbook 2006–2007*, 287. The figures are as at 30 June, 2001, and 30 June, 2006 respectively.

The main reason for the lack of statistical significance appears to be that some quantitative values are either missing or not statistically reliable (SNR). This is evident from Table 6 above, with the statistical outcomes of these missing or SNR values recorded at Table 7 above. Missing[154] or SNR NCLS-2001 and/or NCLS-2006 values for change in attendance (reducing the sample size of weaker non-consultancy churches to n=67, and weaker consultancy churches to n=8), and young adult retention (reducing the sample size of weaker non-consultancy churches to n=59, and weaker consultancy churches to n=3) have negatively impacted the ability to gain overall statistical reliability for these quantitative measures in a way that was not the case for the core quality health indicators (weaker non-consultancy n=74, weaker consultancy n=9).[155] Such data loss particularly renders meaningless the results for young adult retention, so it has been omitted from Figure 6. It is probable that a restoration of the original sample sizes, or larger, would give a statistically significant result for these quantitative measures, as was obtained for most of the core quality health indicators.

The mean growth for all NSW/ACT Baptist churches over the period 2001–06 is 0.56 attenders per church (n=303). This is also outlined in the graph at Figure 5 above. This growth is not reflected in either the consultancy or non-consultancy groups: both groups had a mean change of over twelve attenders for this period.

There are a number of possible explanations for this apparent anomaly. Firstly, that the churches participating in both NCLS-2001 and NCLS-2006 (and thus forming the consultancy and non-consultancy groups in this study) were more inclined to engage in a process of self-evaluation that is consistent with health and growth, than the churches which did not participate in NCLS. If this is the case, the group of non-consultancy churches extracted from NCLS-2001 and NCLS-2006 results would not

---

154. For example, where churches have submitted forms from attenders but have not submitted attendance or other quantitative data for the previous five years on their leader forms.

155. A different set of scores was used for young adult retention in these statistical analyses than was the case for the young adult retention scores on each church's NCLS-2006 Profile. For these analyses, attender's children aged 15 years and over still attending this church were used, which gives a much more dynamic and finer measure, but has the drawback of losing cases in churches where the number of young adults is not sufficient to give statistically reliable results. NCLS-2006 profiles use young people aged 15 to 19 years who have been attending this church for five years or more, as a percentage of all attenders, as the measure for young adult retention.

be representative of all NSW/ACT Baptist churches in health or growth, and most likely exhibit stronger health and higher growth than all NSW/ACT Baptist churches.

Secondly, it is possible that there is a time lag between the improvement of core quality health indicators (that have been clearly demonstrated for consultancy churches in this study), and the improvement of quantitative indicators such as attendance, newcomers, and young adult retention.

The lack of statistical significance for these three NCLS quantitative measures of attendance, newcomers, and young adult retention is quite clear. It is most probable that missing values, causing a reduction in the number of churches (both consultancy and non-consultancy) that could be included in the analysis, has negatively impacted statistical reliability. However, the increase in attendance for consultancy churches relative to all NSW/ACT Baptist churches is also definite. The tentative explanations offered for this anomaly would need further research to validate or refute, which is outside the scope of this study.

5.4 Evaluation and Interpretation of Results

Broadly speaking, the above results are encouraging in terms of the impact of church consultancy on a church's health or core qualities, and on a church's growth. This study is limited by both the number of churches that submitted reliable data for both the 2001 and 2006 NCLS and the number of churches that undertake a church consultancy each year.[156] These factors impacted the significance levels that were able to be obtained in statistical analysis, therefore, the value of a study expanded to include a higher number of churches is indicated.[157]

Statistical reliability was enhanced in the second analysis where only churches with lower overall core qualities or health in 2001 were included. While this analysis is encouraging in that six of the nine core qualities had significance scores smaller than 0.10, p scores for the

---

156. Soden, *NSW and ACT Baptist Churches Handbook 2001–2002*, 217; Soden, *NSW and ACT Baptist Churches Handbook 2006–2007*, 287. The figures are as at 30 June, 2001 and 30 June, 2006 respectively.

157. This could be achieved by including churches from other denominations using the same model of church consultancy, although there may be complexities in obtaining data across denominational lines and in comparing consultancy and non-consultancy churches from various denominational data sets.

three attendance measures (attendance, newcomers, and young adult retention) were less reliable. The significant increase in these six quality characteristics (service, faith-sharing, worship, leadership, belonging, and vision) between 2001 and 2006, along with the stronger significance scores in the second analysis, gives greater scope for asserting that church consultancy has been an important factor in restoring or improving vitality and health. In other words, there is a link between churches that have undertaken a church consultancy and churches that have improved their health through deliberately addressing deficiencies in the various areas of their church life. This is particularly so given that 50 percent of the consultancy churches at that time were struggling with their health and viability, and in receipt of a ministry subsidy.

The interviews confirmed the positive impact of a church consultancy on a church's growth and health. There was a slight variation between the interview responses and the NCLS data for each church regarding health and growth. The interviews validated the role of church consultancies in identifying and addressing areas that were blocking health and growth in the life of each church, resulting in such outcomes as: merging congregations and seeing a resultant growth spurt, gaining a clearer vision and specific strategies for moving forward, addressing relational conflicts that were holding the church back, or identifying strategic opportunities to launch out into new ministries that impact the surrounding community.[158]

While many of the consultancy churches experienced good growth over the four-to-five-year interval, there may be a time-lag between an improvement in qualities and a corresponding improvement in quantities. The reasons a church consultancy was invited (e.g. conflict) could have been a cause of numerical decline, and/or numerical decline triggered the need for a church consultancy. While church health indicators may improve relatively quickly as a response to a consultancy, the church may take some time to grow again. Research indicates a correlation between strong core quality indicators and churches that are growing.[159] And Schwarz asserts that church health is a good predictor of church growth.[160] Therefore, expanding this research for the ten churches in

158. Pastor of Church A, Interview Transcript, 2; Pastor of Church C, Interview Transcript, 3; Pastor of Church F, Interview Transcript, 3; Pastor of Church H, Interview Transcript, 3; Pastor of Church I, Interview Transcript, 2.

159. Bellamy et al., *Enriching Church Life*, 40–51.

160. Schwarz, *Natural Church Development*, 46–48.

the study to include further NCLS findings to evaluate any changes in patterns of growth or decline is recommended.[161] This would enable an evaluation of whether churches that had grown to 2006 since a church consultancy continued to grow, and particularly whether those churches with little growth but strong increases in core quality indicators in NCLS-2006 have broken free of static attendance. Churches with significant health issues may need an interval greater than five years to reverse static or declining attendance.

---

161. Specifically, NCLS-2011 and NCLS-2016.

6

Conclusion

THREE BROAD STREAMS OF church health literature have been examined: systems theory, faithfulness to the biblical purposes of the church, and whether "postmodernity" necessitates the emergence of new forms of church. An analysis of the central place of church health or vitality in the New Testament has also been undertaken, along with some of the theological motifs that contribute to individual spiritual, relational, and church health.

Systems theory has made a significant contribution to understanding how organizations work, and to the fields of organizational development and management consultancy, which in part inform church consultancy. Systems theory recognizes the emotional interconnectedness of a church, and in this sense can often help church leaders, or external interventionists such as consultants, to focus on core or subsurface health issues, and to know how to gain forward movement without "pushback."

However, a critique of both systems theory and the church health movement is the overfocus on the health of the organization/church. The Church Growth Movement and the stream of "faithfulness to the biblical purposes of the church" provide a helpful balancing corrective through understanding that robust health implies replication (or mission). There have been many endeavors to quantify health, but two widely used, multi-country instruments are NCLS/ICLS and NCD, for which NCLS/ICLS has been most affirmed in its rigor.

Local community context, local church internal characteristics, national context and trends (such as the emergence of "postmodernity"), and national denominational characteristics have been examined as they relate to church health and church growth. While external factors have an influence, local church internal characteristics are the most significant determinant of a church's health and growth. The implication of this is that the prime drivers of church health and church growth are meta-cultural. Nevertheless, a church's responsiveness to local demographic characteristics and national trends will be important if it is to be missionally relevant. Indeed, some of the churches included in this study had challenging local contexts but were empowered through the church consultancy process to respond to those settings.

Various aspects of the Church Growth Movement have been criticized for an overfocus on pragmatics, and theological shallowness, and would benefit from some further theological work in the future. However, one of the valuable insights that can be gained from the movement is that faithfulness is not enough: effective churches grow. This idea has been picked up by those researching and writing in the area of church health, such as Schwarz and the NCLS team.[1] The question then arises as to how? How can churches increase their vitality and how can they move from stagnancy or decline into growth?

Church consultancy is one significant catalyst emerging for the growth and health of churches. Drawing from disciplines such as organizational development and theology, church consultancy can be a process-oriented ministry tool for a local church to listen to God and fashion a Godward response to their circumstances. Church consultancy is not the only health strategy that is available to churches, and there may be situations when other approaches such as mediation, an intentional interim pastor, coaching, or mentoring are more appropriate. Church consultancy can make a substantial contribution in either proactively addressing a specific problem or managing a specialized response to difficult situations of transition, recovery from crisis, or conflict.

While the focus of this research is on Baptist churches in NSW/ACT, a brief examination of the interplay between ecclesiology and church consultancy, as well as the current practice of this model of church consultancy in a wide variety of Australian denominations, affirms the use of church consultancy in diverse ecclesiological settings.

In the retrospective study of ten churches that had invited church consultancies, analysis of quantitative data exhibited statistically

1. Schwarz, *Natural Church Development*, 46–48; Bellamy et al., *Enriching Church Life*, 40–51.

significant correlations between church consultancy and church health, particularly in the "weaker churches" analysis of consultancy and non-consultancy groups. Marked improvements in church attendance were evident from the consultancy cohort, but these were not statistically significant. In this respect, the small number of consultancy churches in the study, restricted by the low number of churches having statistically reliable NCLS-2001 and NCLS-2006 data, proved to be a limitation. These results give scope for asserting that a church consultancy has been an important factor in restoring or improving church vitality and health in the consultancy churches group.

This positive impact of consultancy is even more pronounced when it is understood, from interviews, church consultancy reports, and NCLS profiles, that 50 percent of these churches were struggling with significant issues or concerns regarding their ongoing viability such that they were in receipt of a ministry subsidy. The cessation of ministry subsidies, alongside the provision of a church consultancy to such churches, appears to be validated by the growth of 80 percent of the five churches included in this research who were formerly in receipt of such subsidies.

Interviews with some of the pastors of the ten churches which form this research validated increases in health indicators and growth of churches post-consultancy, as hindering issues were addressed by the consultants and the church. The value of church consultancy for churches grappling with growth issues, rather than undergoing significant problems, was also validated.

A theology of church consultancy has been developed in this thesis (in the theological and practical analysis provided in the sections on church health, church growth, and church consultancy). Embedded in a theology of church consultancy, these theological principles inform and represent my convictions about church growth and church health. This theology has carefully articulated theological perspectives on a range of issues. These theological assertions (which surface at key points in this thesis) reveal the following about appropriate measures for assessing the vitality of churches, especially in a Baptist setting.[2]

---

2. It should be noted that in attempting to bring together complex theological paradigms with measures which seek to give shape to the vitality or health, and the growth, of a congregation, care needs to be taken to avoid a reductionist approach, or to pretend that a one-for-one correspondence between theologies and measures is always obtainable. However, these barriers are subsumed by the importance of making such an attempt.

A theology of systems theory will be reflected in the internal core qualities (faith, worship, and belonging) as a church facilitates an environment for attenders' growth and wholeness, and as attenders belong to one another in ways that are interdependent yet differentiated.[3] The openness or permeability of the church's boundaries with the community will be reflected in the outward core qualities of service, faith-sharing, and inclusion, along with the attendance measures of attendance change and newcomers. Such a theology is also connected to a pastor's leadership of the system (core qualities of vision, leadership, and innovation) and the capacity of church health consultants to work with the system for health and growth.

A theology of balanced ecclesiological purpose will be reflected in a lack of eccentricity and balance across the nine core quality indicators. This will neither be to the detriment of church growth (attendance change), nor an unsustainable or exclusive focus on growth that does not attend to church health.[4]

Theologies of sin, sanctification, salvation, and humanity may be demonstrated in a number of core qualities, but most clearly in the quality of an alive and growing faith. The relational dimension is ever present in a church, and the impact of sin on strained relationships will be evidenced by a decrease in the core quality of strong and growing belonging. The opposite is also true; where church attenders are growing in godliness it impacts their relationships in positive ways, increasing their sense of belonging (core quality indicator). As sanctification occurs, a raised concern for others will be demonstrated by increased ministry to others within the church (the core quality of inspiring and empowering leadership includes their involvement in ministry) and the three outward core qualities of service, faith-sharing, and inclusion to those outside the church.

A theology of the church may also be reflected by a number of NCLS core qualities, but particularly in Free Church ecclesiology of mutual ministry to one another[5] (inspiring and empowering leadership reflects this) and missional service, faith-sharing, and inclusion. Attendance growth should be a corollary of this.

---

3. Bowen, *Family Therapy in Clinical Practice*.
4. Warren, *The Purpose Driven Church*, 103–7.
5. Volf, *After Our Likeness*, 217.

A theology of the church's mission and *a theology of church and kingdom*, sees the church as an instrument of God's missional purposes in the world for the establishment of his kingdom. At its ultimate, it is the *being* or living out of the lordship of Christ over all, and the proclamation of that to the world. So, while individual Christians and a local church are agents of that mission in every dimension, including their life together (core quality: belonging), the outward core qualities of service, faith-sharing, and inclusion will be significant markers of that missionality, as will newcomers and growth in attendance. As this mission is communicated clearly and owned by the congregation, the core quality of vision will also be enlivened.

A theology of church and culture recognizes the insufficiency of an ecclesiological-only response to culture. NCLS has endeavored to encapsulate core qualities that embrace a diversity of ecclesiologies, as well as core qualities that are equally meaningful for churches at the "organic movement" end of the spectrum, and those at the "organized institution" polarity.[6] It also affirms the power of a church to work on its health or vitality (reflected in all core quality indicators) on its own or with the assistance of church consultants, rather than being at the mercy of factors external to the church such as local community context, national context and trends, and national denominational characteristics.

A theology of growth and reproduction maintains that these should be the normative experience of healthy churches. While it may be more difficult to capture reproduction, or the planting of another church, in core quality indicators, growth may be seen in newcomers and growth in attendance, faith-sharing in particular, and to some extent in service and inclusion.

A theology of growth with health recognizes the importance of a focus on *both* of these aspects of church life.[7] So rather than focusing on the three measures of attendance *or* the nine core quality indicators of health, in looking at the total picture of a church *both* will be essential. Even the *type* or quality of growth is something that NCLS has attempted to measure: does the inflow of people into a church represent transfers from the same denomination or "switchers" from other denominations? Or, more significantly, does inflow comprise high levels of newcomers to

---

6. Snyder, "The Marks of Evangelical Ecclesiology," 87–88.
7. Schwarz, *Natural Church Development*, 46–48; Borden, *Direct Hit*, 16.

church life?[8] While the theological importance of church growth has been clearly emphasized in this research, growth at any cost, without due attention to the quality of that growth and the core vitality indicators that gauge church health, may be unsustainable and empty.

A *theology of process and capacity-building* will be particularly evidenced internally as leaders build the capacity of attenders for ministry and mission, and be echoed by the core quality of inspiring and empowering leadership. As a church adopts a stance of openness to external capacity-building, the core quality of imaginative and flexible innovation will be stimulated. While this openness to external capacity-building is much wider, it will be reflected specifically in a church's willingness to invite and engage in a church consultancy.

A *theology of interdisciplinary insight* will also be indicated by the core quality of imaginative and flexible innovation. That is, as churches are familiar with insights gained from attenders' study or workplaces, then examine those insights theologically, innovative ideas will be fostered and enacted for carrying out the church's mission, and the church will more closely resemble, in Senge's parlance, a "learning organization."[9]

A *theology of change and transition* may be reflected by a congregation's openness to the inspirational core qualities, vision, leadership, and innovation. Doubtless in times of massive or difficult transition, attenders' sense of connection to the church through the internal core qualities (faith, worship, and belonging) may be more tenuous unless a skilled pastor or consultant is dealing well with the emotional and spiritual aspects of that transition. Such an inward focus may also be reflected in less energy being given to the three outward core qualities at that time.

A *theology of leadership* reflects accountability, contextual to a church, and recognizes the primacy of catalyzing the church to achieve its mission. A helpful starting point in measuring leadership effectiveness is the distillation by NCLS of leadership into three inspirational core qualities: a clear and owned *vision*, inspiring and empowering *leadership*, and open and flexible *innovation*.[10] While governance models, even in a Free Church or Baptist setting, are multifarious, the fundamental task

---

8. Bellamy et al., *Enriching Church Life*, 34–35.
9. Senge, *The Fifth Discipline*.
10. Bellamy et al., *Enriching Church Life*, 10–29.

of governance is ensuring that leaders catalyze and equip the congregation for its biblical mission, which is reflected in each of the nine core qualities.

A theology of conflict and restoration acknowledges the normality of conflict in human communities, that it is not necessarily sin, and that conflict can be an opportunity to clarify direction and navigate change (core qualities of vision and innovation). Sinful behavior associated with conflict can damage relationships (i.e. decrease core quality of belonging) and mar a church's witness (outward core qualities). A pathway to the restoration of relationships is outlined by Halstead:

> For congregations to get unstuck, they need frequent confession, forgiveness and reconciliation taking place at a variety of in-between points—one-to-one between individual members, between pastors and individuals, between pastors and the congregation, between pastors and boards, between congregations and individuals, between congregational groups and members, between local and denominational church systems, and between larger religious groups.[11]

It should be abundantly evident from the theological work above, drawing on theologies embedded throughout this thesis, that the nine NCLS core quality indicators and the three NCLS attendance measures are appropriate for gauging the vitality of churches when used to assess the impact of one model of church consultancy on church health and church growth in NSW/ACT Baptist churches. Church health and church growth are grounded in theological principles, which in turn inform the church consultancy process. This practical means of assisting churches with health and growth is underpinned by the theologies of church health, church growth, and church consultancy, along with corollary and subsidiary theologies expanded on in this thesis.

These theologies intersect with one another, and this has been amply demonstrated in the conclusions of chapters 2, 3, and 4, and elsewhere in the thesis. Such a conversation between these theologies has helped to hone, integrate, and make more explicit the overarching theology presented in this thesis.

---

11. Halstead, *From Stuck to Unstuck: Overcoming Congregational Impasse*, 81.

6.1 Recommendations

1. That an expanded study along similar lines be undertaken, incorporating a larger number of churches, to seek to achieve a greater statistical reliability. This may need to be done cross-denominationally to obtain such church numbers.
2. That a study following the progress of the ten consultancy churches be undertaken to evaluate any changes in patterns of growth or decline, and core quality or health indicators upon the release of NCLS-2011 figures.
3. That a study be undertaken to determine whether a greater impact is achieved through church consultancy on church health and church growth for churches like Church D that are relatively healthy but are seeking assistance to navigate growth issues.
4. That an integrated health strategy, including but not limited to church consultancy, continue to be undertaken by Baptist Churches of NSW/ACT, and that training and policy guidelines for the most appropriate and effective use of church consultancy within this be drawn up, taking into account any results from further study recommendations (1, 2, and 3) above.[12]
5. That regular training courses in areas identified in the discussion of common themes in consultancy objectives at 5.1.1 continue to be offered to pastors and church leaders, thereby lessening the need for church consultancies.
6. That, in conjunction with recommendations 3 and 4, coaching and mentoring of pastors continue to be offered as both an adjunct to and, where appropriate, an alternative to accessing church consultancy.[13]

---

12. Comments were made in chapter 4 regarding Paul Borden's integrated plan for church health and growth. The value of targeting a growing church and helping it with the issues surrounding that growth was affirmed by the impact of consultancy on some of the churches that formed this study. See Appendix F: Diagnostic Flowchart for Intragroup and Individual Intervention, for a model towards such a strategy.

13. Comments were made in chapter 5 that gifted pastors, for one reason or another, did not seem able to identify the changes needed or to implement them, which then resulted in the church consultancy. This may be an area worth exploring in greater depth in another study.

7. Since biblical theologies of church health and church consultancy both inform and underpin the practice of church consultancy, and set it apart from organizational development consultancies conducted in the business world, it is recommended that a higher level of input regarding these theologies be incorporated into church consultancy training for the Baptist Churches of NSW/ACT Consultancy current and future teams.

Appendix A

Interview Questions

A SUMMARY OF THE written information sheet (previously provided) will be given verbally prior to the interview to ensure that the interviewee is fully informed. The form of consent the interviewee has previously provided in writing will also be restated verbally prior to the interview to ensure that the interviewee feels under no obligation to assist with the research. They will also be informed that they may withdraw from the process at any time, and have all information returned to them.

1. What were some of the issues that were present surrounding the health of the church prior to the consultancy being undertaken?
2. How effectively did the consultancy address these health issues at the time? What leads you to that conclusion/what changes did you observe at that time?
3a. Do you think that in the interval since the church consultancy, that attenders' faith has grown, declined, or is about the same? What leads you to that conclusion/what changes do you observe now?
3b. Do you think that in the interval since the church consultancy, that the vitality of worship of the church has grown, declined, or is about the same? What leads you to that conclusion/what changes do you observe now?
3c. Do you think that in the interval since the church consultancy, that peoples' belonging and involvement at the church has grown,

declined, or is about the same? What leads you to that conclusion/ what changes do you observe now?

3d. Do you think that in the interval since the church consultancy, that an active concern for those on the fringe of church life has grown, declined, or is about the same? What leads you to that conclusion/ what changes do you observe now?

3e. Do you think that in the interval since the church consultancy, that care for young people at the church has grown, declined, or is about the same? What leads you to that conclusion/what changes do you observe now?

3f. Do you think that in the interval since the church consultancy, that a focus beyond the church into the community has grown, declined, or is about the same? What leads you to that conclusion/what changes do you observe now?

3g. Do you think that in the interval since the church consultancy, that serving the wider community by the church has grown, declined, or is about the same? What leads you to that conclusion/what changes do you observe now?

3h. Do you think that in the interval since the church consultancy, that discussing faith and inviting others to church has grown, declined, or is about the same? What leads you to that conclusion/what changes do you observe now?

3i. Do you think that in the interval since the church consultancy, that integrating newcomers to the church has grown, declined, or is about the same? What leads you to that conclusion/what changes do you observe now?

3j. Do you think that in the interval since the church consultancy, that a clear, owned vision for the future of the church has grown, declined, or is about the same? What leads you to that conclusion/ what changes do you observe now?

3k. Do you think that in the interval since the church consultancy, that openness to new possibilities of the church has grown, declined, or is about the same? What leads you to that conclusion/what changes do you observe now?

3l. Do you think that in the interval since the church consultancy, that empowering and inspiring leadership of the church has grown, declined, or is about the same? What leads you to that conclusion/what changes do you observe now?

4. Do you think that in the interval since the church consultancy, that the overall health of the church has grown, declined, or is about the same? What leads you to that conclusion/what changes do you observe now?

5. What patterns of growth or decline were present prior to the consultancy being undertaken?

6. How effectively did the consultancy address these growth issues at the time? What leads you to that conclusion/what changes did you observe at that time?

7. Do you think that in the interval since the church consultancy, that attendance at the church has grown, declined, or is about the same? What leads you to that conclusion/what changes do you observe now?

8. Is there anything else that you wish to say or anything else that may assist me in my research?

Appendix B

Request for Permission for Research

- GENERAL SECRETARY BAPTIST CHURCHES NSW/ACT[1]
- CHURCH CONSULTANCY SUPERVISOR[2]
- CHURCHES IN THIS STUDY[3]
- CONSULTANTS OF CHURCHES IN THIS STUDY[4]
- PASTORS OF THOSE CHURCHES WHO WERE INTERVIEWED[5]

21 August 2007

Dear Sir,

I am writing to request permission to conduct the following postgraduate research; *"Explore the impact of one model of church consultancy on church health and church growth in NSW/ACT Baptist Churches."* This

---

1. Permission confirmed by Alan Soden, letter to author, 7 May, 2007.

2. Permission confirmed by Les Scarborough, email message to author, 16 December, 2007.

3. Permission confirmed in various letters or emails to author from churches, dated 2007 or 2008.

4. Permission confirmed in various emails to author from consultants, dated 2007 or 2008.

5. Permission confirmed in various letters or emails to author from pastors, dated 2009. Note that the letter of permission from the church they formerly/currently pastored was attached.

research is being completed as part of my Doctor of Ministry degree under the auspices of the Australian College of Theology in Sydney.

I have been involved in pastoring Baptist churches in NSW/ACT for over thirteen years and I am an accredited church consultant with the Baptist Churches of NSW/ACT. It is my hope that this research, in quantifying the impact of church consultancy, will have significant benefits for the denomination and local churches.

Subject to your approval, I will be using 2001 and 2006 NCLS data and church consultancy reports for ten churches who have undertaken a church consultancy since the 2001 NCLS Survey, as well as interviewing some of those who were pastors of those churches at that time.

In the possible event that completing this research raises issues for those interviewees that are best worked through with a professional counsellor, they will be given contact details for Relationships Australia, Unifam Counselling and Mediation, and The Salvation Army Counselling Service on their Participants Information Sheet.

Any questions that you might have regarding this research can be directed to the researcher, ____ _____, on _____ (home) or _____ (mobile), or to the supervisor, Rev. Dr. John Reid, on 02 9878 0201 at Morling College, 20 Herring Rd, Eastwood NSW 2122.

This study has been approved by the Australian College of Theology's Ethics Committee. In the event that you have a concern or complaint regarding this study, or a query that the researcher or supervisor has not been able to satisfy, you may write to:

Chair, Ethics Committee
Australian College of Theology
Suite 4, Level 6
51 Druitt St
Sydney NSW 2000

Any complaint will be treated in confidence, investigated fully, and you will be informed of the outcome.

Research data collected will be treated in confidence, but may be published or provided to other researchers in a form that does not identify individual churches in any way. Data collected will be held in a locked cabinet for seven years. Churches may withdraw from the process at any time and have all material returned to them. A summary of the project results, when they are available, will be given to you and individual churches upon request.

I look forward to your written response (email should suffice), by no later than 30 September, 2007, to use church consultancy reports for these churches, and to generally undertake this research for the benefit of the denomination and the wider church.

Yours in Christ's Service

Appendix C

Interview Participant Information Sheet[1]

Research Project

Title: Explore the impact of one model of church consultancy on church health and church growth in NSW/ACT Baptist Churches.

(1) What is the research about?

THIS STUDY WILL ATTEMPT to gauge the effectiveness of church consultancy in promoting church health and church growth in NSW/ACT Baptist churches. It will seek to do this by measuring changes in health and growth over time, and interviewing a number of people who observed the church before, during and since the consultancy.

(2) Who can participate?

You must have been at the church before the church consultancy in 2001 or 2002 and for at least one year subsequent to the consultancy. The maximum number of interviews from each church will be limited to one, so as to provide a balance in responses that reflect the various types of consultancies, churches, and contexts where church consultancies were carried out.

---

1. A copy of this information sheet was given to each interviewee.

(3) Who is carrying out the research?

The study is being conducted by Rev. Ian Duncum and will form the basis for the degree of Doctor of Ministry under the auspices of the Australian College of Theology in Sydney. Rev. Ian Duncum is studying through Morling College, under the supervision of Rev. Dr. Graham Hill, DipMinHons, BTheol, PGCertTESOL, CertIV A&WT, MTheol, PhD, Lecturer in Pastoral and Practical Studies, the Director of the Centre for Leadership, the Director of Supervised Field Education, and the Coordinator of Postgraduate Coursework degrees.

(4) What does the research involve?

The study will involve one interview. This will be audiotaped to assist with data gathering.

(5) How much time will the interview take?

Approximately 45 minutes.

(6) Can I withdraw from the research?

Being in this study is completely voluntary—you are not under any obligation to consent. You are free to withdraw your consent and to discontinue your participation at any time without prejudice, and have all data collected up to that point returned to you.

(7) Will anyone else know the results?

Research data collected will be treated in confidence, but may be published or provided to other researchers in a form that does not identify individuals or churches in any way. Data collected will be held in a locked cabinet for seven years. Individuals may withdraw from the process at any time and have all material returned to them. A summary of the project results, when they are available, will be provided to participants upon request.

(8) Will the research benefit me?

It is hoped that this research, in quantifying the impact of church consultancy, will have significant benefits for the denomination, local churches, and persons who attend those churches. Those who participate in this research may have their knowledge of church health enhanced.

In the possible event that completing this research raises issues for you that are best worked through with a professional counselor, the following are organizations that provide such a service (ask for details of your closest center); Relationships Australia (ph) 1300 364 277, Unifam Counselling and Mediation (ph) 02 8830 0777, and The Salvation Army Counselling Service (ph) 02 9743 2831.

(9) What if I require further information?

Any questions that you might have regarding this research can be directed to the researcher, Rev. Ian Duncum, or to the supervisor, Rev. Dr. Graham Hill, on 02 9878 0201 at Morling College, 120 Herring Rd, Macquarie Park NSW 2113.

(10) What if I have a complaint or concerns?

This study has been approved by the Australian College of Theology's Ethics Committee. In the event that you have a concern or complaint regarding this study, or a query that the researcher or supervisor has not been able to satisfy, you may write to:

> Chair, Ethics Committee
> Australian College of Theology
> Suite 4, Level 6
> 51 Druitt St
> Sydney NSW 2000

Any complaint will be treated in confidence, investigated fully, and you will be informed of the outcome.

This information sheet is for you to keep.

Appendix D

Interview Participant Consent Form[1]

I GIVE CONSENT TO my participation in the research project:

TITLE: Explore the impact of one model of church consultancy on church health and church growth in NSW/ACT Baptist Churches.

In giving my consent I acknowledge that:

1. The procedures required for the project and the time involved have been explained to me, and any questions I have about the project have been answered to my satisfaction.
2. I have read the Participant Information Sheet and have been given the opportunity to discuss the information and my involvement in the project with the researcher/s.
3. I understand that I can withdraw from the research project at any time, without affecting my relationship with the researcher(s) now or in the future.
4. I understand that my involvement is strictly confidential and no information about me will be used in any way that reveals my identity.
5. I understand that interviews will be audiotaped to assist data gathering.

Signed:

1. A signed copy of the consent form has been obtained from each interviewee, dated 2009.

INTERVIEW PARTICIPANT CONSENT FORM

Name:
Date:
Address:
Phone:
Email:

Appendix E

NCLS Category by Church

APPENDIX E

NCLS Changes by Church	A'01	A'06	A%Δ	B'01	B'06	B%Δ	C'01	C'06	C%Δ	D'01	D'06	D%Δ	E'01	E'06	E%Δ
Internal Core Qualities															
Alive and Growing Faith	3.9	5.4	38%	5.8	4.3	-26%	6.6	7.9	20%	3.3	5.9	79%	1.2	6.2	417%
Vital and Nurturing Worship	3.1	5.6	81%	6.3	8.8	40%	5.2	6.8	31%	3.9	6.8	74%	3.4	3.4	0%
Strong and Growing Belonging	4.8	6.9	44%	4.7	5.1	9%	6.6	5.5	-17%	3.4	5.8	71%	3.2	2.8	-13%
Inspirational Core Qualities															
Clear and Owned Vision	4.4	8.8	100%	5.5	5.3	-4%	8.7	7.1	-18%	4.9	8.2	67%	3.5	3.2	-9%
Inspiring and Empowering Leadership	3	5.9	97%	6.4	4.9	-23%	5.9	2.2	-63%	2.9	6.4	121%	3.9	5	28%
Imaginative and Flexible Innovation	3.8	4.8	26%	6.3	5	-21%	5.3	3.5	-34%	4.3	6.1	42%	3.4	2.7	-21%
Outward Core Qualities															
Practical and Diverse Service	5.9	6.2	5%	5.5	2	-63%	4.1	3.2	-21%	7.4	7	-5%	2.7	6.5	141%
Willing and Effective Faith-sharing	4.5	5.5	22%	5.5	5	-9%	3.3	2.8	-15%	5	6.5	30%	3.1	2.5	-19%
Intentional and Welcoming Inclusion	1.5	2.3	53%	6.5	4	-38%	3.7	4.8	29%	3.5	6.9	95%	1.9	7.2	285%
Total Qualities	34.9	51.4	47%	52	49.1	-6%	54.8	48.2	-12%	34.1	55.7	63%	27.6	39.9	45%
Attendance Measures															
young adult retention	1	0		2	1		3	4		7	7		6	4	
newcomers	4	2		12	3		8	2		17	13		5	1	
attendance	135	180	33%	50	68	36%	75	76	1%	91	150	65%	68	40	-41%

NCLS Changes by Church	F'01	F'06	F%Δ	G'01	G'06	G%Δ	H'01	H'06	H%Δ	I'01	I'06	I%Δ	J'01	J'06	J%Δ
Internal Core Qualities															
Alive and Growing Faith	4.5	6.9	53%	5.9	4.6	-22%	4.1	3.1	-24%	5.4	5.5	2%	2.4	10	317%
Vital and Nurturing Worship	6.5	8.4	29%	4.8	4.9	2%	3.3	3.8	15%	6.2	10	61%	2.7	5.9	119%
Strong and Growing Belonging	5	7.2	44%	5.9	4.2	-29%	4.3	2.8	-35%	5.3	6.4	21%	2.5	6.7	168%
Inspirational Core Qualities															
Clear and Owned Vision	5	4.6	-8%	6.3	5.5	-13%	4.6	3.7	-20%	6.3	4.5	-29%	4.1	6.9	68%
Inspiring and Empowering Leadership	2.6	6.8	162%	5.3	4.8	-9%	6.1	4.3	-30%	6.3	3.3	-48%	3.5	5.8	66%
Imaginative and Flexible Innovation	2.7	5.4	100%	4.5	5	11%	5.6	3.3	-41%	5.9	8.3	41%	2.7	5.2	93%
Outward Core Qualities															
Practical and Diverse Service	4.4	6.2	41%	7	3	-57%		6.8	100%	6	6	0%	2	8	142%
Willing and Effective Faith-sharing	4.5	5.5	29%	4.7	3.7	-21%	5	4.3	-15%	5	7.2	44%	3.7	8.2	44%
Intentional and Welcoming Inclusion	2.4	5	50%	3.2	4	25%		10			8.3		2	4	136%
Total Qualities	37.6	57.3	52%	46.9	39.8	-15%	45	42.2	-6%	52.6	57.2	9%	27.4	62.5	128%
Attendance Measures															
young adult retention	0	0		5	3		2	1		4	3		0	3	
newcomers	17	9		5	4		3	2		4	16		11	5	
attendance	45	50	11%	140	120	-14%	81	46	-43%	90	98	20%	20	28	40%

Appendix F

Diagnostic Flowchart for Intragroup and Individual Intervention

DENOMINATIONAL EXECUTIVES HAVE A range of intervention tools at their disposal. But with limited resources, the questions they may be asking are: *How can these resources be most effectively deployed for maximum impact? When is it more appropriate to use a particular resource?*

While there is a strong focus on celebrating the achievements of the top one-third of churches, and in remediating the bottom one-third of churches, a proactive intervention facilitating church health and church growth for the middle third of churches may reap the best results for intervention inputs.

Initial Phases

The process of discerning the most effective way forward can be difficult, with churches not always transparent about the reasons for requesting an intervention. So while some churches are upfront about what is occurring in the initial contact, others are less so, meaning that clarity is not gained until later in the process through data gathering and assessment. This raises the issue of designing a tool or series of questions to assist in surfacing the reasons for an intervention request early in the process.

APPENDIX F

INITIAL CONTACT
↓
CONTRACT NEGOTION
↓
PROBLEM DEFINITION
↓
DATA GATHERING
↓
ASSESSMENT

Process Phases*

Diagnosis	Pastoral Transition**— Healthy Leave	Pastoral Transition— Unhealthy Leave***	Pastoral Transition—Church stagnant/ declining	"Simple Conflict"*****
Indicated Process	IIM or Transitional Consultancy may be indicated where pastor has been incumbent 8+ years	IIM or Transitional Consultancy focused on healing. Possibly Recovery Consultancy if ethical misconduct	IIM or Transitional Consultancy focused on revitalization. Emphasis on strategic planning (or parallel Strategic Planning Consultancy) will be key	Mediation for conflict between 2 to 4 families that has not spread to being church-wide, otherwise Conflict Consultancy
Outcome Goal	Church reestablishes own identity and vision before calling new pastor	Church recovers health and hope before calling new pastor	Church is revitalized (e.g. new leadership, vision) before calling new pastor	Agreement/ Transformation of conflict, and policy formation
Closure	Evaluation and closure	Evaluation and closure	Evaluation and closure	Evaluation and closure
Follow-up	Nil	Nil	Nil	Further training in prevention and policy formation

Diagnosis	Leadership Dysfunctions—Pastors	Leadership Dysfunctions—Leadership Team	Systemic Dysfunctions—General	Victimization
Indicated Process	Leadership and Staff Team Review Consultancy. Recommendations for improvement supported by mentoring/coaching. Possibly Recovery Consultancy if ethical misconduct	Governance Consultancy. Possibly Recovery Consultancy if ethical misconduct	General Consultancy, or Strategic Planning Consultancy if warranted, for system-wide intervention	Contact authorities
Outcome Goal	Change or termination	Leadership Team functional	Group decision-making and resolution of issues	Information sharing
Closure	Evaluation and closure	Evaluation and closure	Evaluation and closure	Evaluation and closure
Follow-up	Mentoring or as indicated	As indicated	Further training or as indicated	As indicated

Endnotes

*Adapted from Brubaker, "Diagnostic Flow Chart for Intragroup Intervention," 257.

**While an Intentional Interim Ministry will include the five developmental tasks, the first three columns reflect a different reason for the IIM and therefore a different emphasis in the developmental tasks.

***Of course, a parallel process overseen by a person other than the consultant/IIM may be needed for the pastor.

****It is generally recommended that Church Consultants or IIMs do not work with conflicts of level 4 or above on the Speed Leas scale.

Appendix AA

Church A Consultancy Report Summary[1]

Overview Recommendations

1. That this report be released to the whole church.
2. That all recommendations are implemented within agreed time frames.
3. That the church leadership appoints a three-person group to oversee the implementation of the report, one of the three to be a deacon.
4. That the pastoral team and deacons meet for a half-day conference by [date] to discuss the report and begin planning the implementation process.

---

1. Baptist Churches of NSW and ACT Church Consultancy Team, "Church A Baptist Church Consultancy Report." Church consultancy reports, sometimes running to over thirty pages, have been summarized here and following for the purposes of brevity, and also to minimize opportunities for readers to draw inferences that identify the church and/or its attenders. Observations and reflections pertaining to each objective, the methodology of the consultancy, and appendices such as key leader interview questions have been omitted. The issues facing each church, and the recommended actions to address them, can be determined from the objectives set by each church's leadership team and the recommendations made by the consultants.

Recommendations: Objective 1—To assist the church in the development of a vision for the future

1. That the church appoint a representative Future Directions Taskforce, with an appointed group leader, to facilitate the development of church values and vision statements. Such a process should encourage as much congregational involvement as possible.
2. In this process, a draft statement of core values should be developed first, followed by a draft vision statement, including some specific ministry goals/priorities for [the next three years].
3. The taskforce should provide a draft report to the church leadership and then congregation by the end of [date] at the latest (taking into account the recommended leadership review process—see objective 2 recommendations) with the goal that statements can be adopted by the end of [date] at the latest.

Recommendations: Objective 2—To clarify the congregation's understanding and expectations of the present church leadership and any suggested improvements

1. That the church invite [Associate Superintendent—Ministry] or [Lecturer in Practical and Pastoral Studies, Morling College] to run a workshop for the church, as soon as can be arranged, to assist the congregation develop and affirm a clearer understanding of leadership, authority, and accountability; releasing leaders to lead and people to minister.
2. That the same workshop convener be asked to also facilitate a follow-up open forum to allow people to discuss their expectations and understanding of pastoral leadership and the role of deacons, etc., in light of a biblical and practical understanding of these roles.
3. That out of recommendations 1 and 2, the pastoral team, two deacons and two other suitably gifted members, form a leadership taskforce to review the church's leadership structure in light of present and future needs. Such investigations should reflect on current

structures and any potential changes that could address areas of concern raised in this report.

4. That this same group, in light of the above, also gives consideration to the function of the pastor/s, deacons and/or other suggested leadership positions, including roles, responsibilities, authority, and accountability.

5. That the taskforce present the congregation with a written discussion paper, including recommendations, by no later than the end of [date].

6. In this process, the taskforce should also review present terms of office for deacons and ministry leaders, with the recommendation that such terms be no greater than six years without a one-year time out; to allow for freshness and objectivity within the leadership.

7. That when endorsed, the leadership document be made available to all those who attend [Church A] and incorporated into new members classes, for those who attach themselves to [Church A] in the future. This will prevent confusion and false expectations regarding the roles and functions of the leadership.

8. That the pastoral team and two appointed church members meet with [Joe Smith] to define and articulate [his] role and position within [Church A]. The group should provide a written report to the church by no later than the end of [date], requesting feedback and opportunity for discussion and clarification.

9. That at a church meeting regarding the leadership review (recommendation 5)—the church clarifies and affirm its understanding of the role and position of [Joe Smith].

10. That a mature and godly Christian couple from within [Church A], mutually agreed to by the pastor and his wife meet with the pastor and his wife regularly, to oversee and hold accountable, personal strategies in this regard as recommended by the consultants.

Recommendations: Objective 3—To identify both ministry priorities and potential resources to maximize opportunities in the life of the church

1. That the recently appointed student associate be requested to conduct a resource audit of all present ministries, noting who is involved, where there are personnel needs and providing an overview of ministries to the church leadership. This audit should be complete by the end of (date), with the information provided to the pastoral team, deacons and Future Directions Taskforce.

2. That following the acceptance of the Church Vision Statement the church leadership consider present and future pastoral team needs, including the potential appointment of an associate pastor (in a specific, identified ministry area).

3. That to assist in the development of ministry priorities, a small group of people (say three or four suitably gifted people) be asked to carry out some basic community research, focusing on age and community profile demographics and the apparent ministry strengths of other local churches.

Recommendations: Objective 4—To enable the church to implement a leadership development process, including training, support and communication strategies

1. That over the next twelve months the church leadership develop and/or clarify an intentional ministry incorporation and leadership development strategy for implementation in 2003. This strategy should be consistent with the church's mission and vision.

- Follow-up of visitors/new attenders
- New Christians/nurture groups
- Introduction to vision/life of [Church A]/newcomers welcome
- Identification of spiritual gifts
- Discovering a place of ministry

- Leadership training and skilling.
2. That from [date] the pastoral team facilitate quarterly gatherings of all those involved in ministry leadership in the life of the church. These leadership community gatherings should allow for encouragement and sharing, communication across ministries, visioning and prayer support.
3. That the Network or SHAPE course be used at least once a year in the life of the church to assist people in the identification of spiritual gifts and ministry heart.[2]
4. Wherever possible, young adults and younger leaders in the life of the church be assisted to develop meaningful mentoring relationships with mature, ministering members of the congregation.

Recommendations: Objective 5—To explore creative decision-making processes

1. That the church clearly establishes the basis (values and vision) from which decision-making finds its reference and priority.
2. That the church examine the type of decisions that take up the majority of time at church members meetings, and determine what decisions need to come to a church members meeting and which decisions can be made by those entrusted with both the responsibility and leadership of that area.
3. That the church empowers people they entrust in leadership to have the authority to make decisions within their areas of responsibility and function.
4. That the church leadership explore some of the following decision-making process suggestions in the big decisions—to include people, and opportunities for listening and feedback:

- Detailed discussion papers clarifying the decision to be made, giving background and reasoning, biblical support and understanding where necessary, and other relevant information—and asking for

---

2. Bugbee, What You Do Best in the Body of Christ; Rees, S.H.A.P.E.: Finding and Fulfilling Your Unique Purpose for Life.

and allowing time for, feedback and input, before decisions go to a members meeting.
- Small group discuss papers presented at small groups by leaders to receive feedback and free and open discussion.
- Providing open forums for the whole church family (members and non-members)—where decisions aren't made, but information, feedback, input, etc. can be gained, and people given a place where they can express their thoughts and opinions. Then reflecting all the input back to the church family in a paper so that people know they have been heard.
- Congregational mapping exercises (e.g. like those carried out during consultancy), to allow people to interact and wrestle with decisions together.
- Enlisting the support of outside facilitation to provide impartiality and objectivity (again like seen in the consultancy process).
- Establishing task groups around a specific purpose, issue, decision, with designated task group leaders—who can bring recommendations.
- Having defined trial, assessment, testing periods to see how something works and gain feedback.

Appendix BB

Church B Consultancy Report Summary[1]

Overview Recommendations

1. That this report be released to the whole church.
2. That all recommendations be implemented within agreed time frames.
3. That the church leadership appoints a three-person group to oversee the implementation of the report, one of the three to be a deacon.
4. That the church participates in a further consultancy in two years.
5. That in conjunction with the implementation of this report, the church reviews its present assets in line with its ministry needs and investment return.

Recommendations: Objective 1—To clarify the church's vision for the future

1. That the church holds an externally-facilitated vision forum in the next three months to discuss and clarify the church's vision and future direction.

---

1. Baptist Churches of NSW and ACT Church Consultancy Team, "Church B Baptist Church Consultancy Report."

2. That the church develops a vision statement focusing on a multicultural emphasis, with some specific, tangible ministry goals for the next three years.
3. That following the completion of objectives 1 and 2, the church leadership review its pastoral/ministry team needs and develop a strategic pastoral/ministry team plan for the next three years. In such a process an emphasis should be placed on community contact and outreach/evangelism.

Recommendations: Objective 2—To assist the congregation in encouraging greater personal spiritual maturity

1. That in home groups and other forums, the opportunity for people to talk about their personal experience of God be encouraged.
2. That those in home groups be given the regular opportunity in services (say once a month) to share the benefits of being in a home group, particularly how it encourages their spiritual growth.
3. That the training of new home group leaders and multiplying existing groups be given priority in this stage of the church's life.
4. That the church seriously explore prayer for spiritual renewal, including the possibility of prayer triplets and other appropriate prayer initiatives.
5. That consideration be given to running Christianity Explained or Alpha for the whole church family (this will also help give confidence in faith sharing).

Recommendations: Objective 3—To assist the church in motivating greater involvement in ministry

1. That in conjunction with the review of the church's vision (objective 1 recommendations) the church discuss and identify ministry priorities and personnel needs.

2. That the church conduct a spiritual gifts/heart for ministry seminar in the next four months.

3. That the church leadership seek to implement an informal ministry mentoring strategy in the life of the congregation.

4. That over the next six months the church leadership review the present membership policy, and in particular the links between membership and church leadership, and report back to the church by the end of the year.

Recommendations: Objective 4—To identify appropriate community outreach strategies and ways of building people into the life of the church

1. That church attenders be trained and equipped to build authentic relationships with non-Christians of different ethnic and religious backgrounds.

2. That intentional outreach prayer initiatives be implemented in the life of the church (e.g. prayer triplets, prayer walks, evangelism prayer cards).

3. That small group relationship-building activities such as small dinners/BBQs with some level of personal spiritual sharing (e.g. testimony, the difference Jesus makes now, etc.) by an attender be explored.

4. After checking the availability of similar programs in the area and suitable leaders, consideration be given to commencing an ESL class.

5. That the church leadership consult with Australian Baptist Missionary Society as to potential learning and support strategies for the development of [cross-cultural] outreach ministries.

6. That a partnership with a mission agency be explored, such as that between the [MANCA] and [Happy Plains] Baptist Church.

Recommendations: Objective 5—Assist the leadership in developing effective ministry training strategies

1. One or two people in the life of the church be invited to be responsible for training strategies in the life of the church.
2. That the church leadership invite one or two suitably gifted people to develop a worship/music training strategy for the next twelve months.
3. That those currently working among children in the life of the church, along with other interested people, plan to visit at least three other churches (with an effective children's ministry) over the next nine months to gain insight into the development of children's ministry strategies.
4. That the church commence ministry leaders community nights once a term from [date], with a focus on vision, skilling, encouragement, and prayer.[2]

---

2. Baptist Churches of NSW and ACT Church Consultancy Team, "Church B Baptist Church Consultancy Report."

Appendix CC

Church C Consultancy Report Summary[1]

Overview Recommendations

1. That an oversight group be appointed to oversee the implementation of this report, in accordance with a mutually agreeable time frame. The oversight group should consist of three people appointed by the diaconate. One member of the group should be a deacon.
2. That the report be released to the whole church.

Recommendations: Objective 1—To examine the respective processes for communication and conflict management in the church

A) Communication

1. Church members be encouraged to read the church newsletter and to take note of announcements and other information published on the church notice board.

---

[1]. Baptist Churches of NSW and ACT Church Consultancy Team, "Church C Baptist Church Consultancy Report."

2. Hold quarterly members "forums" for church attenders where leaders can raise issues and seek feedback from the congregation. This could be done by a question/answer time or through group discussion and questionnaires.
3. Small group leaders be responsible to remind their group of important notices published in the LINK or special announcements passed on by the pastors.
4. A copy of the LINK to be sent to members who have been away for two weeks.

B) Conflict management

1. That the church develop a comprehensive conflict management policy and subsequently train all members in healthy conflict management processes by [date].
2. All new attenders be given a copy of the church's conflict management policy and subsequently train all members in healthy resolution processes.
3. That healthy conflict management be taught from the pulpit and in small groups.
4. That church leaders develop a covenant that includes:

- All leaders be accountable to resolve conflicts within twenty-four hours of a conflict occurring (or to make arrangements within that time for the conflict to be resolved at a specific time).
- A ministry philosophy that expressly places relationship before task.
- All leaders being trained in conflict mediation.

Recommendations: Objective 2—To identify the unmet needs and aspirations of the church attenders

1. That the above unmet needs list and aspiration list be used by the leadership team as it considers future ministry priorities.

2. That the leadership team undertake an audit of the ministry resources (people, facilities, finance) of the church by [date]. And use this data to prioritize the allocation of resources to:
     a. enhance present ministries, and to
     b. support new ministry initiatives.
3. That external resource people such as the Associate Superintendents of the Baptist Churches NSW and ACT be engaged to facilitate the meeting of the expressed needs.
4. That the leadership team assist each ministry group, to develop its objectives with measurable outcomes in relation to the church's mission and vision statements and the church's annual goals and objectives.
5. That the "Strategic Issues Outcomes" document be used to develop measurable outcomes.
6. That the church leadership develops an ongoing training and equipping strategy for people to both discover and utilize their giftedness. And this process while ongoing be initiated immediately. Developing and adapting material such as "Network" from the Willow Creek Church or "SHAPE" from the Saddleback Church could provide a place to begin.[2]

Recommendations: Objective 3—To explore strategies to facilitate the growth of the youth ministry both spiritually and numerically

1. That the church continue to work on its strengths (e.g. ministry with young families) with the long-term goal of building a youth group.
2. That the church focuses resources on the primary school years 4–6 and develops a five year plan for growth.
3. That the church leadership accesses the denominational resources for youth ministry development by the [date].

---

2. Rees, S.H.A.P.E.: Finding and Fulfilling Your Unique Purpose for Life; Bugbee, What You Do Best in the Body of Christ.

Recommendations: Objective 4—To discover the attitude of the clients of the ministries of Church C toward the church and to explore strategies to more effectively incorporate them into the church

1. That the leadership team immediately initiates discussions with the leaders of the playtime ministry team and the leaders of the craft ministry team. As a part of these discussions, the following should be addressed:

- the purpose and vision of the ministry in relation to the vision of the church
- strategies to strengthen links between the church and ministry
- strategies to maximize use of the mission opportunities.

2. Matters that could be included in the strategizing discussions might involve:

    a. The church host at least two intentional bridge-building events each year specifically aimed at the people participating in these two ministry areas.

    b. That a special newsletter (broadsheet) be developed at least quarterly targeted for these groups including news about upcoming events in the church and the community. Especially highlighting possible entry points for people into other church-related activities and other church ministries. This newsletter should also be distributed through the opportunity shop.

3. That a process for the recruitment and training of a group of people with the specific role of developing relationships with the clients be initiated immediately. The use of material such as "Contagious Christianity" for this training would be essential.

Appendix DD

Church D Consultancy Report Summary[1]

Overview Recommendations

1. That three people be appointed by the leadership team to oversee the implementation of the recommendations in this report. Only one of the three appointed is to be a member of the leadership team.
2. That this report be released to the whole church.
3. That the leadership mutually agree to a time frame for the implementation of this report subsequent to the acceptance of the recommendations in the report.

Recommendations: Objective 1—Develop and implement appropriate communication processes within the church

1. That a strategic task force be formed comprising the leadership team, plus one representative from the management team and one from the congregation. This task force is to be formed no later than

---

1. Baptist Churches of NSW and ACT Church Consultancy Team, "Church D Baptist Church Consultancy Report."

[date]. This is the same task force as referred to under objective 3, recommendation 1 below. Its purposes will include:

    a. Clarify who is responsible for communicating what to whom.

    b. Establish who is responsible for which decisions and what authority they have to make them without reference to another body.

    c. Express this to the decision-makers and communicators in the form of a flow chart.

    d. Monitor and evaluate communication so as to ensure that the established channels are being effectively used and new means of communication are set up as needed.

2. That the "Leadership Community," composed of all leaders of all home groups and activities of the church be established as a means of improving communication between various leadership and ministry groups. See recommendations (2) and (3) under objective 3 below.

Recommendations: Objective 2—Define and share a vision in a way that the church owns it

1. That the leadership team meets to establish core values and to reexamine the vision of the church in order to affirm or modify it.
2. That the leadership team, in close collaboration with the pastoral team, develops strategies to promote ownership by the church of the core values and vision.
3. That the refined vision and core values statements be presented first to the leadership community for their acceptance and comments at the first leadership community meeting.
4. That, once the leadership community has come to own the vision and core values, they be presented to the church as recommended by the leadership team and endorsed by the larger leadership community.
5. That individual members of the leadership community do all in their power to propagate the vision so as to create ownership by the church members.

6. That once the church agrees to own the vision, ownership be strengthened by constant communication of the vision in as many different forms as possible. For example, in the bulletin, via overhead projection before or during church services, through banners, posters, wall hangings, and by highlighting some aspect of the vision in the church service say once a month, using interviews, PowerPoint presentations, and the like.
7. That a central part of the leadership community meetings (see objective 3, recommendation 2) be imparting the vision of the church.

Recommendations: Objective 3—Design the most effective structures and strategies to achieve the church's vision

1. That a strategic task force be formed comprising of the leadership team plus one representative from the management team and one from the congregation. This task force is to be formed no later than [date]. This is the same task force as referred to under objective 1, recommendation 1 above. Its purposes will include:
    a. Review the effectiveness of the current structure and make recommendations for changes where necessary.
    b. Develop strategies to achieve the church's vision.
2. That all leaders of all ministries and home groups and activities of the church be identified and known as "The Leadership Community."
3. That the Leadership Community meet once a term for three hours, possibly commencing with a light meal, with the following objectives:
    a. Vision sharing
    b. Communication, cohesion and coordination
    c. Encouragement, support and prayer
    d. Equipping
    e. The first meeting of the Leadership Community is to take place sometime in [date].
4. That consideration be given to forming a separate management team for [XYZ Childcare Centre]. It may be beneficial to include those outside the church such as parents and staff.

5. That the existing management team be released to focus on managing the church, while monitoring meeting length and frequency.

6. That a greater priority and visibility be given to the expansion and development of the home group ministry and that a team of three be appointed by the leadership team to oversee the home groups ministry.

7. That those with gifts in personal evangelism be identified by the leadership team and released to train and equip church attenders in sharing their faith (using tools such as Contagious Christianity), thereby complementing the existing outreach events/programs. Relational and smaller scale evangelism tools such as Alpha and Hospitality evangelism (e.g. using existing home groups) may prove to be more effective in your demographic context.

Appendix EE

Church E Consultancy Report Summary[1]

Overview Recommendations

1. That an oversight group be appointed to oversee the implementation of this report, in accordance with a mutually agreeable time frame. The oversight group should consist of three people appointed by the diaconate. One member of the group should be a deacon. No more than two members of this oversight group should be deacons.

2. That this report be released to the whole church.

Recommendations: Objective 1—To identify ministry strategies to take up the opportunities presented by existing and potential contacts in the light of current church activities and services

1. That the church move to identify a Coordinator of Outreach (possibly a younger person from outside the present diaconate), specializing in the areas of evangelism, outreach, and community contact, to work with the pastor and diaconate to develop the community contacts already in place and implement new strategies.

---

1. Baptist Churches of NSW and ACT Church Consultancy Team, "Church E Baptist Church Consultancy Report."

2. That the Coordinator of Outreach facilitates a ministry audit in the church's catchment area to ascertain unmet ministry opportunities and the ministry strengths of other evangelical churches in the area. As well as the ministry strength of Church E Baptist Church to provide a framework for outreach activities.

3. That the Coordinator of Outreach, in conjunction with the pastor, immediately initiates a process for the recruitment and training of a group of people with the specific role of intentionally developing relationships with church contacts, in addition to friends and neighbors. The use of material such as "Contagious Christianity" for this training would be essential.

4. That the Coordinator of Outreach initiates discussions with the leaders of the toddler time ministry team and the leaders of the brigade's ministry team to develop a strategy to build on the contacts already established with families in the community.

5. That the leadership of the church utilize the resources of the denomination, particularly the Associate Superintendent—Church Development, to assist in developing this outreach strategy.

Recommendations: Objective 2—To evaluate the level of fatigue amongst church workers and provide suggestions for the way forward

1. That the church adopt the 1x1x1 principle as a guide for a balanced involvement in church life and ministry:

- 1 worship service
- 1 key ministry
- 1 small group.

2. That the principle of the sabbatical be adopted by the diaconate—following six years of service, a deacon would take twelve months break from the role. During this time, prayerful consideration would be given to continuing in the role and to other directions that God may be calling the person to.

3. That the Network Gift Discovery course be offered to the whole church on at least an annual basis.

4. That Bible study groups set aside time towards the end of each year for each group member to prayerfully consider the question, "How is God calling me to use my spiritual gifts in the coming year?" Groups would then provide encouragement for their members to pursue the implications of God's call, including the identification of new ministries and new leaders.

Recommendations: Objective 3—To identify levels of conflict in the life of the church and develop a process to implement a biblical conflict resolution strategy

1. That the church develops a comprehensive conflict management policy and subsequently trains all members in healthy conflict management processes by [date]. To achieve this, the church should engage on external facilitator/trainer to assist in implementing this recommendation. A recommended facilitator would be the Associate Superintendent—Pastoral Development from the denomination.

2. That all new attenders be given a copy of the church's conflict management policy and subsequently train all members in healthy resolution processes.

3. That healthy conflict management be taught from the pulpit and in small groups and be modeled by the diaconate.

4. That all leaders be trained in conflict mediation.

5. That subsequent to the conflict management policy being implemented in the church, a reconciliation strategy be developed by the diaconate to deal with the unresolved issues from previous pastorates.

Appendix FF

Church F Consultancy Report Summary[1]

Overview Recommendations

1. That three people be appointed by the leadership team (pastor and deacons) to oversee the implementation of the recommendations in the report. One of whom to be a deacon.
2. That this report be released to the whole church.
3. That the church request another consultancy in two years.

Recommendations: Objective 1—To explore ways of encouraging non-members to take the step into membership

1. That the church establish a taskforce of three [people] to research how other churches in NSW and beyond are working with this issue.
2. That the taskforce bring recommendations back to the church leadership within six months.
3. Task force to consist of one deacon and two others.

---

1. Baptist Churches of NSW and ACT Church Consultancy Team, "Church F Baptist Church Consultancy Report."

Recommendations: Objective 2—To encourage and support the Aboriginal leadership in the growth and development of their fellowship, within the life of the church

1. That [pastor of the Aboriginal Fellowship and his wife] identify a suitable spiritual mentor and role model for their ongoing spiritual nurturing. They may access the two consultants for assistance in this process.
2. That [pastor of the Aboriginal Fellowship and his wife] be accountable to the two consultants to implement recommendation 1 by June 30th, 2001.
3. That the church leadership make representation to the General Superintendent on [pastor of the Aboriginal Fellowship's] behalf, to facilitate the confirmation of his accreditation in NSW.
4. That a taskforce of up to five people, including a deacon and two members of the Aboriginal Fellowship, be established to explore ways of securing funding from government and non-government agencies including ABMS, to financially support [pastor of the Aboriginal Fellowship] in ministry, at least part-time.
5. That the same taskforce explore ways of securing funding from government and non-government agencies for the purchase of a bus to assist in the welfare and pastoral care of Aboriginal people in the region.
6. That this taskforce report back to the leadership within six months.
7. That the Aboriginal Fellowship approach the fellowship of Baptist Churches of NSW and ACT (through the General Superintendent's e-mail mailout) for donations of suitable musical instruments.

Recommendations: Objective 3—To develop the corporate prayer life of the church

1. That the church begin a process of spiritual retreats for all interested participants. Refer to appendix D for process [not here reproduced].

2. That participation in spiritual retreats be a requirement of availability of the elected leadership.
3. That the church begin prayer triplets with growth targets set as a result of objective 4, recommendation 3.
4. That the church access prayer resources as listed at appendix D [not here reproduced].

Recommendations: Objective 4—To develop mission strategies that will lead to effective church growth

1. That the church participate in the upcoming NCLS to be held on Sunday [date] as a means of gaining valuable information for outreach purposes.
2. That the church establish prayer triplets as per objective 3, recommendation 3 and appendix D [not here reproduced].
3. That the church set a church growth prayer target for the next twelve months of 15 percent growth per year to be prayed for each time folk gather together.
4. That the church give consideration to other medium and longer-term strategies as per appendix E [not here reproduced], in twelve months to two years following successful implementation of recommendations 1–3 above.

Recommendations: Objective 5—To enhance the overall music ministry of the church

1. That the church give consideration to using tapes and CD music resources for worship services.
2. That the church give consideration to forming a worship team of three to five people, under the direction of the pastor, to be trained to assist in the leading of worship and the leading of the singing.
3. That the church give itself permission to consider alternative venues for worship.

4. That the church establish a task force of three to five people, one of whom to be a deacon, to investigate the availability of another worship venue that could convey a more welcoming and contemporary feel, and to report back to the leadership within three months.

Recommendations: Objective 6—To become a financially [self] sufficient church under the guidance of God

1. That the church focus on prayer, evangelism and worship rather than on the lack of funds.
2. That the church prepare a five-year financial plan with anticipated growth rate of 15 percent per year as per prayer triplets.
3. That this financial plan be reviewed in two years.

Appendix GG

Church G Consultancy Report Summary[1]

Overview Recommendations

1. That this report be released to the whole church, on the Sunday following its presentation to the appointed leadership.
2. That three people be appointed by the diaconate to oversee the implementation of the recommendations in this report, and that one of the three be a deacon.
3. That subsequent to the acceptance of these recommendations the appointed leadership agree to a time frame for the implementation of this report.
4. That in nine months' time, there be a review of the implementation of this consultancy's recommendations.

---

1. Baptist Churches of NSW and ACT Church Consultancy Team, "Church G Baptist Church Consultancy Report."

Recommendations: Objective 1—To develop and train present and potential leaders

1. That the church develops an intentional and integrated strategy for training present and potential leaders. This strategy may include the following:

- A seminar concerning general leadership principles;
- Reexamine the training program of the church to consider what skills could be taught, what sort of character should be nurtured, and training in issues such as the structure and organization of the Church G Baptist Church;
- The church continues to promote or organize and subsidize training for specific ministries such as: youth ministry, worship leading, pastoral care, small group leading, and evangelistic programs.

2. That a taskforce of five persons (no more than two from the present leadership team) be appointed to implement recommendation 1.
3. That this taskforce brings recommendations to the leadership team no later than [date].
4. That members of the pastoral team and elder(s) meet with ministry leaders and deacons on a regular basis (three to four times a year), to discuss their ministry area, and to offer encouragement, support and care.
5. That leaders of different departments meet together bimonthly to communicate, plan, and pray together.
6. That the second last of these bimonthly meetings includes an evaluation of the current year, as well as involve planning for the following year, and that the final meeting be a time for celebration and thanksgiving for the year.
7. That the leadership develops (including a calendar of children's and youth activities—see objective 2, recommendation 7) a corporate calendar which can be presented to the church each term.
8. That the church reviews the following:

- [pastor's] and [associate pastor's] job descriptions, giving rough time allocation to each aspect of their roles;

- the role descriptions of the elders and deacons;
- reallocation of the more mundane tasks that currently fall to the pastor and deacons.

Recommendations: Objective 2—To explore the current practices and outcomes of children's and youth ministries

1. That a person or three persons be appointed to:
- identify the gaps and distribution of children's ministries across the age groups;
- examine the needs of children from five years to twelve years to determine ways in which those needs might be most effectively met whilst reducing the potential for tension between different ministries (this might include setting up a forum with older children, say nine to twelve years, to discuss with them what they perceive their needs to be and how these needs might be met).
2. That this person or three persons bring recommendations to the leadership team no later than [date].
3. That a person or three persons be appointed to review the current youth ministries to:
- identify the gaps and distribution of ministries/programs across all age groups
- to set up a forum of some description to discuss with teenagers and young adults what they perceive their needs to be and how these needs might be met
- to outline a strategy which will allow the church to actively and deliberately pursue its intention to strengthen the senior teens and young adult ministries.
4. That this person or three persons bring recommendations to the leadership team no later than [date].
5. That the persons appointed (to undertake recommendations 1 through 4 above) liaise with regard to the appropriate overlap of and transition between children's and youth ministries.

6. That subsequent to the recommendations that arise from 1 to 5 above, a person or persons be appointed with the permanent responsibility for overall oversight of the children's and/or youth ministries.
7. That a combined calendar of children's and youth ministry activities be developed and included as part of the corporate church calendar (see objective 1, recommendation 7).
8. That those responsible for the holiday program consider possible strategies to follow up children who are contacted through this program.

Recommendations: Objective 3—To continue to develop ownership and commitment to Church G Baptist Church

1. That the church leadership implement strategies designed to develop and strengthen the corporate worship and relational aspects of church life and that these strategies include:

- reviewing pastoral care;
- training of home group leaders (see objective 1, recommendation 1);
- a teaching series (4 to 6 weeks) exploring and building into the corporate life of the church a variety of biblical notions of worship.
- a teaching series (4 to 6 weeks) exploring and building into the corporate life of the church a variety of biblical notions of community.

2. That people be encouraged to explore and express their giftedness in the life, ministry, and worship of the church.
3. That in order to maintain a healthy sense of ownership and commitment into the future, the church engage in a series of workshops by suitably skilled resource people in order to develop strategies for:

- managing differences
- conflict negotiation and resolution
- a process of mediation.

4. That the leadership of the church gives opportunity for anyone still holding hurts from conflicts in the past to acknowledge and discuss this with the pastor or pastoral care worker.

5. That the above recommendations 1 to 4 be oversighted by the pastor.

Appendix HH

Church H Consultancy Report Summary[1]

Overview Recommendations:

1. That this report be released to the whole church.
2. That all recommendations be implemented within agreed time frames.
3. That the church leadership appoints a three-person oversight group to oversee the implementation of the report, one of the three to be a deacon.
4. That the church leadership meet for an extended period within the next month to discuss in detail the implications and implementation of the report.
5. That the senior pastor and deacons invite Associate Superintendent—Pastoral Development to meet with them as soon as possible to discuss the pastoral/leadership matters raised above. This meeting should take place and an agreed strategy be implemented before any other recommendations in this report are acted upon (with a summary report on this process to be communicated to the church).
6. That the church leadership appoint a Future Directions Group to facilitate vision development in the church.

1. Baptist Churches of NSW and ACT Church Consultancy Team, "Church H Baptist Church Consultancy Report."

7. That the Future Directions Group prepare a draft [years] vision plan to be presented to the church by the end of [date]. The plan should seek to provide a clear sense of direction for the church and specific, tangible ministry goals for [years].

Recommendations: Objective 1—To explore ways to sharpen the church's spiritual focus

1. That the church commence the [year] calendar year with an intentional focus on heightening congregational spiritual passion (this could include a Sunday morning/evening message series, home group studies, individual reading and reflection and exploration of other means of creative spirituality.)
2. That people from across the church's three congregations covenant to come together to pray for the church's future direction.
3. That this commence with a "Day of Prayer" to be held in [date] and continue with an intentional monthly corporate prayer strategy throughout [year] (including some creative initiatives such as local prayer walks, etc.).
4. That the church appoint a person[s] to coordinate the church's prayer ministry.
5. That home group leaders commence meeting together on a quarterly basis from [date] for mutual encouragement, resource/idea sharing, communication, pastoral care networking, goal-setting, and prayer.
6. That a forum be held in early [year] for Sunday night attenders to discuss issues such as the style, structure, format, location, and vision of the evening service, with specific reference to reaching singles/young professionals/young couples within a postmodern context/cafe culture.

Recommendations: Objective 2—To suggest appropriate outreach strategies, including potential target groups within the community

1. That the proposed vision plan (overview recommendations 6 and 7) gives specific reference to strategic church outreach plans for [years], including:
    a. identification of specific outreach targets and strategies
    b. creative and effective use of the church's unique physical location
    c. the future direction of current worship services.

2. In the process of developing the vision plan, a church discussion-forum be held to consider options raised in appendix 1—*Some Possible New Directions* [not here reproduced].

3. That in identifying specific outreach strategies, the church commission the Christian Research Association to prepare a more detailed demographic profile of those living within a 5km and 10km radius of the church and a 5km radius of the church preschool.

4. Further that two members of the Future Directions Group are to prepare a brief report on the ministries of other evangelical churches within the [suburb] and [suburb] areas.

5. That in the development of the vision plan, the Future Directions Group and church leadership give serious and prayerful consideration to the potential appointment of:

- an associate pastor, with specific oversight for outreach/evangelism and families' ministry
- a Sunday evening service pastor/staff-worker.

(This recommendation, including the ministry load and appointment time of such roles would need to be considered as part of an overall review of pastoral team roles and responsibilities, including the future plans of the current student team members.)

Recommendations: Objective 3—To identify ministry priorities that effectively utilize the church's present resources [people, facilities, finances, etc.]

1. That the above observations and reflections [not here reproduced, but revolving around people, facilities, and finances] be considered in the development of the [years] vision plan.
2. That current ministry personnel opportunities be identified, and a spiritual gifts/ministry identification seminar be held in first term [year] with particular encouragement of members of the evening congregation to be involved.
3. That the senior pastor and deacons meet with older members of the congregation to discuss long-term pastoral care and fellowship needs and expectations.
4. That the diaconate appoint as soon as possible a small property management team (suggested no more than two to three people—with some property and/or financial experience).
5. That when formed, this team meet with the senior pastor and deacons to discuss a range of identified property maintenance and management issues.
6. That the church leadership, in conjunction with the property management team, review the present lease arrangements on the Church Ministry Center to allow for greater ministry usage in [year] and beyond.

Recommendations: Objective 4—To review present leadership roles, responsibilities and structures and recommend any changes that will enhance the effectiveness of leadership in the life of the church

1. That the present diaconate structure be replaced in advance of the [year] Annual General Meeting, with the appointment of deacons (or ministry coordinators) in specific functional (portfolio) ministry areas.

2. That the present diaconate bring a recommendation on the proposed portfolio areas to the church by the end of [date] and any consequential constitutional changes.
3. That following the implementation of the proposed new diaconate structure, the potential benefit of the appointment of elders be considered by the leadership and congregation.
4. That an external facilitator meets with the pastoral team before the end of the year to discuss ways of improving teamwork processes.
5. That an external facilitator be engaged for team building/relational exercises as part of the appointment process of any future pastoral team member[s].
6. That the senior pastor, church secretary and church treasurer meet in early [year] with the church's office administrator to review his responsibilities, with the goal of enhancing support to the pastoral team and church leadership and clarifying expectations on both sides.
7. That the senior pastor meet with a person outside the congregation to implement the strategies maintained in the confidential personal ministry report provided to him.
8. And further that he meets with Associate Superintendent—Pastoral Development by the end of March [year] to discuss in confidence the implementation of these strategies.

Recommendations: Objective 5—To identify any barriers to belonging in the life of the church and to recommend strategies to strengthen community and enhance integration into the congregation

1. That there be an intentional focus on building the church's home group/small group ministry over the next few years (see objective 1, recommendation 5).
2. That combined congregational worship gatherings be held in [month] to launch the new ministry year and in [month] to celebrate the ministry year.

3. That each congregation be invited to plan and host one special social event for the whole church in [year].

4. That occasional "Sharing Spots" be introduced, where representatives from the three congregations share some points of encouragement and prayer at the other services.

5. That the senior pastor meet with a small group of people from both the morning and evening service to facilitate the development of a more intentional welcoming and follow-up strategy (including seeking feedback of those who may leave the church).

6. That the church engage an appropriate consultant to consider ways of maximizing the church welcoming space, signage, and overall property aesthetics, given the street context it finds itself in.

Appendix II

Church I Consultancy Report Summary[1]

Overview Recommendations

1. That four people be appointed by the diaconate, including two from each congregation, to oversee the implementation of the recommendations in this report.
2. That a mutually agreed time frame be agreed to for the implementation of the report, subject to the acceptance of recommendations.
3. That the report be released to the whole church.
4. That the morning church leadership team consider inviting the consultants back again in the next four months to assist the church to process the report.

Recommendations: Objective 1—To review and assess the congregation's growth and any barriers to growth

No recommendations are made under this objective given subsequent recommendations made.

---

1. Baptist Churches Of NSW and ACT Church Consultancy Team, "Church I Baptist Church Consultancy Report."

Recommendations: Objective 2—To review and assess the congregation's ownership of the church's vision and future ministry direction

1. That the current vision to impact [suburb], by building a multicultural church, be kept before the people.
2. That the morning congregation leadership team review, clarify, and prioritize the current evangelistic strategies for that congregation (apart from the seeker-sensitive services), in place to achieve the church vision.
3. That the above review be completed by [date].
4. That in the above review, the morning congregation leadership team consider involving an external resource person to assist the process (i.e. a member of the Evangelism and Church Planting Taskforce, or Associate Superintendent—Church Development).
5. That the above review considers, as a part, the church's ability to reach young families.
6. That those in the morning service affirm the Romanian ministry and their strong desire to reach their people.

Recommendations: Objective 3—To review and assess the congregation's present and projected financial situation toward self-reliance

1. That there be teaching given on the subject of financial giving, especially from the pulpit.
2. That the above teaching be complemented by Bible study groups using study material on the topic.
3. That attenders be encouraged to see personal giving as part of their discipleship and commitment to the Lord and his church.
4. That both congregation leadership teams set goals in relation to the church becoming self-supporting, in the light of the goal of becoming self-sufficient.

5. That these goals be presented to a congregational forum of the whole church, occurring no later than [date].
6. That consideration be given to using an external facilitator for this congregational forum.

Recommendations: Objective 4—To review and assess the church's leadership structure

1. That the pastor meet with the morning congregation leadership team to review ways of better supporting ministry leaders.
2. That this review should consider such things as
- the expectations placed upon leaders
- the care of leaders
- the accountability structures for leaders.
3. That a leadership community be commenced once a quarter for the purposes of
- encouragement
- networking
- planning
- evaluation
- brainstorming.
4. That the leadership community include
- the diaconate
- ministry leaders
- home group leaders.
5. That the first leadership community meeting be held in [month].

Appendix JJ

Church J Consultancy Report Summary[1]

Overview Recommendations

1. That three people be appointed by the leadership to oversee the implementation of the recommendations in this report; one of the three appointed to be a deacon.
2. That this report be released to the whole church.
3. That the leadership mutually agree to a time frame for the implementation of this report subsequent to the acceptance of the recommendations in the report.
4. That a second consultancy be requested no later than [date].

Recommendations: Objective 1—Identify ways to improve the spiritual life of the church

1. That the church organize a spiritual retreat with an outside trained facilitator.
2. That a group of three people be appointed to stimulate and oversee a coordinated prayer ministry within the church.

---

1. Baptist Churches Of NSW and ACT Church Consultancy Team, "Church J Baptist Church Consultancy Report."

3. That the prayer ministry coordinator consider suggestions along the following lines:

   a. Call for people to enlist as private prayer partners who undertake to pray faithfully for needs shared with them by means of a regularly distributed prayer list.

   b. Establish prayer triplets to undertake to pray daily for common needs and to meet once a week for combined prayer.

   c. Determine effective ways to regularly collect and distribute prayer points to the partners, prayer triplets, and home groups on a weekly or monthly basis.

   d. Establish a contact person, other than the pastor, to be contacted whenever there is a need for emergency prayer.

   e. Consider reactivating the prayer tree that has functioned to some degree in the past.

   f. Encourage people to share testimonies in church concerning prayers answered and spiritual lessons learnt.

4. That existing small group leaders meet to consider how small groups could be further developed and extended within the church and people motivated to attend in order to assist their spiritual growth.

Recommendations: Objective 2—Develop strategies for the church to own and implement the vision

1. That the church prayerfully considers the above five options regarding its future in order to clarify its vision.[2]
2. That the diaconate organize a forum in the first quarter of [year] to begin consideration of these five options.
3. That the second consultancy be requested no later than [date] next year to primarily focus on addressing these options.

---

2. a. Continue as is.
b. Pastor to continue.
c. Pastor to conclude.
d. Explore a relationship with _____ Baptist Church.
e. Close down.
See Baptist Churches of NSW and ACT Church Consultancy Team, "Church J Baptist Church Consultancy Report," 11.

4. That in the meantime, the church adopts the proposed mission and vision statement in principle with a view to determining some definite strategies for implementation of the vision in the light of the proposed consultancy next year.

Recommendations: Objective 3—Identify ways whereby the church can support and assist our pastor through his loss

1. That a confidential strategy to support and bring health to the pastor be implemented. This strategy has been outlined to the pastor.
2. That this strategy be oversighted by the Associate General Superintendent, plus a member of the diaconate who is appointed by the diaconate in mutual agreement with the pastor.
3. That the church meets the cost of any counselling that is part of this strategy.
4. That the pastor submits to an objective review process in relation to his ministry and options for his future.
5. That the diaconate liaises with the two consultants to implement this objective review process.
6. That this review process be completed during the months from March to June [year].

Recommendations: Objective 4—Develop and implement a strategy for effective pastoral care

1. That a group of three people, gifted in pastoral care, be appointed to oversee a pastoral care ministry. One of these people should be an elder or deacon.
2. That this group liaise closely with the prayer oversight group referred to in objective 1, recommendation 2 above, in order to learn of pastoral needs as soon as prayer is requested.

3. That this group prayerfully searches out others who are willing to be involved in pastoral care and implements a strategy to engage them as pastoral needs arise, according to their availability.
4. That this group relates closely to the pastor in order to keep him regularly informed of ministry undertaken and to discuss ways of assisting his pastoral care load.
5. That the existing home group leaders, when they meet in terms of recommendation 4 in objective 1 above, also consider how training could be offered in order to help facilitate pastoral care within the home groups.
6. That Lifecare be approached to facilitate this training course.

Bibliography

Abernathy, Alexis. *Self-Care for Pastors, Attending to the Mind, Body, and Spirit. Ministry Enrichment Seminar.* Pasadena, CA: Fuller Theological Seminary, Office of Field Education, 2008.
ABS Census of Population and Housing. *Suburb Profiles—Demographics.* Sydney: Domain, 2006. https://www.domain.com.au/suburb-profile/.
ABS Census of Population and Housing, 1986, 1996, and 2006.
Adam, Barbara, and Stuart Allan, eds. *Theorizing Culture: An Interdisciplinary Critique After Postmodernism.* New York: New York University Press, 1995.
Anderson, Leith. *A Church for the 21st Century.* Minneapolis, MN: Bethany House, 1992.
Anderson, Neil T., and Charles Mylander. *Extreme Church Makeover.* Ventura, CA: Regal, 2005.
Arn, Win. *The Church Growth Ratio Book: How to Have a Revitalized, Healthy, Growing, Loving Church.* Monrovia, CA: Church Growth, 1990.
———, ed. *The Pastor's Church Growth Handbook.* Pasadena, CA: Church Growth, Institute for American Church Growth, 1979.
Arn, Win, and Donald McGavran. *Back to Basics in Church Growth.* Wheaton, IL: Tyndale House, 1981.
Astley, J. "Reviews the Book 'Natural Church Development: A Practical Guide to a New Approach,' by Christian A. Schwarz." *Journal of Beliefs and Values: Studies in Religion and Education* 19, no. 2 (October 1998) 260–1.
Bandy, Thomas G. *Kicking Habits: Welcome Relief for Addicted Churches.* Nashville, TN: Abingdon, 2001.
Baptist Churches of NSW and ACT Church Consultancy Team. "Church A Baptist Church Consultancy Report." Epping, NSW, 2001.
———. "Church B Baptist Church Consultancy Report." Epping, NSW, 2001.
———. "Church C Baptist Church Consultancy Report." Epping, NSW, 2001.
———. "Church D Baptist Church Consultancy Report." Epping, NSW, 2001.
———. "Church E Baptist Church Consultancy Report." Epping, NSW, 2001.
———. "Church F Baptist Church Consultancy Report." Epping, NSW, 2001.
———. "Church F Baptist Church Consultancy Report." Epping, NSW, 2003.
———. "Church G Baptist Church Consultancy Report." Epping, NSW, 2001.
———. "Church H Baptist Church Consultancy Report." Epping, NSW, 2001.
———. "Church I Baptist Church Consultancy Report." Epping, NSW, 2001.
———. "Church J Baptist Church Consultancy Report." Epping, NSW, 2001.

Barna, George. *New Statistics on Church Attendance and Avoidance*. Ventura, CA: Barna Group, 2008. https://www.barna.com/research/new-statistics-on-church-attendance-and-avoidance/.

———. *Turn-Around Churches*. Ventura, CA: Regal, 1993.

———. *Unchurched Population Nears 100 Million in the U.S*. Ventura, CA: Barna Group, 2007. https://www.barna.com/research/unchurched-population-nears-100-million-in-the-u-s/.

Begbie, Jeremy S. "The Shape of Things to Come?—Wright Amongst Emerging Ecclesiologies." In *Jesus, Paul and the People of God: A Theological Dialogue with N. T. Wright*, edited by Nicholas Perrin, and Richard B. Hays. Downers Grove, IL: IVP, 2009, 183–210.

Bell, Rob. *Velvet Elvis: Repainting the Christian Faith*. Grand Rapids, MI: Zondervan, 2005.

Bellamy, John, et al. *Enriching Church Life: A Practical Guide for Local Churches*. Adelaide, South Australia: NCLS, 2006.

———. *Why People Don't Go to Church*. Adelaide, South Australia: NCLS and Openbook, 2002.

Bellamy, John, and Keith Castle. *2001 Church Attendance Estimates*. NCLS Occasional Papers. Sydney South, NSW: NCLS Research, 2004.

Bennis, Warren. *Beyond Bureaucracy: Essays on the Development and Evolution of Human Organization*. Jossey-Bass Management Series. San Francisco: Jossey Bass, 1993.

Bennis, Warren, and Robert Townsend. *Reinventing Leadership: Strategies to Empower the Organization*. New York: Morrow, 1995.

Bertalanffy, Ludwig von. *General System Theory: Foundations, Development, Applications*. New York: G. Braziller, 1969.

Blomberg, Craig L. *Matthew. The New American Commentary*, vol. 22. Nashville, TN, Broadman, 1992.

Bonhoeffer, Dietrich. 1937. *The Cost of Discipleship*. London: SCM, 2001.

Borden, Paul D. *Direct Hit: Aiming Real Leaders at the Mission Field*. Nashville: Abingdon, 2006.

Bosch, David J. *Transforming Mission: Paradigm Shifts in Theology of Mission*. American Society of Missiology Series, no. 16. Maryknoll, NY: Orbis, 1991.

Bowen, Murray. *Family Therapy in Clinical Practice*. New York: J. Aronson, 1978.

Branson, Mark Lau. *Memories, Hopes, and Conversations: Appreciative Inquiry and Congregational Change*. Herndon, VA: Alban Institute, 2004.

Bridges, William. *Managing Transitions: Making the Most of Change*. Reading, MA: Addison-Wesley, 1991.

Bromiley, Geoffrey W. In *The International Standard Bible Encyclopedia*, edited by Geoffrey W. Bromiley et al., 518–25. Grand Rapids: W. B. Eerdmans, 1979–88.

Brown, Raymond E. *The Churches the Apostles Left Behind*. London: Geoffrey Chapman, 1984.

Browning, Don S. "Integrating the Approaches: A Practical Theology." In *Building Effective Ministry: Theory and Practice in the Local Church*, edited by Carl S. Dudley, 230–7. San Francisco: Harper, 1983.

Brubaker, David. edited by Carolyn Schrock-Shenk, A

Bruce, Deborah, et al. "An International Survey of Congregations and Worshipers: Methodology and Basic Comparisons." *Journal of Beliefs and Values: Studies in Religion and Education* 27, no. 1 (April 2006) 3–12.

Bruce, Deborah, et al. "Fast-Growing Churches: What Distinguishes Them from Others?" *Journal of Beliefs and Values: Studies in Religion and Education* 27, no. 1 (April 2006) 111–26.

Bruce, Steve. *God Is Dead: Secularization in the West*. Oxford, UK: Wiley-Blackwell, 2002.

Bryant, Philip. "Do Church Health Consultancies Assist Local Churches to Become Healthier? Two Western Australian Case Studies." DMin thesis, Vose Seminary, 2009.

Bugbee, Bruce. *What You Do Best In the Body of Christ: Discover Your Spiritual Gifts, Personal Style, and God-Given Passion*. Grand Rapids, MI: Zondervan, 1995.

Buono, Anthony F., and Kerber, Kenneth W. "Intervention and Organizational Change: Building Organizational Change Capacity." In *Consultation for Organizational Change*, edited by Anthony F. Buono and David W. Jamieson, 81–112. Research in Management Consulting Series. Charlotte, NC: Information Age, 2010.

Burtonshaw-Gunn, Simon A. *Essential Tools for Management Consulting: Tools, Models and Approaches for Clients and Consultants*. Chichester, West Sussex: John Wiley and Sons, 2010.

Campbell, Dennis G. *Congregations as Learning Communities: Tools for Shaping Your Future*. Washington, DC: The Alban Institute, 2000.

Caragounis, Chrys C. *Peter and the Rock*. Berlin: W. de Gruyter, 1990.

Carson, D. A. "Matthew, Mark, Luke." In *The Expositor's Bible Commentary: With the New International Version of the Holy Bible*, edited by Frank E. Gaebelein. Grand Rapids: Zondervan, 1992.

Carter, Louis, et al. *Best Practices in Leadership Development and Organization Change: How the Best Companies Ensure Meaningful Change and Sustainable Leadership*. San Francisco, CA: Pfeiffer, 2005.

Carver, John. *Boards That Make a Difference: A New Design for Leadership in Nonprofit and Public Organizations*. Jossey-Bass Nonprofit Sector Series. San Francisco, CA: Jossey-Bass, 1997.

Carver, John, and Miriam Carver. *The Policy Governance Model and the Role of the Board Member*. A Carver Policy Governance Guide, Adjacent Leadership Roles. San Francisco, CA: Jossey-Bass, 2009.

Chait, Richard P., et al. *Governance as Leadership: Reframing the Work of Nonprofit Boards*. Hoboken, NJ: John Wiley and Sons, 2005.

Chester, Andrew. "The Pauline Communities." In *Vision for the Church: Studies in Early Christian Ecclesiology*, edited by Bockmuehl, Markus, and Michael B. Thompson, 105–20. Ebook. London: Continuum International, 1998.

Claiborne, Shane. *The Irresistible Revolution: Living as an Ordinary Radical*. Grand Rapids, MI: Zondervan, 2006.

Clendinning, Ken H. *Report on the Current State of Baptist Churches in NSW and ACT*. Epping, NSW: Baptist Union of NSW and ACT, 2008.

Collinson, Sylvia Wilkey. *Making Disciples: The Significance of Jesus' Educational Methods for Today's Church*. Paternoster Theological Monographs. Milton Keynes, UK: Paternoster, 2004.

Comiskey, Joel. *Cell Church Solutions: Transforming the Church in North America*. Moreno Valley, CA: CCS, 2005.

———. *From 12 to 3: How to Apply G-12 Principles in Your Church*. Houston, TX: Touch, 2002.

———. *Home Cell Group Explosion: How Your Small Group Can Grow and Multiply*. Houston, TX: Touch, 2002.

———. *Leadership Explosion: Multiplying Cell Group Leaders to Reap the Harvest*. Houston, TX: Touch, 2000.

———. *Planting Churches That Reproduce: Starting a Network of Simple Churches*. Moreno Valley, CA: CCS, 2009.

Cosgrove, Charles H., and Dennis D. Hatfield. *Church Conflict: The Hidden Systems Behind the Fights*. Nashville: Abingdon, 1994.

Cronshaw, Darren. "Fresh Forms of Church for Today." *Opportunities for Mission— Conversation Paper* no. 1, 6 October 2009. Conference Proceedings, Australians Beyond the Church: Growing Fresh Expressions of Church Today, 5-7 October 2009. ANU, University House, 1 Balmain Crescent, Canberra, ACT. http://www.freshexpressions.org.au/LinkClick.aspx?fileticket=d%2BZwJ%2BdJUtI%3D&tabid=62&mid=427.

Croucher, Rowland. "Measuring a Church's Health." Wantirna, VIC: John Mark Ministries, 2005. http://jmm.aaa.net.au/articles/15776.htm.

———. "Best Practices in a Healthy Church." Wantirna, VIC: John Mark Ministries, 2008. http://www.jmm.org.au/articles/21803.htm.

Davies, Peter. "Consultancy Master List Numerical 070919 (Version 2).xls." Excel Sheet of All Church Consultancies to Date. Baptist Churches of NSW/ACT Church Consultancy Team. Epping, NSW, 2007.

Dearborn, Tim. *Beyond Duty Leader's Guide: A Passion for Christ, a Heart for Mission*. Federal Way, WA: World Vision; Monrovia, 1997.

Derrida, Jacques. *The Gift of Death; and, Literature in Secret*. Translated by David Wills. Chicago: University of Chicago Press, 2008.

———. *Jacques Derrida: Basic Writings*. Edited by Barry Stocker. New York, NY: Routledge, 2007.

Dever, Mark E. *Nine Marks of a Healthy Church*. Washington, DC: Center for Church Reform, 1998.

———. *What is a Healthy Church?* Wheaton, IL: Crossway, 2007.

Dobson, Edward G., et al. *Mastering Conflict and Controversy*. Mastering Ministry Series. Portland, OR: Multnomah; Christianity Today, Inc., 1992.

Dollard, Maureen F., et al., eds. *Occupational Stress in the Service Professions*. London; New York: Taylor and Francis, 2003.

Driscoll, Mark. "A Pastoral Perspective on the Emergent Church." *Criswell Theological Review* n.s. 3, no. 2 (Spring 2006) 87-93.

Dudley, Carl S., ed. *Building Effective Ministry: Theory and Practice in the Local Church*. San Francisco: Harper, 1983.

Dudley, Carl S., et al. "Insights Into: Congregational Conflict." *Faith Communities Today*. Hartford, CT: Faith Communities Today and the Cooperative Congregational Studies Partnership, Hartford Institute for Religion Research, Hartford Seminary, 2007. http://faithcommunitiestoday.org/.

Dudley, Carl S., and Carl Roozen. "A Report on Religion in the United States Today." *Faith Communities Today*. Hartford, CT: Faith Communities Today and the

Cooperative Congregational Studies Partnership, Hartford Institute for Religion Research, Hartford Seminary, 2001. http://faithcommunitiestoday.org/.

Dyer, Tim. "Biblical and Theological Basis for Consulting." Handout at Consultancy Training Day. Epping, NSW, 2009.

———. "Church Consultancy Training." Sheffield, TAS: John Mark Ministries, 2011. http://johnmark.net.au/jm/?page_id=733.

———. "Standard and Specialist Consultancies." Personal Communication. Sheffield, TAS, 2011.

———. "Types of Proactive Consulting." Handout at Consultancy Training Day. Epping, NSW, 2009.

Easum, Bill, and Bil Cornelius. *Go Big: Lead Your Church to Explosive Growth*. Nashville: Abingdon, 2006.

Easum, William, M. *Sacred Cows Make Gourmet Burgers: Ministry Anytime, Anywhere, By Anybody*. Nashville: Abingdon, 1995.

———. "Transformation and Reproduction Across Denominational Lines." The Great Commission Network, Columbus, Ohio. Port Aransas, TX, 2008.Ellul, Jacques. *The Subversio of Christianity*. Grand Rapids, MI: Eerdmans, 1986.

Encyclo Online Encyclopedia. Health. UK: Encyclo Online Encyclopedia, n.d. http://www.encyclo.co.uk/search.php.

Erickson, Millard J. *Christian Theology*. Grand Rapids, MI: Baker, 1987.

Erwich, René. "Missional Churches: Identical Global 'Plants' or Locally Grown 'Flowers?' Christian A. Schwartz's 'Natural Church Development' Revisited." *Transformation* 21, no. 3 (2004) 180–91.

Fee, Gordon D. *The First Epistle to the Corinthians*. The New International Commentary on the New Testament. Grand Rapids, MI: Eerdmans, 1987.

Fletcher, Michael. *Overcoming Barriers to Growth*. Minneapolis, MN: Bethany House, 2006.

Friedman, Edwin H. *Generation to Generation: Family Process in Church and Synagogue*. The Guilford Family Therapy Series. New York: Guilford, 1985.

Frost, Michael. *Exiles: Living Missionally in a Post-Christian Culture*. Peabody, MA: Hendrickson, 2006.

Frost, Michael, and Alan Hirsch. *ReJesus*. Peabody, MA: Hendrickson; Erina, NSW: Strand, 2009.

———. *The Shaping of Things to Come: Innovation and Mission for the 21st-Century Church*. Peabody, MA: Hendrickson, 2003.

Fryling, Alice. *Seeking God Together: An Introduction to Group Spiritual Direction*. Downers Grove, IL: IVP, 2009.

Gaede, Beth Ann, ed. *Size Transitions in Congregations*. Harvesting the Learnings Series. Bethesda, MD: The Alban Institute, 2001.

Gales, R. *Diagnostic Review—Training Teams to Assess the Ministry of Local Churches*. Berwick: Church Resource Ministries Australia, 1992.

Galindo, Israel. *The Hidden Lives of Congregations: Understanding Congregational Dynamics*. Herndon, VA: Alban Institute, 2004.

Galloway, Dale, et al. *Making Church Relevant*. Beeson Pastoral Series. Kansas City, MO: Beacon Hill, 1999.

Garrison, David. *Church Planting Movements: How God is Redeeming a Lost World*. Midlothian, VA: WIGTake Resources, 2004.

Geiger, Eric, and Thomas S. Rainer. *Simple Church: Returning to God's Process for Making Disciples.* Nashville, TN: Broadman, 2006.

Gibbs, Eddie. *ChurchMorph: How Megatrends Are Reshaping Christian Communities.* Allelon Missional Series. Grand Rapids, MI: Baker, 2009.

———. "The Emerging Church." *The Bible in Transmission* (Summer 2002) 1–4. Gibbs, Eddie

Gibbs, Eddie, and Ryan K. Bolger. *Emerging Churches: Creating Christian Community in Postmodern Cultures.* Grand Rapids, MI: Baker, 2005.

Goodman, Denise W. *Congregational Fitness: Healthy Practices for Layfolk.* Bethesda, MD: Alban Institute, 2000.

Greenfield, Guy. *The Wounded Minister: Healing from and Preventing Personal Attacks.* Grand Rapids, MI: Baker, 2001.

Grenz, Stanley J. *A Primer on Postmodernism.* Grand Rapids, MI: Eerdmans, 1996.

Guinness, Os. *Dining with the Devil: The Megachurch Movement Flirts with Modernity.* Grand Rapids, MI: Baker, 1993.

Gutiérrez, Gustavo. *A Theology of Liberation: History, Politics and Salvation.* Maryknoll, NY: Orbis, 1973.

Hadaway, C. Kirk. *Church Growth Principles: Separating Fact from Fiction.* Nashville, TN: Broadman, 1991.

———. "The Demographic Environment and Church Membership Change." *Journal for the Scientific Study of Religion* 20, no. 1 (March 1981) 77–89.

———. "Do Church Growth Consultations Really Work?" In *Church and Denominational Growth*, edited by David A. Roozen, and C. Kirk Hadaway, 149–54. Nashville: Abingdon, 1993. http://hirr.hartsem.edu/bookshelf/Church&Denomgrowth/ch&dngrw-ch6.pdf.

———. *FACTs on Growth. A New Look at the Dynamics of Growth and Decline in American Congregations Based on The Faith Communities Today 2005 National Survey of Congregations.* Faith Communities Today. Hartford, CT: Faith Communities Today and the Cooperative Congregational Studies Partnership, Hartford Institute for Religion Research, Hartford Seminary, 2006. http://faithcommunitiestoday.org/.

———. "From Stability to Growth: A Study of Factors Related to the Statistical Revitalization of Southern Baptist Congregations." *Journal for the Scientific Study of Religion* 30, no. 2 (June 1991) 181–92.

———. "Is Evangelistic Activity Related to Church Growth?" In *Church and Denominational Growth*, edited by David A. Roozen, and C. Kirk Hadaway, 169–87. Nashville: Abingdon, 1993. http://hirr.hartsem.edu/bookshelf/Church&Denomgrowth/ch&dngrw-ch8.pdf.

Hadaway, C. Kirk, and Penny Long Marler. "Growth and Decline in the Mainline." In *Faith in America*, edited by Charles H. Lippy, 1–24. Westport, CT: Praeger, 2006.

Hagner, Donald A. *Matthew 14–28.* Word Biblical Commentary, vol. 33B. Dallas, TX: Word, 1995.

Halstead, Kenneth A. *From Stuck to Unstuck: Overcoming Congregational Impasse.* Washington: Alban, 1998.

Hanson, Rebecca. "Healthy Church or Unhealthy Church?" Rochester Hills, MI: Ministry Health, n.d. http://www.ministryhealth.net/mh_articles/196_hc_healthy_church.html.

Hart, Archibald. "Building a Healthy Church." Masters/Doctor of Ministry Course "Minister's Personal Growth and Skill Development." Wollongong Church of Christ, 2004.

———. "Unhealthy Trends in the Church." Masters/Doctor of Ministry Course "Minister's Personal Growth and Skill Development." Wollongong Church of Christ, 2004.

Hemphill, Ken. *The Antioch Effect: 8 Characteristics of Highly Effective Churches.* Nashville, TN: Broadman, 1994.

Hirsch, Alan, and Dave Ferguson. *On the Verge.* Grand Rapids, MI: Zondervan, 2011.

Hoge, Dean R., and David A. Roozen, eds. *Understanding Church Growth and Decline, 1950–1978.* New York: Pilgrim, 1979.

Holy Bible: Containing the Old and New Testaments, New Revised Standard Version. Nashville: T. Nelson Publishers, 1989.

Hopewell, James F. *Congregation: Stories and Structures.* Philadelphia, PA: Fortress, 1987.

Hotchkiss, Dan. "Borrowing from Business: How Church Boards Can Benefit from Secular Practices." *Congregations* 31, no. 2 (Spring 2005) 28–33.

———. *Governance and Ministry: Rethinking Board Leadership.* Herndon, VA: Alban Institute, 2008.

Hough, Joseph C. "Theologian at Work: Theological Ethics." In *Building Effective Ministry: Theory and Practice in the Local Church*, edited by Carl S. Dudley, 112–32. San Francisco: Harper, 1983.

Hughes, Philip. *Natural Church Development—The Schwarz Method.* Melbourne, Australia: Christian Research Association. http://www.cra.org.au/pages/00000135.cgi.

Hughes, Philip, et al. *Exploring What Australians Value.* Adelaide: Openbook, 2004.

Hull, Bill. *The Disciple-Making Church: Leading a Body of Believers on the Journey of Faith.* Grand Rapids, MI: Baker, 2010.

———. *Seven Steps to Transform Your Church. Can We Save The Evangelical Church?* Grand Rapids, MI: F. H. Revell, 1993.

Hunter, George G., III. "Examining the 'Natural Church Development' Project." *Journal of The Academy for Evangelism in Theological Education* 22 (2006–7) 6–22. http://journals.sfu.ca/witness/index.php/witness/issue/download/8/28.

———. "The Legacy of Donald A. McGavran." *International Bulletin of Missionary Research* 16, no. 4 (1992) 158–62.

Hutcheon, Linda. "Postmodern Afterthoughts." *Wascana Review of Contemporary Poetry and Short Fiction* 37, no.1 (2002) 5–12. https://tspace.library.utoronto.ca/bitstream/1807/9479/1/TSpace0030.pdf.Iannaccone, Laurence R. "Reassessing Church Growth: Statistical Pitfalls and Their Consequences." *Journal for the Scientific Study of Religion* 35, no. 3 (September 1996) 197–216.

Iannaccone, Laurence R. "Why Strict Churches Are Strong." In *Sacred Companies*, edited by Demerath, N. J., III, et al., 269–91. Oxford, UK: Oxford University Press, 1998.

Iannaccone, Laurence R., et al. "Religious Resources and Church Growth." *Social Forces* 74, no. 2 (December 1995) 705–31.

Johnson, David, and Jeff VanVonderen. *The Subtle Power of Spiritual Abuse.* Minneapolis, MN: Bethany House, 2005.

Kaldor, Peter, et al. *Build My Church: Trends and Possibilities for Australian Churches.* Adelaide, SA: Openbook/NCLS, 1999.

Kaldor, Peter, et al. *Shaping a Future: Characteristics of Vital Congregations.* Adelaide: Openbook, 1997.

Kaldor, Peter, and Rod Bullpitt. *Burnout in Church Leaders.* Adelaide, SA: Openbook, 2001.

Kärkkäinen, Veli-Matti. *Introduction to Ecclesiology: Ecumenical, Historical and Global Perspectives.* Downers Grove, IL: InterVarsity, 2002.

Kelley, Dean M. *Why Conservative Churches Are Growing: A Study in Sociology of Religion.* New York: Harper, 1972.

———. "Why Conservative Churches Are Still Growing." *Journal for the Scientific Study of Religion* 17, no. 2 (July 1978) 165–72.

Kierkegaard, Søren. "Attack Upon Christendom." In *A Kierkegaard Anthology,* edited by Robert Bretall, 434–68. Princeton, NJ: Princeton University Press, 1946.

Kierkegaard, Søren. "Training in Christianity." In *A Kierkegaard Anthology,* edited by Robert Bretall, 372–417. Princeton, NJ: Princeton University Press, 1946.

Kirk, J. Alex, et al. *Small Group Leaders' Handbook: Developing Transformational Communities.* Downers Grove, IL: IVP Connect, 2009.

Koehn, Dennis. "Considerations for the Consultant." *Conciliation Quarterly* 7, no. 1 (Winter 1988) 2–3. us.mcc.org/../1%20Group%20Consulting%20and%20 Intervention%20- %20Winter%201988.pdf.

Kruse, Axel. "After Postmodernism: Literary Theory, Culture and the New HSC English Syllabus." *Sydney Studies in English* 27 (2001) 1–14. https://openjournals.library. sydney.edu.au/index.php/SSE/article/view/561/530. Kubr, Milan, ed. *Management Consulting: A Guide to the Profession.* Geneva: International Labour Office, 2002.

Lane, William L. *Hebrews 1–8.* Word Biblical Commentary. Dallas, TX: Word, 1991.

———. *Hebrews 9–13.* Word Biblical Commentary. Dallas: TX; Word, 1991.

Leas, Speed B. *Discover Your Conflict Management Style.* Washington, DC: Alban Institute, 1997.

———. *Leadership and Conflict.* Creative Leadership Series. Nashville: Abingdon, 1982.

———. *Moving Your Church through Conflict.* Washington, DC: Alban Institute, 2002.

Lehr, Fred. *Clergy Burnout: Recovering from the 70-Hour Work Week and Other Self-Defeating Practices.* Minneapolis: Fortress; Edinburgh: Alban, 2006.

Lewin, Kurt. *The Complete Social Scientist: A Kurt Lewin Reader.* Edited by Martin Gold. Washington, DC: American Psychological Association, 1999.

Lewis, Christopher Alan, et al. "Clergy Work-Related Psychological Health, Stress, and Burnout: An Introduction to This Special Issue of Mental Health, Religion and Culture." *Mental Health, Religion and Culture* 10, no. 1 (January 2007) 1–8.

Logos Bible Software 4.2. Electronic Resource. Oak Harbor, WA: Logos Research Systems, 2000–2010.

London, H. B., and Neil B. Wiseman. *Pastors at Risk.* Wheaton, IL: Victor, 1993.

———. *Pastors at Greater Risk.* Ventura, California: Gospel Light, 2003.

Longenecker, Richard N. *Galatians.* Word Biblical Commentary, vol. 41. Dallas, TX: Word, 1990.

Louw, Johannes P., and Eugene A. Nida. Vol. 1: *Greek-English Lexicon of the New Testament: Based on Semantic Domains.* Electronic Ed. of the 2nd Edition. New York: United Bible Societies, 1996.

Lovell, George. *Consultancy Modes and Models*. Calver, UK: Cliff College, 2005.
MacArthur, John. *Ashamed of the Gospel: When the Church Becomes Like the World*. Wheaton, IL: Crossway, 2010.
Macchia, Stephen A. *Becoming a Healthy Church: 10 Characteristics*. Grand Rapids, MI: Baker, 1999.
MacNair, Donald J. *The Practices of a Healthy Church: Biblical Strategies for Vibrant Church*. Phillipsburg, NJ: Presbyterian and Reformed, 1999.
Mallory, Sue. *The Equipping Church: Serving Together to Transform Lives*. Grand Rapids, MI: Zondervan, 2001.
Malony, H. Newton. *Church Organization Development: Perspectives and Processes*. Pasadena, CA: Integration, 1986.
Malphurs, Aubrey. *Strategic Disciple Making: A Practical Tool for Successful Ministry*. Grand Rapids, MI: Baker, 2009.
Mancini, Will. *The 2010 Church Consulting Future Trends Report*. Louisville, KY: Church Central. http://www.willmancini.com/wpcontent/uploads/2011/01/FT_Executive_Summary.pdf.
Mann, Alice. *The In-Between Church: Navigating Size Transitions in Congregations*. Alban Institute Publication. Bethesda, MD: Alban Institute, 1998.
———. *Raising the Roof: The Pastoral-to-Program Size Transition*. Alban Institute Publication. Bethesda, MD: Alban Institute, 2001.
Martin, Ralph P. *2 Corinthians*. Word Biblical Commentary, vol. 40. Waco, TX: Word, 1986.
Maula, Marjatte, and Flemming Poulfelt. *Knowledge Transfer, Consulting Modes and Learning: Do the Codes of Conduct and Ethics Reflect Reality in Management Consulting?* Working Papers. Copenhagen Business School, Department of Management, Politics and Philosophy, 2000.
McDowell, Josh, and Bob Hostetler. *The New Tolerance: How a Cultural Movement Threatens to Destroy You, Your Faith, and Your Children*. Wheaton, IL: Tyndale House, 1998.
McGavran, Donald Anderson. *The Bridges of God: A Study in the Strategy of Missions*. London: World Dominion, 1955.
———. *Church Growth and Mission in Jamaica*. Lucknow, India: Lucknow, 1962.
———. *Church Growth in West Utkal*. Indianapolis, IN: United Christian Missionary Society, 1956.
———. *How Churches Grow: The New Frontiers of Mission*. London: World Dominion, 1959.
———. *Multiplying Churches in the Philippines*. Church Growth in the United Church of Christ in the Philippines, vol. 1. Manila: United Church of Christ in the Philippines, 1958.
———. "My Pilgrimage in Mission." *International Bulletin of Missionary Research* 10, no. 2 (1986) 165–72.
———. *Understanding Church Growth*. Grand Rapids: Eerdmans, 1970.
———. "Wrong Strategy: The Real Crisis in Missions." *International Review of Mission* 54, no. 216 (1965) 451–61.
McGavran, Donald Anderson, et al. *Church Growth in Mexico*. Grand Rapids: Eerdmans, 1963.
McGavran, Donald Anderson, and Winfield C. Arn. *How to Grow a Church*. Glendale, CA: Regal, 1973.

McGavran, Donald Anderson, and Winfield C. Arn. *Ten Steps for Church Growth.* San Francisco: Harper, 1977.

McIntosh, Gary L. *Biblical Church Growth: How You Can Work with God to Build a Faithful Church.* Grand Rapids, MI: Baker, 2003.

———. *Staff Your Church for Growth: Building Team Ministry in the 21st Century.* Grand Rapids, MI: Baker, 2000.

———. *Taking Your Church to the Next Level: What Got You Here Won't Get You There.* Grand Rapids, MI: Baker, 2009.

McIntosh, Gary L., ed. *Evaluating the Church Growth Movement: Five Views.* Counterpoints. Grand Rapids, MI: Zondervan, 2004.

McIntosh, Gary L., and Samuel D. Rima. *Overcoming the Dark Side of Leadership: The Paradox of Personal Dysfunction.* Grand Rapids, MI: Baker, 1997.

McLaren, Brian D. *A New Kind of Christian: A Tale of Two Friends on a Spiritual Journey.* San Francisco: Jossey-Bass, 2001.

———. *Reinventing Your Church.* Grand Rapids, MI: Zondervan, 1998.

McMinn, Mark R., and Amy W. Dominguez, eds. *Psychology and the Church.* New York: Nova Science, 2005.

Mead, Loren B. "Seeking Significant Intervention." In *Building Effective Ministry: Theory and Practice in the Local Church*, edited by Carl S. Dudley, 155–9. San Francisco: Harper, 1983.

Mead, Loren B. *A Change of Pastors and How It Affects Change in the Congregation.* Herndon, VA: Alban Institute, 2005.

Merriam-Webster Online Dictionary. "Postmodern." Springfield, MA: Merriam-Webster Incorporated. https://www.merriam-webster.com/dictionary/postmodern. Microsoft Office. Microsoft Office Home and Business 2010. Computer File. Redmond, Washington: Microsoft, 2010.

Miller, Kevin A. "What Pastors Are Saying." *Leadership* (2001) 1–2.

Mittelberg, Mark, et al. *Becoming a Contagious Christian: Leader's Guide: Communicating Your Faith in a Style That Fits You.* Contributions by Wendy Seidman and Don Cousins. Grand Rapids, MI: Zondervan; Barrington, IL: Willow Creek Resources, 2007.

———. *Becoming a Contagious Christian: Participant's Guide: Communicating Your Faith in a Style That Fits You.* Contributions by Wendy Seidman and Don Cousins. Grand Rapids, MI: Zondervan; Barrington, IL: Willow Creek Resources, 2007.

Moltmann, Jürgen. *The Church in the Power of the Spirit: A Contribution to Messianic Ecclesiology.* London: SCM, 1992.

Mounce, William D. *Pastoral Epistles.* Word Biblical Commentary, vol. 46. Nashville: TN: Nelson, 2000.

Murray, Stuart. *Post-Christendom: Church and Mission in a Strange New World.* Carlisle, England: Paternoster, 2004.

Myers, Ched. *Binding the Strong Man: A Political Reading of Mark's Story of Jesus.* Maryknoll, NY: Orbis, 1988.

NCLS Research. *Church Life Profile—Church A Baptist Church.* Sydney South, NSW: NCLS Research, 2006.

———. *Church Life Profile—Church B Baptist Church.* Sydney South, NSW: NCLS Research, 2006.

———. *Church Life Profile—Church C Baptist Church.* Sydney South, NSW: NCLS Research, 2006.

———. *Church Life Profile—Church D Baptist Church.* Sydney South, NSW: NCLS Research, 2006.
———. *Church Life Profile—Church E Baptist Church.* Sydney South, NSW: NCLS Research, 2006.
———. *Church Life Profile—Church F Baptist Church.* Sydney South, NSW: NCLS Research, 2006.
———. *Church Life Profile—Church G Baptist Church.* Sydney South, NSW: NCLS Research, 2006.
———. *Church Life Profile—Church H Baptist Church.* Sydney South, NSW: NCLS Research, 2006.
———. *Church Life Profile—Church I Baptist Church.* Sydney South, NSW: NCLS Research, 2006.
———. *Church Life Profile—Church J Baptist Church.* Sydney South, NSW: NCLS Research, 2006.
———. *Regional Church Life Profile—Baptist Church NSW/ACT.* Sydney South, NSW: NCLS Research, 2006.
Nicholson, Roger S., ed. *Temporary Shepherds: A Congregational Handbook for Interim Ministry.* Washington, DC: Alban Institute, 1998.
Oden, Thomas C. *Life in the Spirit.* San Francisco, CA: Harper, 1992.
Olson, Mark A. *Moving Beyond Church Growth: An Alternative Vision for Congregations.* Prisms. Minneapolis: Fortress, 2002.
Oswald, Roy M. "Getting Feedback on Your Ministry: Three Ways to Do Evaluation Without Risking a Public Flogging." *Congregations* 28, no. 2 (March/April 2002) 16–18.
Oswald, Roy M., et al. *Beginning Ministry Together: The Alban Handbook for Clergy Transitions.* Bethesda, MD: Alban Institute, 2003.
Oswald, Roy M., and Speed B. Leas. *The Inviting Church: A Study of New Member Assimilation.* Washington, DC: Alban Institute, 1987.
Pastor of Church A. Interview Transcript. Sydney, NSW, 2009.
Pastor of Church C. Interview Transcript. Sydney, NSW, 2009.
Pastor of Church F. Interview Transcript. Sydney, NSW, 2009.
Pastor of Church H. Interview Transcript. Sydney, NSW, 2010.
Pastor of Church I. Interview Transcript. Sydney, NSW, 2009.
Pattison, E. Mansell. *Pastor and Parish: A Systems Approach.* Creative Pastoral Care and Counseling Series. Philadelphia: Fortress, 1977.
Phillips, William Bud. *Pastoral Transitions: From Endings to New Beginnings.* Washington, DC: Alban Institute, 1988.
Pickett, J. Waskom. *Christ's Way to India's Heart: Present Day Mass Movements to Christianity.* London: The United Society for Christian Literature, 1938.
———. *Christian Mass Movements in India: A Study with Recommendations.* New York: Abingdon, 1933.
———. *The Dynamics of Church Growth.* New York: Abingdon, 1963.
Pickett, J. Waskom, et al. *Christian Missions in Mid India: A Study of Nine Areas with Special Reference to Mass Movements.* Jubbulpore, India: The Mission, 1938.
———. *Church Growth and Group Conversion.* Lucknow: India, Lucknow, 1956.
Powell, Ruth. *NCLS Research Fact Sheet: Why Innovation is Needed in Church Life.* Sydney South: NCLS Research, 2010. http://www.ncls.org.au/default.aspx?sitemapid=6516.

———. *NOVUS: Innovations in Australian Church Life.* Sydney South: NCLS Research, 2006. http://www.ncls.org.au/download/doc4264/NOVUSMagazine.pdf.

Pratt, Jonathan. *Baptist Churches of NSW and ACT Directions 2012 Research Project—"Awaken O Sleeper": Disturbing a Denomination at the Crossroads—Working Paper No. 1.* Epping, NSW: Baptist Churches NSW/ACT Directions 2012 Research Steering Group, 2009.

Rainer, Thom S. *The Book of Church Growth: History, Theology, and Principles.* Nashville, TN: Broadman, 1993.

———. *Breakout Churches: Discover How to Make the Leap.* Grand Rapids, MI: Zondervan, 2004.

———. *Surprising Insights from the Unchurched and Proven Ways to Reach Them.* Grand Rapids, MI: Zondervan, 2001.

Rairdin, Craig. QuickVerse for Windows 3.0h. 1992. Omaha, NE: Parsons Technology Inc., 1994.

Rediger, G. Lloyd. *Clergy Killers: Guidance for Pastors and Congregations Under Attack.* Inver Grove Heights, MN: Logos Productions, 1996.

Rees, Erik. *S.H.A.P.E.: Finding and Fulfilling Your Unique Purpose for Life.* Grand Rapids, MI: Zondervan, 2006.

Rendle, Gilbert R. *Leading Change in the Congregation: Spiritual and Organizational Tools for Leaders.* Bethesda, MD: Alban Institute, 1998.

Rendle, Gilbert R., and Alice Mann. *Holy Conversations: Strategic Planning as a Spiritual Practice for Congregations.* Bethesda, MD: Alban Institute, 2003.

Richardson, Ronald W. *Creating a Healthier Church: Family Systems Theory, Leadership, and Congregational Life.* Creative Pastoral Care and Counseling Series. Minneapolis: Fortress, 1996.

Robson, Colin. *Real World Research: A Resource for Social Scientists and Practitioner-Researchers.* Oxford, UK: Blackwell, 2002.

Roozen, David A. "Oldline Protestantism: Pockets of Vitality Within a Continuing Stream of Decline." In *Why Liberal Churches Are Growing*, edited by Martyn Percy and Ian Markham, 119–42. London: T. & T. Clark, 2006.

Roozen, David A., and Jackson W. Carroll. "Recent Trends in Church Membership and Participation: An Introduction." In *Understanding Church Growth and Decline 1950–1978*, edited by , 21–41. New York: Pilgrim, 1979. Rorty, Richard. *Objectivity, Relativism, and Truth.* Philosophical Papers, vol. 1. Cambridge: Cambridge University Press, 1991.

———. *Truth, Politics and "Post-Modernism."* Spinoza Lectures. Assen: Van Gorcum, 1997.

Rosenau, Pauline Marie. *Post Modernism and the Social Sciences: Insights, Inroads, and Intrusions.* Princeton, NJ: Princeton University Press, 1992.

Rothwell, William J., and Roland Sullivan, eds. *Practicing Organization Development: A Guide for Consultants.* Pfeiffer Essential Resources for Training and HR Professionals. San Francisco: Pfeiffer, 2005.

Roukema, Richard W. *Shepherding the Shepherd: Negotiating the Stress of Ministry.* Enumclaw, WA: Pleasant Word, 2003.

Rudaityte, Regina, ed. *Postmodernism and After: Visions and Revisions.* Newcastle, UK: Cambridge Scholars, 2008.

Saarinen, Martin F. *The Life Cycle of a Congregation.* Alban Institute Publication. Washington, DC: Alban Institute, 1990.

Savage, Sara B. "Psychology Serving the Church in the United Kingdom: Church Consultancy and Pastoral Care." *Journal of Psychology and Christianity* 22, no. 4 (Winter 2003) 338–42.

———. *Psychology and Pastoral Theology Resource for Pioneer and Traditional Ministry*. Norwich: Canterbury, 2007.

Scarborough, Les, et al., eds. *Church Consultancy Manual*. Epping, NSW: Baptist Churches of NSW and ACT, 2007 (revised).

Scazzero, Peter, and Warren Bird. *The Emotionally Healthy Church: A Strategy for Discipleship That Actually Changes Lives*. Grand Rapids, MI: Zondervan, 2003.

Schaller, Lyle E. *The Interventionist: A Conceptual Framework and Questions for Parish Consultants, Intentional Interim Ministers, Church Champions, Pastors Considering a New Call, Denominational Executives, the Recently Arrived Pastor, Counselors, and Other Intentional Interventionists in Congregational Life*. Nashville, TN: Abingdon, 1997.

Schein, Edgar H. *Process Consultation. Volume II: Lessons for Managers and Consultants*. Addison-Wesley Series on Organization Development. Reading, MA: Addison-Wesley, 1987.

Scherer, John J., et al. "Whole System Transformation—The Consultant's Role in Creating Sustainable Results." In *Consultation for Organizational Change*, edited by Anthony F. Buono and David W. Jamieson Research in Management Consulting Series. Charlotte, NC: Information Age, 2010.Schwarz, Christian A. *Natural Church Development: A Guide to Eight Essential Qualities of Healthy Churches*. Carol Stream, IL: ChurchSmart Resources, 1998.

Searcy, Nelson, and Jennifer Dykes Henson. *Ignite: How to Spark Immediate Growth in Your Church*. Grand Rapids, MI: Baker, 2009.

Senge, Peter M. *The Fifth Discipline: The Art and Practice of the Learning Organization*. New York: Currency Doubleday, 1990.

Shelley, Bruce, and Marshall Shelley. *The Consumer Church: Can Evangelicals Win the World Without Losing Their Souls?* Downers Grove, IL: InterVarsity, 1992.

Shelley, Marshall. *Well-Intentioned Dragons: Ministering to Problem People in the Church*. Minneapolis: Bethany House, 1994.

Shenk, Wilbert R., ed. et al. *The Challenge of Church Growth, a Symposium*. Institute of Mennonite Studies. Missionary Studies, no. 1. Elkhart, IN: Institute of Mennonite Studies, 1973.

Siebert, Steven. *Nota Bene 8.0*. Computer File. 1982. New York, NY: Nota Bene, 2006.

Simons, Herbert W., and Michael Billig, eds. *After Postmodernism: Reconstructing Ideology Critique*. Inquiries in Social Construction. London; Thousand Oaks, CA: Sage, 1994.

Smalley, Stephen S. "The Johannine Community and the Letters of John." In *Vision for the Church: Studies in Early Christian Ecclesiology*, edited by Craig L. Blomberg et al., 95–104. Ebook. London: Continuum International, 1998.

Snyder, Howard A. "The Marks of Evangelical Ecclesiology." In *Evangelical Ecclesiology: Reality or Illusion?*, edited by John G. Stackhouse, 77–103. Grand Rapids, MI: Baker, 2003.

Soden, A, ed. *NSW and ACT Baptist Churches Handbook 1995–1996*. Forest Lodge, NSW: Executive Committee, Baptist Union of NSW, 1996.

———. *NSW and ACT Baptist Churches Handbook 2001–2002*. Forest Lodge, NSW: Executive Committee, Baptist Union of NSW, 2002.

———. *NSW and ACT Baptist Churches Handbook 2003-2004*. Forest Lodge, NSW: Executive Committee, Baptist Union of NSW, 2004.

———. *NSW and ACT Baptist Churches Handbook 2004-2005*. Forest Lodge, NSW: Executive Committee, Baptist Union of NSW, 2005.

———. *NSW and ACT Baptist Churches Handbook 2005-2006*. Forest Lodge, NSW: Executive Committee, Baptist Union of NSW, 2006.

———. *NSW and ACT Baptist Churches Handbook 2006-2007*. Forest Lodge, NSW: Executive Committee, Baptist Union of NSW, 2007.

———. *NSW and ACT Baptist Churches Handbook 2007-2008*. Forest Lodge, NSW: Executive Committee, Baptist Union of NSW, 2008.

———. *NSW and ACT Baptist Churches Handbook 2008-2009*. Epping, NSW: Executive Committee, Baptist Union of NSW, 2009.

———. *NSW and ACT Baptist Churches Handbook 2009-2010*. Epping, NSW: Executive Committee, Baptist Union of NSW, 2010.

Spiro, Melford E. "Postmodernist Anthropology, Subjectivity, and Science: A Modernist Critique." *Comparative Studies in Society and History* 38, no. 4 (1996) 759–80.

Spitzer, Lee B. *Making Friends, Making Disciples: Growing Your Church Through Authentic Relationships*. Living Church Series. Valley Forge, PA: Judson, 2010.

Stanley, Andy, and Ed Young. *Can We Do That? 24 Innovative Practices That Will Change the Way You Do Church*. West Monroe, LA: Howard, 2002.

Stedman, Thomas Lathrop. *Stedman's Medical Dictionary*. Philadelphia: Lippincott Williams and Wilkins, 2006.

Steinke, Peter L. *Healthy Congregations: A Systems Approach*. 1996. Herndon, VA: Alban Institute, 2006.

———. *How Your Church Family Works: Understanding Congregations as Emotional Systems*. Herndon, VA: Alban Institute, 2006.

Sterland, Sam, et al. "Attracting and Integrating Newcomers into Church Life: Research in Four Countries." *Journal of Beliefs and Values: Studies in Religion and Education* 27, no. 1 (April 2006) 39–52.

Stetzer, Ed. "The Evolution of Church Growth, Church Health, and the Missional Church: An Overview of the Church Growth Movement from, and Back to, Its Missional Roots." American Society for Church Growth—50th Anniversary of "Bridges of God." Alpharetta, GA, 2005. http://lci.typepad.com/leaders_resourcing_leader/files/EvolutionOfChurchGrowthHealthMissional.pdf.

———. *First-Person: Understanding the Emerging Church*. Alpharetta, GA: Baptist, 2006. http://www.bpnews.net/22406/firstperson-understanding-the-emerging-church. Stetzer, Ed, and Thom S. Rainer. *Transformational Church: Creating a New Scorecard for Congregations*. Nashville, TN: B and H, 2010.

Stevens, R. Paul, and Phil Collins. *The Equipping Pastor: A Systems Approach to Congregational Leadership*. Washington, DC: Alban Institute, 1993.

Stierstorfer, Klaus, ed. *Beyond Postmodernism: Reassessments in Literature, Theory, and Culture*. Berlin: W. de Gruyter, 2003.

Stott, John R. W. *The Spirit, the Church and the World*. Bible Speaks Today. Leicester, England: InterVarsity, 1990.

Stringer, Martin. "Putting Congregational Studies to Work: Ethnography, Consultancy and Change." In *Congregational Studies in the UK: Christianity in a Post-Christian Context*, edited by Mathew Guest, et al, 203–14. Explorations in Practical, Pastoral, and Empirical Theology. Aldershot, Hants, England; Burlington, VT: Ashgate, 2004.

Sturgis, Paul W. "Institutional Versus Contextual Explanations for the Growth of the Jehovah's Witnesses in the United States, 1945–2002." *Review of Religious Research* 49, no. 3 (March 2008) 290–300.

Surratt, Geoff. *Ten Stupid Things That Keep Churches from Growing: How Leaders Can Overcome Costly Mistakes*. Grand Rapids, MI: Zondervan, 2009.

Tenny-Brittian, Bill. *The Complete Ministry Audit vs. Natural Church Development*. Columbia, MO: 21st Century Strategies. http://churchconsultations.com/resources/faqs-resources-and-info/c/complete-ministry-audit/complete-ministry-audit-vs-natural-church-growth/.

Thomas, Jeremy N., and Daniel V. A. Olson. "Testing the Strictness Thesis and Competing Theories of Congregational Growth." *Journal for the Scientific Study of Religion* 49, no. 4 (December 2010) 619–39.

Thompson, W. L., et al. edited by Dean R. Hoge, and David A. Roozen,

Thorndike, Jeanie M. *Gratitude and Human Flourishing: Examining the Benefits of Gratitude on Effective Coping, Resilience and Well-Being*. Pasadena: Fuller Theological Seminary, School of Psychology, 2007.

Train, Philip L. *A Strategy of Maintaining Personal Care in Ministry*. 2005, 2004. http://www.worldcat.org/title/strategy-of-maintaining-personal-care-in-ministry/oclc/69374967.

Van Rheenen, Gailyn. "Contrasting Missional and Church Growth Perspectives." *Restoration Quarterly* 48, no. 1 (2006) 25–32.

Volf, Miroslav. *After Our Likeness: The Church as the Image of the Trinity*. Grand Rapids, MI: Eerdmans, 1998.

Wagner, C. Peter. *The Healthy Church*. Ventura, CA: Regal, 1996.

———. *Strategies for Church Growth: Tools for Effective Mission and Evangelism*. Ventura, CA: Regal, 1987.

Wagner, C. Peter, ed., et al. *Church Growth: State of the Art*. Wheaton, IL: Tyndale House, 1986.

Walsh, J. Richard, and Brian J. Middleton. *Truth Is Stranger Than It Used to Be: Biblical Faith in a Postmodern Age*. Downers Grove, IL: InterVarsity, 1995.

Warren, Rick. "Interviewed by Ed Rowell and Kevin Miller (1997). 'Comprehensive Health Plan: To Lead a Healthy Church Takes More Than Technique.'" *Leadership* 18, no. 3 (Summer 1997) 23–29.

———. *The Purpose Driven Church: Growth Without Compromising Your Message*. Grand Rapids, MI: Zondervan, 1995.

Warren, Yvonne. *The Cracked Pot: The State of Today's Anglican Parish Clergy*. Stowmarket: Kevin Mayhew, 2002.

Webb, Heather P. *Small Group Leadership as Spiritual Direction: Practical Ways to Blend an Ancient Art into Your Contemporary Community*. El Cajon, CA: Youth Specialties, 2005.

Werning, Waldo J. *12 Pillars of a Healthy Church: Be a Life-Giving Church and Center for Missionary Formation*. St. Charles, IL: ChurchSmart Resources, 2001.

Whitney, Diana, and Amanda Trosten-Bloom. *The Power of Appreciative Inquiry: A Practical Guide to Positive Change*. San Francisco, CA: Berrett-Koehler, 2003.

Woods, C. Jeff. *Congregational Megatrends*. Alban Institute Publication Once and Future Church Series. Bethesda, MD: Alban Institute, 1996.

Woolever, Cynthia, and Deborah Bruce. *Beyond the Ordinary: Ten Strengths of U. S. Congregations*. Louisville, KY: Westminster John Knox, 2004.

———. *A Field Guide to U. S. Congregations: Who's Going Where and Why?* Louisville, KY: Westminster John Knox, 2010.

———. *Places of Promise: Finding Strength in Your Congregation's Location*. Louisville, KY: Westminster John Knox, 2008.

Wright, N. T. *Jesus and the Victory of God*. Christian Origins and the Question of God. London: Society for Promoting Christian Knowledge, 1996.

———. *Simply Christian: Why Christianity Makes Sense*. San Francisco, CA: HarperSanFrancisco, 2006.

Yeakley, Flavil R., Jr, and John W. Ellas. "Natural Church Development: A Guide to Eight Essential Qualities of Healthy Churches." *Journal of the American Society for Church Growth* 10 (Spring 1999) 83–92.

Yoder, John Howard. "A People in the World." In *The Royal Priesthood*, edited by Michael G. Cartwright, 66–101. Grand Rapids, MI: Eerdmans, 1994. Yoder, Perry B. *Shalom: The Bible's Word for Salvation, Justice, and Peace*. Nappanee, IN: Evangel, 1998.

Yust, Karen Marie. "Playing with Mirrors: Narrative Inquiry and Congregational Consultation." *Religious Education* 104, no. 1 (January–February 2009) 84–93.

www.ingramcontent.com/pod-product-compliance
Lightning Source LLC
Chambersburg PA
CBHW052058230426
43662CB00036B/1366